BLITZKRIEG
IN THEIR OWN WORDS

BLITZKRIEG
IN THEIR OWN WORDS

FIRST-HAND ACCOUNTS FROM
GERMAN SOLDIERS 1939–1940

FOREWORD BY
GENERAL HEINZ GUDERIAN

TRANSLATED BY PROFESSOR ALAN BANCE

Pen & Sword
MILITARY

The accounts featured in this book first appeared in Mit Den Panzern In Ost Und West *in 1942. The opinions expressed in this translation are those of the original authors, and not those of the translator or publisher.*

First published in Great Britain in 2005 by
Pen & Sword Military
an imprint of
Pen & Sword Books Ltd
47 Church Street
Barnsley
South Yorkshire
S70 2AS

© 2005 Amber Books Ltd

ISBN 1 84415 276 6

A CIP catalogue record for this book is
available from the British Library

Pen & Sword Books Ltd incorporates the Imprints of Pen &
Sword Aviation, Pen & Sword Maritime, Pen & Sword Military,
Wharncliffe Local History, Pen & Sword Select, Pen & Sword
Military Classics and Leo Cooper.

For a complete list of Pen & Sword titles please contact
PEN & SWORD BOOKS LIMITED
47 Church Street, Barnsley, South Yorkshire, S70 2AS, England
E-mail: enquiries@pen-and-sword.co.uk
Website: www.pen-and-sword.co.uk

Editorial and design by
Amber Books Ltd
Bradley's Close
74–77 White Lion Street
London N1 9PF
www.amberbooks.co.uk

Consultant: Will Fowler
Project Editor: Michael Spilling
Designer: Hawes Design

Printed and bound in China

All pictures supplied by Will Fowler

Contents

Publisher's Note

Published in Germany in 1942, *Mit den Panzern in Ost und West* reflects the attitudes of a militarized Germany that even after the defeat at Moscow in the winter of 1941–1942 was still confident of victory.

Though the ethnic and political prejudices of the period are woven into some of the accounts of the fighting in France and Poland, many of the accounts are just straightforward front-line soldiers' stories. The book is therefore in part history and in part propaganda – propaganda for the new Nazi Germany and also for the *Panzerwaffe*, the tank arm that had delivered the resounding victories in the first years of the war.

Foreword

When they crossed the eastern frontier of the Reich on that memorable 1st of September day in 1939 to launch their attack on Poland, the tank crews had years of laborious preparation behind them. But it was not only hard work they faced: it had been a tough struggle to build up this new branch of the armed forces. Opinions about ways to deploy it were divided, and there was little faith in its effectiveness. The baby was born into a world more inclined to reject it than offer it a loving welcome.

It was not surprising that officers and men looked forward with eager anticipation to the coming events. They were proud of their tanks and they knew their power. For years they had done nothing but practise the assault – they had shrugged off the nightmare of defeat in 1918, and they believed in victory. With wonderful élan the armoured regiments roared into action against the enemy, achieving the decisive victory and completing follow-up operations with unprecedented speed to accomplish the total defeat of the Polish forces.

The tank crews did not fight alone. From the inception of the new weapon, its creators' thinking about modern tank warfare led to the close involvement of support units that were fully motorized and to some extent armoured. The German Army created tank divisions that formed large, self-contained units which included all arms of the service. After reconnaissance, in combat the tanks and the supporting riflemen and motorcycle troops, artillery, engineers and signal corps, could exploit their joint successes instantly, thanks to the mechanization common to all these arms. Further backing was given to the tank divisions by motorized infantry.

The tank divisions became the natural partners of the air force, with whom they soon formed the closest bonds of comradeship. The enforced delay imposed upon the forces by the winter conditions of 1939-40 was utilized to build up the tank formations. In May 1940, they advanced with renewed vigour in the west. Their achievements exceeded all expectations. One can only look back with deep pride and gratitude to those days of spring and summer that saw our victorious breakthroughs to the Channel coast and the Swiss frontier. Such élan, such boldness, such readiness for sacrifice!

In this book, men who saw combat with me in the east and the west, and who are drawn from every arm of our tank formations, relate their experiences. They are men of the sword, not the pen. But it is precisely the plainness of their language that makes the book so gripping and forceful. It paints a picture of our great victories in Poland and France, and will help to keep alive their memory. It tells of the heroism of our dead and wounded, of true comradeship, and of loyalty to the Reich and the Führer.

And so this small book is a contribution to victory!

Guderian
Generaloberst

Heinz Guderian (1888–1954)

Born in Kulm on 17 June 1888, Heinz Guderian was the son of a Prussian general. During the 1920s and 1930s, Guderian had developed deep-penetration armoured tactics and formed the nucleus of a mechanized force. In 1939, he was given command of the XIX Corps, which fought in Poland and France.

Guderian, a former signals officer, realized that with reliable radio communications he could command from armoured vehicles on the move. In his SdFfz 251 command halftrack, he led his corps from the front. His forces punched through the thin French lines at Sedan on 14 May and crossed the Meuse. Though they were actually outnumbered, his panzers were able to the break through to the Channel coast and cut off Allied troops in northern France. The corps covered the 234km (151 miles) to the Channel in eight days at an average speed of 30km (19 miles) per day, and on one day achieved a remarkable 90km (56 miles). Guderian was able to bluff Hitler into believing that they had halted by using a field telephone link that was run back to a static radio station as the tanks pushed west.

On 28 May, Hitler gave Guderian command of the group south from near Sedan, moving as far as Pontarlier on the Swiss border and then turned left, driving north to capture Belfort. Following the fall of France, he was promoted to *Generaloberst*. For the Soviet campaign he was given one of the four *Panzergruppen*, part of Army Group Centre, with its vehicles emblazoned with the letter 'G'. However, Guderian was relieved of his command when he withdrew his *Panzergruppe* under the intense pressure of Soviet attacks in December 1941.

He was brought back from retirement in February 1943 and made Inspector of Armoured Troops. In July 1944, Guderian was promoted to army chief of staff and held this post until 22 March 1945. On 10 May 1945, Guderian surrendered to the Americans. After the war he was exonerated of any war crimes by the Allies and released from internment in Neustadt in June 1948 on his 60th birthday. He died in Bavaria on 15 May 1954.

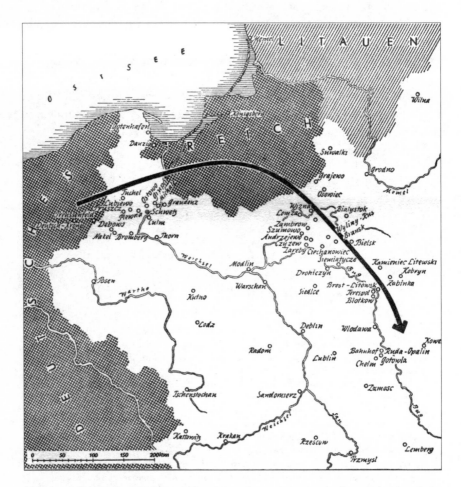

The attack led by the XIX Panzer Corps carved its way across northern Poland to Brest-Litovsk on the River Bug. This ancient fortress town became the meeting place of German and Soviet forces on 19 September 1939.

INVASION OF POLAND

The Men in the Fighting Machines
– A band of conspirators

Camouflaged against air or ground attack, the heavy tanks stand among the scrubby, head-high trees. To provide cover, the dull grey barrels of their guns point in the direction of the enemy. The crews, in their black uniforms with death's heads insignia on the lapels, have checked their vehicles over once more, topped up the fuel, and loaded fresh ammunition into the bellies of their grey-black monsters. But they are monsters only for the enemy, whom they are designed and destined to push over, destroy, and crush. Hence the names: *Griffin, Eagle, Falcon, Condor, Tiger, Panther*. These outwardly inanimate steel fortresses are living beings for us; protection and fire-power in battle, home when at rest.

The men of my platoon lie under the bushes and sleep. For sleep is a duty. Every free moment must be devoted to it, to allow our tensed bodies to conserve their vigour and stamina. I call out a subdued order:

'First platoon, to me!'

They all leap to their feet and cluster round me in the shadow of a bush. With a few brief words I outline the situation, give a few orders, suited to the nature of the terrain, about the platoon's position, order of march, and battle tactics, and then order them to mount up. The next moment, engines growl into life to our right and left, and from further back there is the whining and howling and clattering of the smaller combat vehicles. The tank brigade is ready to attack!

The platoons pull out on to the road; the company sets off in file. We have to get through a village first. The sound of fighting ahead of us, single shots, machine-gun fire, the dull thud of artillery fire. The tank commanders are still peering out from their turrets to get their bearings and snatch a last look at the terrain. Howitzers have taken up position and are firing in the direction of the sound of battle. There's a noise in our headphones; order from the chief over the radio:

'Battle stations!'

Heads are pulled back down into the tanks; hatches and covers are closed. The tanks are ready to strike up with their rumbling voices.

We have put the village behind us. The company turns off the road to the left, into open country, fording a stream and then fanning out. On a broad front and in loose formation, the tanks roll towards the enemy.

Looking out through the narrow slits of my turret, I see the tanks of my platoon travelling to right and left of me. I concentrate hard on the terrain ahead. There is still no sign from the enemy. Everything looks dead. But he has got to be there; in the scrubland, behind the hills, in the farmsteads among the clumps of trees. Then suddenly my crew and I hear a hard clanging blow that reverberates faintly through the whole tank. We've been hit by an anti-tank gun! It has probably caught one of our tracks. The other tanks push ahead at full speed. They have located the anti-tank gun and are engaging with it. This means that piece of artillery is no threat to us! So, out of the tank we jump! One man stays on the machine-gun to cover us, while the others repair the damaged track. We have got away with it again! Twenty centimetres (8 inches) further to the left, and this would have been our last attack.

Within a few minutes the damage is made good, and travelling at full speed we soon catch up with the lead tanks. We have still not fired off a shot in this skirmish; no worthwhile target has presented itself so far. But look there, 500 metres (547 yards) ahead, brown figures moving about – Polish infantry! They cannot stand up to the concentrated might of a tank assault, and a dense crowd of them take flight. That's a real gift for us! I yell out the direction and range to my gunner, and then bawl to my loader what type of shell to load. I order my driver through the intercom: 'Forward, faster, close in on the enemy!' I give the command over the radio to my platoon: 'To our left, ten o'clock, single tree, enemy infantry, destroy!'

Now our tanks open up, just a few shells at first among the densest groups to set the ball rolling! I observe the effect: fabulous! On the edge of the wood some try to reach cover. They are caught in our machine-gun fire. Knocked out! A small detachment has disappeared into a house, from whose windows and roof they are soon blasting fierce fire at us. One shell aimed at the roof and another at the front of the house, and the survivors are driven out into the open again. Our machine gun takes loving care of them. A few columns of earth fly up among our tanks. Aha! The Polish artillery wants to let us know they're still there. Let them shoot! We are shooting too – and we're hitting our target! A machine-gun nest, putting up stubborn resistance, is favoured with a shell. It falls silent. Guns, machine guns, shells, long bursts of machine-gun fire, and more shells!

The loader is sweating. He can hardly keep up with the gunner's rate of fire. Smoke pours out of the breech and blackens our sweating faces. Our shirts stick to our bodies. Altogether, the noise of our engine, the racket of our gun and machine gun, the heat, the fumes, and the inevitable battlefield excitement, combined with the enjoyment of our obvious successes, produce an atmosphere known only to the tank-man, one he is used to, and has grown to love for its wild, primitive quality. To all this you have to add the half-light of the crew compartment, the flashing of the little coloured lamp that enables me to communicate with our wireless operator, the constantly changing orders and reports to and from the company, and the unbroken radio contact with the tanks of my platoon.

Meanwhile, unperturbed, our trusty driver has been bumping our heavy crate across the terrain. Within his restricted vision, ahead of him he can see fields, meadows, ditches, streams, and the many obstacles that suddenly loom up in open country and confront him with rapid decisions. He bears the heavy responsibility of maintaining the vehicle; he sits in the hottest place, he has to steer the heavy tank, and change gear quickly and frequently; keep a steady eye on the instruments; with my help, find his way through the terrain; manoeuvre the tank into the right firing position to give the gunner the best line of fire; and, in addition, help me to identify targets.

The driver is always alert, always 'on his toes'! He drives in action; he drives on the march, day and night. The entire crew of the tank sleeps during marches, while the tank commander remains in the turret – and the driver drives! With us men in the crew compartment it is true that to be a successful fighting force requires inseparable comradeship in battle and faultless co-operation, where every crew member must utterly devote himself to operating the equipment entrusted to him, and carrying out the procedures acquired in rigorous training. But, even if he does not always do so directly, it is the driver who contributes most to our success.

It is now late afternoon. The hours seem to have flown by in the wild push forward, the chase and the shooting. It's a shame for our tireless tanks to be held up by a wide stream that forces them to take an involuntary rest while Pioneers locate crossing points or fords. The enemy has been routed or destroyed. Instead of the villages and farmsteads picturesquely scattered across the landscape, which had served as strong points for the Polish troops or hiding places for treacherous sharpshooters, there are now just bare chimneys jutting up from the smoking ruins of broken beams; sad testimony to the criminal insanity of the Poles.

Now, with the day's bloody work over, it is a matter of holding on to the conquered territory until our own infantry, left behind by the pace of the tank attack, can take over our watch.

Within a short while, parts of our division take up concealed positions facing the enemy, with a good field of fire. The main body of tanks stays back under cover and rests.

It is only now that the hatches and covers open, and the crew crawl out. We look at each other and laugh; because of our successful attacks and the achievements of the tanks, but also because of our appearance. We look like Negroes, blackened by the smoke and sprayed oil from the guns; only the whites of our eyes and the lighter channels traced across our cheeks by the trickling sweat shine out from the men's sooty faces. And yet their look beams with proud satisfaction. Pride at the glorious comradeship that embraces the whole crew; officers, NCOs and men. Pride above all at the invincible might of this young German weapon we love so much: our tanks.

By *Oberleutnant* Rudolf Behr

Baptism of Fire

I t is the 31st of August 1939. We are situated close to the eastern frontier. The regiment's objectives are clear: to break through the Polish border east of Preussenfeld, and reconnoitre north of the Notec River towards Naklo.

Not much is known about Poland. The commanders of the armoured reconnaissance unit have been briefed. Every man in the regiment knows what his task is, and the anticipated route of the regiment.

Now we are just waiting …

While a few last jobs are carried out on the vehicles, the men are kept fit and tough with drill and sport. They are all young people, facing their first combat mission. Not many of the officers have seen active service, either. The tension for all of us is at breaking point. Will we be sent into action at all? Will the Poles put up a fight? Will they be crazy enough to try to defy the might of the new German nation? But whatever happens, we are ready. We know that the whole German army is behind us, and that if needs be it will show that the years of peacetime work have not been in vain.

At last, late in the afternoon, we finally get our order to advance. Early tomorrow morning! From 04.45 hours, we will be using live ammunition. No quarter given from now on.

Instantly, the tension disappears. There is now only anticipation; an inner calm, confidence, even unaccustomed cheerfulness takes hold. The night is pitch black. The regiment lies in wait in a wood near Preussenfeld. Without lights and almost in silence, all sections manoeuvre themselves into position in the narrow corridor through the forest. The motorcycle troops, supported by the first wave of armoured reconnaissance cars and the heavy guns, will be the first to cross the frontier. They will take the customs post and thus create a gap through which the regiment can slip. During the night they are already moving right up to the border.

It is 04.30 hours, and the sky is getting lighter in the east. A thin mist covers the countryside. It is unlikely that anyone slept during the night. All thoughts are focused on what lies ahead. Punctually at 04.45 hours, the regiment is on the move. It all goes according to plan, as though on manoeuvres. Polish resistance is slight, and quickly overcome by motorcycle troops. There is nothing to hold the regiment up as it pushes on through the captured Polish position. The motorcycle troops remount and join the regiment again.

At the Polish customs post we see our first casualty, a wounded man being attended to by a medical orderly. The soldier looks at us, eyes wide with astonishment. He is badly wounded, and says nothing. It is as much as he can do to wave a hand, wishing us well as we push on with our long journey, in which he will take no further part.

Behind the customs post we turn off the highroad, to find our way to our objective, Naklo, using back roads and farm tracks. It is not our job to look for a fight. It would not be helpful for our reconnaissance work. But where we meet resistance, we sweep it aside with all the force at our disposal.

That is what happens in Dembovo, for example. Having skirted round roadblocks and obstacles to penetrate 40 kilometres (25 miles) into Polish territory, our advance guard runs into resistance. We must get through. We go into action for the first time. The Poles holding the village are not intimidated by the armoured reconnaissance cars that are supposed to mop up the place. Once again, the motorcycle troops move in to the attack, with support provided by our heavy guns.

I am standing with the commanding officer by the side of the road. The first ricochets whistle overhead. The commanding officer smiles; he is a veteran of the Great War. Then he says quietly, lost in thought: 'There you go again, my little birdies.'

In precise stages, the motorcycle troops advance to the edge of the village, and then push further in towards the centre. Reconnaissance cars use their guns to eliminate a Polish machine-gun nest in the church tower. After half an hour the unit reports that they have taken the village. A formation of Polish cycle troops has been driven out; the way is clear.

A reconnaissance unit reports that there is no serious resistance in Naklo, and no roadblock on the west side of the town. The commanding officer has only one order for his regiment: 'I'll see you in Naklo.'

We reach the town without incident. There is not a Pole in sight. One or two civilians slip away into their houses. We are standing in the market square. All exits have been closed. The Poles are positioned south of the Notec, preventing access to the bridges. But they won't be getting across, either. We will blow up the bridges.

Then shots rip through the streets. Instantly, all hell breaks loose. From every window, door, skylight and cellar opening there are flickers and flashes, clattering and cracking as we come under machine-gun and rifle fire. Hand grenades explode near our vehicles.

We are boxed in. The Poles are invisible, but we are sitting ducks out on the street. Next to the railway crossing by the northern exit from the town there is a clear space. Thanks to some storage sheds, we have some cover from the houses in the town. Here at least we are not threatened from the rear, and we can pull our vehicles clear of enemy fire. There is a hellish din in the town. The armoured reconnaissance cars, shooting with all the firepower they've got and rotating their turrets in every direction, provide cover for the unarmoured part of our column. Our anti-tank guns and light artillery have been unhitched and are pouring direct fire into the houses. Fires are burning in a number of places. It does not take our men long to develop an excellent technique; one shell aimed low at the corner of the house, one above it in the middle of the building, and one into the roof. That's enough to bring the whole Polish construction clattering down…

In this way, we manage to escape the worst. The regiment assembles at the northern exit from the town, and the pioneers start to clear away the tree-trunk roadblock. But we cannot rest here for long, either. With our small detachment we cannot hope to clean up a town like Naklo. The people we are fighting here are not the Polish military. Civilians and soldiers out of uniform are engaging in nasty, criminal warfare.

It is already dark when we leave this inhospitable town. Behind us the darkening sky is lit up by the red glow of our first day of war.

By *Rittmeister* Freiherrn von Esebeck

Tanks Break into the Corridor

I n the last glimmer of twilight on 1 September 1939, we crowd round the loudspeaker on the commanding officer's vehicle and listen to a repeat broadcast of the speech made by the Führer that afternoon. It is by his orders that we stand here, on ancient German soil, in the [Danzig] Corridor, a few miles west of the Brda River, whose course is indicated by a dark fringe of trees in the east. Burning villages and towns light up the horizon all around like torches. They have partly been fired by the fleeing Poles, and partly set alight by German tracer fire in the early fighting.

Things have quietened down now in the large field where our detachment has halted after achieving its first objectives. From the early afternoon onwards, endless columns of motorized troops, artillery, motorized machine-gun battalions, even echelon and medical units had been trundling towards the Brda, giving us a vivid idea of the irresistible power of our army. After skirmishes involving the advance guard, it was here on the Brda that German troops first ran into serious resistance. As far as we know, a group from our 1st Regiment is engaged in securing a crossing-point over the river.

We are still listening to the Führer's voice and his message of deep seriousness and implacable determination, when the regiment is alerted by the familiar cry: 'Action stations! Company leaders to commanding officer!'

The crews go to their vehicles. Orders are buzzing around in the darkness. For a while there is busy activity and purposeful movement everywhere. The company commanders have collected their maps and message pads from their map cases and are hurrying towards the command post. After a few minutes everything is in place.

Flashlights are switched on, and we find the commanding officer in consultation with the adjutant. What we hear makes our pulses race with anticipation. At last a job for us to do, after being forced to spend the entire morning almost without action, bringing up the rear behind other detachments! We are told that the 1st Regiment has opened up the Brda section and secured a crossing for the German advance. Our 2nd Regiment's task is to link up with the 1st, cross the Brda and, proceeding via Pruszcz, to secure the important lake narrows east of the Brda near Sviakatova and Jania-Goria for the advance of the regiment.

While the orders are still being issued, engines are already warming up here and there. The last preparations for the start are being made. In the meantime, the darkness is total; it looks as though it will be a clear starlit night.

The company commanders return to their units. I do not have far to go. The regiment's HQ vehicles, which are under my command as intelligence officer and head of the HQ Company staff, are close at hand. Their crews are already in position and waiting for me. I summarize the detachment's position and objective.

Shortly before we set off, the driver of an armoured car from the regiment's reconnaissance platoon returns to me to report. Under the command of a platoon sergeant, he had been sent out towards Lubnów, where, together with sections of our neighbouring regiment, he had become involved in heavy fighting. He gives a brief report on the course of the battle, in which among other things three Polish anti-tank guns had been destroyed. The platoon commander, whose own tank had also been damaged, is still trying to rescue one of his vehicles. A driver has been killed, and a rifleman wounded in the arm – he has already been evacuated. Today has seen our first brush with death. I briefly report what I have just heard to the commanding officer, and the regiment gets under way, with lights switched off, towards the Brda.

We make only fitful progress. A number of columns are creeping forward during the night on the narrow road, often several side by side. As soon as I am given permission to break radio silence, I contact the reconnaissance platoon leader, asking him for his position, and giving him instructions. Progress gets slower all the time, but the way is cleared for us by repeated shouts of 'Let the tanks through!' At times the commanding officer walks ahead of his vehicle, waving aside vehicles causing obstructions and opening the path for us.

Towards midnight, just west of the Brda, we finally catch up with the tail end of the reconnaissance platoon. We reach the bridge at Sokolc-Kuznica. It is eerily illuminated by the distant glow of burning farmsteads. Our vehicles rumble across the planks. The oily, sluggish river slides away beneath us. Beyond the river there is a climb through wooded terrain, over churned-up earth. Passing bogged-down vehicles, we reach a paved highway, and we finally see our road clear ahead. At a brisk pace the armoured regiment races through the night behind the faster armoured reconnaissance vehicles of the intelligence unit. Finally halting at about 03.00 hours, the main body of the regiment is ordered to close up. The commanding officer takes his adjutant and me back with him in his command car to the front, to make contact with the commander of the reconnaissance platoon. He finds him at the eastern approach to Gora. A few reconnaissance troops push forward on the main routes to the east in order to spy out the lie of the land. In the process they shoot up a truck with Polish soldiers, and blow up an important rail link.

At first light, the reconnaissance platoon moves on towards the Vistula sector, and a reinforced tank regiment takes over the defence of the lake sector. The command post stays in the Sviekatovo area. The artillery battery assigned to us has positioned itself nearby and is laying down intermittent fire on the roads and tracks running down from the north, on the eastern side of the railway line. The shells land with a dull thud, producing no echo in the damp misty morning.

I am hanging half out of the car, dosing gently after the exhausting night, but still wearing my headphones, when suddenly I hear a strange sound in the headset. It is faint and indistinct, but it sounds like a frenzied outbreak of shooting. Startled, I hear a forceful expletive coming through my headphones – one that is not to be found in the wireless operator's manual. But the required explanation follows immediately, in the tones of 5 Company's leader, 'Polish attack, strength unknown, from north, north-west and west!' I shout this out to the commanding officer, who immediately reaches for the handset, and orders me to radio 6 Company, providing cover out on the right flank of 5 Company, to lend support. However, with the mist getting thicker all the time, neither 6 Company nor the battery assigned to it has any chance of joining in the battle. In any case, half an hour later there is a further report, to the effect that the attempted Polish breakthrough has been beaten off with heavy enemy losses. From now on, at short intervals, the Poles mount many further attempts to break out to the south through the increasingly menacing pincer grip we have on them.

By about 09.00 hours, things are quiet again. The regimental staff arrives with the 3rd Regiment. We are pulled out of our sector and take up a new position on the flat ground on top of the rise running along the road from Jania-Gora to Stazki. We spend the day beating back ever-renewed Polish attempts to break through to the south. At 15.00 hours the 3rd Regiment goes over to the attack, destroying numerous enemy columns and forcing the enemy back towards the north. An hour later we receive a radio command from the brigade, which is expecting a Polish tank attack. With feverish haste the regiment takes up firing positions around Jania-Gora, its guns pointing north. However, the attack fails to materialize. Meanwhile, 5 Company is pulled out of the defensive line and, reinforced with an 8 Company tank, directed towards Tuszyny to protect the right flank of the regiment. On the road just in front of the town, it meets and destroys a fairly strong enemy force equipped with anti-tank weapons.

Our 6 Company, moving up behind the 3rd Regiment, advances at about 17.00 hours on the burning town of Sviekatovo, putting two anti-tank guns out of action and taking a number of prisoners. I myself do not see very much of this exciting action because as intelligence officer I am confined to the commanding officer's car. I can hear the increasing noise of battle and reports of gains made by the different companies, and at this moment I long to be an ordinary trooper in a front-line tank.

A short while later, the radio reports that 5 Company is advancing further northwards and that it has knocked out two anti-tank guns. Their progress allows us to recover our own battle-damaged tanks from the firing line and relieve a platoon of 4 Company deployed there. They have used up all their ammunition, and for a while they faced the enemy without firepower. The conduct of the leader of 5 Company makes a particularly deep impression on us. When the attack is beginning to falter under the first harsh, unaccustomed impact of battle, he jumps out of his tank under enemy fire and passes on his orders to the platoon commanders personally, before taking his place at the head of the company and propelling his men forward by the sheer force of his determined example.

In the meantime, 8 Company has also been drawn into the battle, thus extending the attacking front of 5 Company to the left. It is about 18.30 hours and already getting dark as orders from the regiment send the rest of the detachment, too, into the attack against Tuszyny. Just an hour later, the left wing of 6 Company, placed alongside the railway line, penetrates the west flank of the enemy forces confronting 5 Company. The lethal firepower of our now reunited regiment once more destroys enemy machine guns and anti-tank weapons.

The landscape is broad and flat, with burning villages standing out ever more clearly in the twilight as bright marker points for us. The horizon before us is dissected by a long dark line. It is the heavily defended Tuszyny railway embankment. From that quarter the attacking companies are met with fierce fire from weapons of every calibre, to which we respond with every barrel blazing. I take a radio message from the regiment ordering us to suspend the attack, secure positions on both sides of Tuszyny, and link up to our left with the 3rd Regiment. Meanwhile, night has descended completely. We see more and more disarmed Poles flooding singly and in groups towards the rear – for me the first visible evidence of the success of our attack. Enemy dead lie scattered all around. The burning town of Tuszyny makes the surrounding countryside as light as day.

Using radio and signal pistols the companies are withdrawn from the railway embankment and allocated to the sectors they are to hold for the night. The adjutant's tank rattles ceaselessly from one company to the other, carrying orders and instructions from the commanding officer. After two hours, the dispositions are essentially complete, but our position remains somewhat uncomfortable. Our right flank is completely exposed, and on our left flank, although we have made contact, the distance involved makes it impossible to link up. Not far ahead of us is the fortified embankment. We cannot count on any reinforcements by other divisional troops.

It is during this night that most of us young soldiers begin to grasp what war is really about. The groaning of wounded Polish soldiers fills the darkness around. Somewhere in this darkness lurks an enemy whose intentions are unknown to us, but who in his desperation seems capable of anything. Locked in the sheds of burning farms, the cattle bellow helplessly. German artillery shells howl overhead. Here we lie with our senses alert and tense, waiting for the hours to come.

The regiment radios through to announce the imminent arrival of fuel tankers and field kitchens. What is more, there is the prospect of a company being sent to reinforce our holding operation.

After we have appeased the first pangs of nagging hunger with our hard rations and apples from the gardens of burning villages, the promised and eagerly awaited vehicles arrive. Food has seldom tasted better to us than the field kitchen's aromatic bacon and peas, and rarely more fully deserved. No less welcome is the fuel for our vehicles; an almost exhausted commodity after the day's many attacks. The officer from the echelon formation tells that during the fighting around Jania-Gora and Sviekato we had at times been completely cut off from the division, because the Poles had temporarily succeeded in breaking through along the Brda at Sokolc-Kuznica. As he speaks Polish, he interrogates a few prisoners who all concur that a Polish attack is planned for dawn, supported by light tanks.

Somewhat later the promised reinforcements arrive. It is 4 Company, who remain in the vicinity of the regimental HQ as a reserve against possible Polish attacks. At dawn we pick up numerous wounded Poles. They make a truly demoralized impression and confirm that next to the German planes it is the tanks that have caused them most distress. To sharpen their appetite for the assault, they had actually been persuaded by their officers that the German tanks were made of cardboard and could be fought with bayonets!

Daylight comes without the expected attack. Isolated Polish patrols are driven off by machine-gun fire. Around 08.00 hours the regiment pulls us out of our previous sector and sent in as the third wave of the assault on Ostovo…

By the evening of the following day the advanced guard of German troops is outside Grudziadz. We have completed the encirclement of the Polish armies in the Corridor. Next day we ourselves see the towers of Grudziadz looming above the silver ribbon of the Vistula.

Two days later we have the privilege of welcoming the Führer, visiting his troops in Grupa Dolna, the old German training round of Gruppe.

The Corridor is German again!

By *Oberleutnant* Lossen

I Have Always Had Faith in the Tanks!

O ur tanks rolled along, penetrating ever further into Polish territory, on the heels of an enemy fleeing in panic. The motorized infantry mopped up the remnants of large cavalry forces dispersed over the Tuchola Heath and the Brda woods. By the evening of the third day, our tanks had reached the stretch of the Vistula between Gniev and Culm, achieving their objective in an extremely short time. The tank men had a chance to check over their vehicles to get ready for the next advance. After being on the move for three days, this was the first opportunity to enjoy a night's sleep. Until now, the watchword had been 'Keep pushing on, and don't let the enemy out of your sight!'

We had halted with our corps headquarters staff in Lubievo, on the eastern side of the Brda woods. When we arrived, the village seemed completely dead, but by the next morning the peasants were swarming in from the woods, their carts groaning with household goods, to settle back into their cottages again. During this time the Führer was visiting his troops at the front. With great interest, we followed the route taken by Führer Headquarters. With a mixture of anxiety and confidence, we all hoped it was true that the Führer intended to pay a visit to his 'men in black', too. Excited expectation gave way to celebration when finally, on the morning of 6 September, the report was confirmed: 'The Führer is coming to see us today!'

We had orders to move off at 10.00 hours. Our general was due to present his army corps to the Führer at 14.00 hours. We loaded up in a

25

feverish hurry, and left Lubievo punctually, heading for Plevno. The sun smiled upon us: we had really lovely 'Hitler weather'. There was not the smallest cloud in the brilliant blue sky.

Throwing up dense clouds of dust behind us, we made our way over the poor Polish country roads. When we arrived, a meal was handed out. It was a feast: rice and meat stew.

However, our surroundings did not look exactly festive. We stopped just outside Plevno at a crossroads on the main road from Tuchola to Sviecie, the chief route for the Polish retreat across the Tuchola Heath. It was here that our tanks had scored a resounding success in thwarting the attempts of the Polish Army in the Corridor to link up with their army of the Vistula. The road presented the most powerful testimony to that wild flight from our 'dummy tanks'. The bodies of dead Poles lay piled up among a chaotic litter of baggage wagons, motor vehicles and numerous guns, whose teams of horses lay dead in their harnesses. Heaps of munitions lay next to countless hurriedly discarded rifles, bayonets, gasmasks and all kinds of other equipment. It was a sombre, doom-laden sight. Perhaps it was here at this spot that the Führer recalled the quotation he was later to use in his speech after the overthrow of Poland:

'Mit Mann und Ross und Wagenhat
sie der Herr geschlagen ... '
[Man and horse and wagon
The Lord smote them all ...]

At last, dispatch riders announce the approach of the Führer's column. A few front-line infantry companies have joined us in the meantime, and are drawn up in formation. Eagerly anticipating the Führer's arrival, we too fall in, our eyes fixed on the grey stretch of road leading to Tuchola. In front of us stands our general, Guderian, with his staff officers. Then the advance car appears bearing its yellow standard: *the Führer has arrived!* On our left we can already hear the shouts of 'Heil!' from our infantry comrades.

Immediately afterwards the Führer's car stops at the crossroads. General Guderian presents his Panzer corps to him, and reports on the great success of this young branch of the service.

Now our Supreme Commander is stepping out of his car and shaking his tank general's hand with the words: 'My dear General, what a magnificent achievement by you and your troops! I thank you and your soldiers! You know that *I have always had faith in the tanks!*

Meanwhile, we are pressing in ever closer to the Führer – the highest soldier of our nation – and cutting his car off from the rest of the column. We, who are mostly from the Ostmark [annexed Austria], are especially thrilled to be so close to the Führer. For many of us, in fact, it is the first time in our lives that we have had a chance to salute the Führer. We are delighted beyond words to stand face to face with him as soldiers after proving ourselves for the first time in battle. Our hearts swell in his presence – in the presence of the liberator of the Ostmark, the Sudetenland, Bohemia and Moravia, the Memel lands, Danzig, and now of the former Polish Corridor. But his look is stern, and we can read in his countenance the inexorable, iron will to see this struggle to win worldwide recognition for the Greater German Reich through to its final objective.

By now, the Führer has greeted the general staff officers of our Panzer corps. Not far from him we see Major-General Keitel and SS Lieutenant-General Schaub.

Soon the Führer is getting back into his car and trying to address us soldiers; he is prevented for a few minutes by our cheers. But when he raises his hand, there is total silence, and he speaks: 'Soldiers! You have put the Berliners' minds at rest – the Poles won't get to Berlin, after all. But what has been won at the cost of German blood will stay forever German. Sieg Heil, soldiers!'

With a roar we thank the Führer for his words. Our men capture every moment of this unique experience on countless cameras. General Guderian joins the Führer in his car for the visit to the tank regiments on the Vistula that is to follow. Accompanied by our shouts of 'Heil', the Führer takes his leave of us. We are left only with the memory of these unforgettable minutes, and the certainty that Adolf Hitler will pass our way again on his return journey ...

From nearby Plevno, women appeared with their children to wait with us for the return of the Führer. They have picked the last flowers from their gardens and took up positions standing at the roadside, which suddenly looks colourful and reminiscent of springtime. These ethnic Germans, having gone into hiding from the bestial brutality of murderous gangs of Poles, have now escaped a terrible fate. Hearing our penetrating cheers from a distance, they had been tempted out of their hiding places. And then, when they recognized that it was the Führer's column driving past, they were blessed with the certainty that they could once more set foot upon the soil of their native land as free, upright people. Their intense joy had rendered them all completely silent.

And in the late afternoon we share with them the sight of the Führer returning from his visit to the front, which has taken him in a large triangular route from Plevno via Sviecie and along the Vistula levels to Michale, opposite Grudziadz. Girls and mothers from Plevno cover the Führer with flowers. Many of the women are quietly sobbing with happiness. The Führer holds out his hand to many of them.

The echo of our 'Sieg Heils' is still hanging in the air, the women and girls are still staring as though spell-bound at the spot where the Führer had just stood in front of them, and the children are still holding up their flowers – long, long after the Führer has driven on …

But we have enshrined this picture in our hearts, and it will go with us into future battles.

By *Unteroffizier* Pries

Hedgehog

– all-round defence

We have been pushing the Poles back for four days now. Ahead of us, a tank division is engaged in a fight with this tough enemy. The Poles have committed all their available reserves to try to halt our deep advance into their territory. About midday we are ordered to the front. The situation is urgent. Our tank division is sent in on the left of the division ahead of us. The tank regiments are being thrown into combat just in the order in which they appear on the battlefield.

Everyone realizes the decisive significance of this moment. The finest hour has come for our tanks – a deep thrust into the heart of Poland. The enemy must be allowed no rest, we must go on fighting, pushing on with all possible speed.

Thus committed, the regiment moves out of the main column to join the battle. Our regimental commander leads from the front, followed by 1 and 2 Detachments, their leaders heading up their units.

The attack meets no opposition. Only 2 Detachment radios through a report that its company out on the left flank has run into some resistance, at the edge of a forest. The company attacks immediately, driving its opponent into the forest, and so averting the threat to our flank.

The regimental staff are the first to reach our immediate objective. The next task is to block an important crossroads 10 kilometres (6.5 miles) to the north. I ask my commander's permission to press on in that direction with my light platoon, and receive the corresponding orders from him. A short while later he tells me that a plane has spotted Polish tanks ahead of us. I radio back: 'Will attack Polish tanks.'

We drive on northwards. Passing two villages, we reach the road. But there is not a Polish tank in sight. The pilot no doubt mistook a few German vehicles for Polish ones. Now we use the road to advance quickly, two tanks always giving us fire cover to either side. A small village lies ahead of us, eerily silent. Perhaps it harbours a treacherous enemy. We stop just outside it – one burst of fire from our machine gun ... but nothing stirs, although a few of the lightly built houses immediately burst into flames. So we reach the next small town without enemy contact. A German-speaking Polish girl tells us that there are no more Poles around. They had murdered her employer, the German proprietor of a brickyard. His wife had fled with the children. While we are interrogating her, tanks are reconnoitring towards the east, north and west. We report to the regiment: 'Crossroads held, clear of enemy.'

At this moment the tank scouting to the west begins firing. Its target is an enemy car that races across the roadside ditch after the first round, and gets stuck in a field. A man crawls out sideways and escapes. We cannot investigate further for the moment, because our tank is firing again. This time it is shooting at a bicycle-mounted Polish field-telephone unit. The Poles make off at top speed, abandoning telephones and bikes. We are just about to take a look at this meagre booty, when a three-man enemy bicycle reconnaissance unit appears from the east. I take a shot at one of them with my pistol. Completely taken aback, they all disappear into the ditch, and get away under cover of the rapidly increasing darkness, leaving their bicycles and equipment behind. We are beginning to feel a bit uncomfortable out here with our few tanks, 10 kilometres (6.5 miles) ahead of the regiment. We take up all-round defence by placing our tanks with hulls touching, so that each one covers a different sector of the compass. We remove the covers from the headlamps so that we can light up the ground in front of us if need be. Our caution is immediately rewarded.

From the east, we suddenly hear the sound of an engine. We see a Polish truck heading towards us. He has his lights on, as it is now really dark. At 25 metres (27 yards) we blind him with our headlights, and as he is braking our first machine-gun burst hits the driver. A man jumps out, and we can see other Poles on the lorry. I loose off a shell from my gun at the vehicle; the fuel tank explodes, and a tall jet of flame shoots up. Instantly, the truck is on fire, and we hear the cries of its burning occupants, but we cannot help them because we are now under a veritable hail of explosive materials. There must have been masses of explosives and ammunition on the lorry, now blown sky-high. It gets so hot that we have to move our 'armoured hedgehog' 20 metres (21 yards) further back.

The fire, accompanied by constant detonations, lasts about two hours. The whole area is as bright as day. We report to the regiment, which promises to send us a relief force. But it takes so long to arrive that I have no choice but to decide to stay on the spot until dawn. So that is how we spend the night. One man keeps watch in every tank while the others sleep. We change the watch every two hours.

At first light we examine our booty. In the burnt truck we find a number of machine guns and rifles, and the remains of a large store of ammunition. The trailer had carried petrol cans. We have the impression that this unit had been tasked with bridge demolition. The Poles had obviously only expected an advance from the west, and completely failed to notice the danger from the south. In the car we had previously destroyed, we found the bodies of a paymaster complete with cashbox, together with his driver. About 06.00 hours we are relieved by sections of a reconnaissance unit, and proceed straight to the regiment, which is just moving forward on its next advance.

By *Oberleutnant* Guderian

[Oberleutnant Heinz Günther Guderian was Generaloberst Heinz Guderian's son.]

A Prisoner for Ten Minutes

O n the second day of our advance into the [Danzig] Corridor, our platoon receives orders to reconnoitre the strip of land alongside a railway embankment. We are in the middle of the Tuchola Heath. The misty weather gives way to rain. Visibility is limited. My armoured car is held up by a few obstacles in the terrain. It does not take long for me to lose contact with the man ahead. Now foraging on my own account, criss-crossing the terrain, I soon encounter 4 Platoon, caught up in a fire fight behind the village of Klonovo.

Without hesitating, I take up my position and throw in everything my good old machine guns can deliver. The result is that shortly afterwards two horses appear, leaping forward wildly with an anti-tank gun in tow. But what is this? In the ditch ahead of me I see two black-clad figures. Those are our people! Now I notice that one car has been badly hit. The two men in front of me just managed to escape. At lightning speed they disappear into the turret of the heavy vehicle, which is still capable of movement.

A quick about-turn, to retreat through an abandoned village! But this village is not nearly as deserted as it looks from the outside. There is an immediate banging and crashing against the armour. With a jerk, the car stops; it has lost a wheel. The next second, my driver slumps noiselessly sideways over the gear-stick. I think: 'the enemy is using special ammunition'. A blow to my left arm shocks me, but I can still move it. I try in vain to help my comrade who has been hit.

Rifle-butt blows are raining down on the armour! 'Open up!', I hear somebody shouting outside in Polish. A confusion of voices tells me that a number of the enemy are gathered around my vehicle. Is this the end? After a moment's thought I raise the turret roof. Instantly, I find a Polish mug grinning at me. I am dragged to the nearest farmyard, lie still and act as though dead.

When I look up again after 10 minutes, I cannot believe my eyes! The man the Poles had detailed to guard me has disappeared. There is nothing to be seen in the farmyard except poultry and army horses. I make a decision and carry it out immediately. I take off over fences and hedges as fast as I can go. Another few hundred metres and I find myself in a potato field. Throw yourself down and lie still! After less than five minutes, it is as though all hell has broken loose. Our artillery is trained on the village I have just left. A Polish patrol notices me as it passes, but leaves me unscathed.

Even the approach of night does not bring the chance of escape I had hoped for. The glow of the burning villages, together with the moonlight and the Polish flares, illuminate the landscape with a fantastic, unreal light. Machine-gun fire ranges across the terrain to cover the Polish infantry's retreat. A whole night – endless – of dreadful uncertainty – and cold!

The sun's first rays bring new hope. It is 3 September – a Sunday.

Over there, the distant drone of an engine! The familiar-sounding noise gets closer all the time. It must be a German vehicle. The sound could not have been more welcome to me if it had been the ringing of the church bells at home. Now I must concentrate all my strength. I need to drag myself as far as the road. Two armoured cars are in sight, sent out on a reconnaissance mission. Thank God, the crews recognize me as a German soldier. So I am saved.

One of the reconnaissance cars is taking me back to our infantry lines. As we drive off, I take a last look at my shot-up armoured car, and think of my good comrade, hit by a fatal bullet. How does the battle-song of the men in black go? [*der Panzerlied*]

'ruft uns das Schicksal ab,
dann ist unser Panzer ein ehernes Grab!'
[If we are called away by fate,
then our tank is an iron grave!]

By *Unteroffizier* Helmut Baier

An Unforgettable Night

Eight days in action without a break! Day and night, night and day on reconnaissance. The men are tired, drivers cannot keep their eyes open, our faces are covered in grime, and in the hot September weather we are constantly tormented by thirst.

It is 8 September 1939 when we – a reconnaissance unit reinforced with motorcycle troops – return to our detachment around 15.30 hours after successfully completing our mission. I report to my commander; he does not want to hear from me at all, but greets me with the words: 'How soon can you go out again?' I quickly calculate the time needed to eat and to replace fuel and ammunition, and reply: 'In 30 minutes, Colonel!'

I am briefed about my new mission on the spot. Our motorcycle company, reinforced with armoured cars, has just reported the complete destruction of two horse-drawn Polish gun batteries. I am ordered to join this unit, reconnoitring the terrain as I go.

Back to the reconnaissance troop immediately! Hurried orders are issued. For a moment my men are disappointed that they will not be enjoying a well-earned rest. But they are soon back 'on their toes', stimulated by the prospect of new action, and after a 30-minute pause for eating, drinking and refuelling, we head out into no-man's-land again.

We arrive at a village, drive slowly round it, probing, moving slowly in: nothing to be seen. We get through the village, and suddenly come across our 3 Company. The sight that greets us here is incredible: horses shot to pieces, shattered guns and ammunition trucks, among them dead and wounded Poles, medical orderlies treating and transporting the wounded. It is a picture that immediately conveys to us the meaning of the word 'war'. But there is no time for reflection, because the unit's commanding officer is already giving me my new orders, just received over the radio from the detachment. I am to push through to the next big river and establish whether or not a bridge there, very important for our advance, is being held by the enemy, and report on its condition.

I glance at my men, who are once again overcome by fatigue and are sleeping in every kind of posture on or near their vehicles. My reconnaissance unit has been supplemented by two motorcycle groups, a mortar troop and an armoured car. At any rate, I have now assembled a considerable fighting force! I quickly take my leave of my comrades, who shake my hand and wish me luck, and then, in staggered formation, my reconnaissance unit sets off along Polish tracks towards the river.

It is 17.00 hours. A glance at the map tells me that I have 25 kilometres (16 miles) to cover. Twenty-five kilometres through completely unknown enemy territory, crossed by hedgerows, copses and treacherous villages! We might stumble upon the enemy at any moment. So my patrol inches carefully forward, watching out anxiously wherever there is cover. The minutes pass in intense concentration.

A village looms up in front of us. Small, dirty thatched houses, in a state of semi-collapse, with enormous barns next to them. Preceded by the motorcyclists, we comb through the village. We find no Polish soldiers. But we do discover a few refugees, whom we question about the whereabouts of the enemy, using sign language and the few words of 'Polish' we have picked up. But they know nothing, either; they are just glad to be left alone.

Darkness has gradually set in. What to do? I decide to spend the night some way beyond the village, to make an early start and reach my objective by daybreak. This tricky terrain is impossible to reconnoitre at night. But I must give my men at least a few hours of sleep, so that they will be fresh tomorrow for the most difficult part of our task.

A farmstead about 200 metres (218 yards) from the village seems to me the most suitable place to spend the night, drawn up in all-round defence. I post a group of motorcyclists about 100 metres (109 yards) further forward to provide cover by the road. I also place an armoured car with its gun trained on the entrance to the village, and the two other cars under cover behind a large barn. The rest of my group stay in the middle of the position with their weapons and vehicles.

I myself take over standing guard, and allocate every man his arcs of fire. I radio my decision through to the detachment. Then I make my rounds from sentry to sentry.

Hours pass. Nothing happens. The wide landscape seems to be sleeping peacefully.

Suddenly one of the sentries draws my attention to a dull sound in the distance; it sounds like metal-shod wheels rumbling over a poor quality, gravel-coated road.

At first I think it is the refugees we stopped a few hours earlier, who have now resumed their restless wanderings during the night. But the suspicious noise becomes louder and louder, closer and closer. To be on the safe side, I rouse my unit. They instantly take up their stand-to positions. I myself go over to the armoured car covering the entrance to the village. I have hardly got to it when the sentry there switches on the headlights, and in the bright beam penetrating the darkness we clearly make out a column of Polish troops, marching in closed ranks and pouring out of the village. Without hesitating, the sentry empties two volleys from his machine gun into the solid mass. We hear the loud cries of the wounded, and the next moment the Poles have set fire to two barns, lighting up the landscape as bright as day.

My whole unit has now opened fire. The mortar crew drop their bombs in the midst of the enemy column, who break up in panic, only to present a target for our machine guns in the glare of the burning buildings. Their losses must be enormous.

But the Poles soon recover from the shock, and open fire in their turn. They have obviously located our position from the flashes of our guns, and are peppering our farmstead with machine-gun fire. Thank goodness, in their excitement they do not notice that they are aiming much too high, so that the shots meant for us pass high above our heads. I have ordered my men to cease firing. The Poles fall silent too, a rather eerie silence after that hellish racket. Then, to our right, way off on our flank, a Polish machine gun starts to hammer. Simultaneously, another enemy machine gun begins firing into our left flank. They are trying to pin us down! We give as good as we get. But now the Polish fire is more accurate.

We suffer our first casualty. 'Private M., wound to the chin!', someone shouts out to me. Somebody else asks: 'Where is Corporal W.?' We soon find him lying in the road dead with two shots to the head, but we cannot recover the body yet, because the Poles are raining fire on us.

The barns that were burning like torches earlier have now collapsed into a red glowing mass. But another house is going up in flames. Once more the landscape is lit up as bright as day, and our every movement attracts murderous fire.

Suddenly there is a massive detonation – a bang that makes us think it's all over with us. 'God, they're using artillery on us! Direct fire – from 300 metres (330 yards)!'

It is high time to clear out of here. From where I placed him to cover our left flank, with a few short bursts our machine gunner has succeeded in putting out of action the enemy machine gun that was causing us the most trouble. As it is no longer firing, I seize the moment to withdraw the whole reconnaissance unit. My vehicles open up a furious barrage of fire. Meanwhile, the motorcycle troops drive out from the cover of the buildings. I had told them to assemble by my covering machine gun. To left and right the artillery shells are crashing down. All hell has broken loose! The driver of an armoured car drives it into a deep ditch. Bring up my eight-wheel armoured car! Pull him out again! The others are shooting with everything they've got. There is mad confusion. The vehicle won't budge. Decision: blow it up!

Then comes another blow. The logistics echelon vehicle carrying our fuel is suspended over the ditch. Under fierce machine-gun fire, one man courageously drags over a towline and attaches it to my eight-wheeled vehicle. It slowly pulls away – and with a jolt, the wretched car is free! The driver puts his foot down and roars off to the rear. I cover the retreat of the unit with my eight-wheeler.

Back with my troop, I order the motorcyclists to push their machines to cut out engine noise, and the armoured vehicles to engage their lowest gear and travel at reduced speed only. I myself walk on ahead to look for a path anywhere in the terrain where we can leave the road and strike off into the scrub. Meanwhile, the Poles continue to hit the farmstead with undiminished artillery and machine-gun fire. Flames are pouring out of the roof. They have not noticed our retreat. We are lucky to have escaped from that hell, even though it is with heavy hearts that we leave behind our dead comrade and one of our cars.

Looking for a place of safety, after 3 kilometres (2 miles) we finally hit upon a track leading away from the road and into the fields. I go scouting ahead and find that about 500 metres (547 yards) further ahead it enters a small wood that seems to me a suitable hiding place. The vehicles are camouflaged, defensive positions taken up, and then we wait again. It is completely quiet. The Poles have stopped shooting. By now they have obviously discovered that the juicy morsel has escaped them. Tense in every nerve, we listen out for sounds in the quiet night. Two riderless horses gallop past very close to us. A glance at my watch: it's only 23.30 hours! And we thought the dawn was due any minute.

From our hiding place we are now privileged to view a scene that few soldiers will ever see in such proximity to the enemy. Hour after hour one Polish troop unit after another passes us on the road heading east: artillery, logistic support, cavalry, infantry, and company after company – endless columns. For six hours, until daybreak. A defeated army.

They travelled across 'our' bridge, the one we were sent to reconnoitre. So my mission was completed, and I was able to report the enemy's movements by radio back to the detachment for hours on end. It was a night we will never forget!

By *Oberleutnant* **von Bünau**

A Special Mission for our General

O n 7 September we cross the Polish border from East Prussia for the second time. On the extreme left wing of the German forces, our job is to push forward past Grajevo and reconnoitre towards the River Narev at Lomza. We fail to take Grajevo. The motorcycle squadron suffers heavy losses in its attack on a heavily fortified Polish position. None the less, we must go on and reconnoitre. So we have to leave Grajevo to the following troops. Only by deploying all of our armoured reconnaissance cars do we succeed in pulling the motorcycle troops out of the attack. We lose one car, and almost all the others return with flat tyres. They have been torn to ribbons by machine-gun fire.

There is nothing for it. The division is waiting for the results of our recce. We have already lost half a day. Without hesitation, the commander decides to press on. In tight formation, we skirt round Grajevo.

Now we find ourselves advancing once again into the wide open Polish landscape. Our objective for today is the Narev. We leave kilometre after kilometre of dusty Polish country paths behind us. We scatter a Polish cavalry squadron. We must make up for lost time. Then a new order reaches us: to take the bridge over the Narev at Vizna and to try to open up the strongpoint of Lomza by a surprise attack from the rear. But things do not always go according to plan. Right under our noses, the bridge is blown sky high. On the far side of the wide, marshy Narev valley, there are Polish defensive bunkers. We are now forced to stand idly by – a terrible experience for reconnaissance people – until the division has secured the crossing. But the way is now clear, and we are about to embark on the finest mission we will experience in Poland.

We have been travelling for about an hour. During that time, we have not seen any of our troops. The infantry regiment that spearheaded the Narev crossing operation must be somewhere ahead of us. I am driving out in front with the detachment commander to establish contact with this advance regiment. Our objective is to scout from the south towards Lomza, which is still putting up a tough fight.

Then, by the roadside, we come across our own General Guderian with a radio transmitter and armed only with a pistol, completely alone! For a moment the general reviews the situation. 'Show me your map.' On my map-board I always have my map folded so that it displays the area we might cover in a good day's march. 'No, no,' says the general, 'unfold the whole map.' Then, pointing at the map, now hanging down to the ground: 'Can you see the bridge over the Bug down there? That's the one I've got to have – by early tomorrow morning.' I cannot believe my ears. A hundred kilometres (62 miles) as the crow flies! … and it is already beginning to get dark. A short outline of the situation follows. 'When can the detachment be ready to leave?' 'Immediately.' 'Well then, good luck with it.'

We put scouts out ahead, one to the right and one to the left, moving forward in short tactical bounds, with the rest of the detachment following in close formation. Our objective is the bridge over the River Bug at Tonkiele. We drive through Zambrov at dusk. It was captured by our infantry half an hour ago. Fires are burning near the church. The inhabitants, a few Jews among them, timidly scuttle out of sight around corners. Just outside the southern exit from the town, large barrack blocks stand next to the road. Well? But nothing stirs.

It is now dark. On a road that is quite good by Polish standards, we drive south without headlights. The next little town we get to, Czyzevo, has been burnt to the ground. There is literally not a house left standing. Eerily, the still-intact chimneys point into the night sky. Our bombers have done a thorough job here.

In Ciechanoviec we turn away from the main road. Our lead scouts report that the town is completely undamaged and still inhabited. No troops, no roadblocks. With lights blazing we drive through the place, so that we have a clear view ahead. The detachment does not turn off into the narrow, winding streets, and any potential attackers will be blinded. Civilians, mostly Jews, scatter away from us in fright. It all seems to be going well, as not a shot has so far been fired.

Damn it – we spoke too soon. The major part of the detachment is already out of the place; it can only be the baggage train that is still inside the town. Then flares shoot up and splutter down again. Some completely confused shooting breaks out behind us in the darkness. We move on with the bulk of our force, and the support echelon catches up with us again. Nobody really knows what happened just now. A Polish dispatch rider was caught, and that probably triggered off the whole panic.

In the meantime it has become pitch black. Our lights are switched off again. Just let the Polacks try to find us in this darkness.

But this 'civilized' nation has not made it easy for us to progress. What is a solid road according to the map is in reality a sandy channel. We can mostly drive only in first and second gears. Sometimes the path widens to unknown dimensions, and then it becomes even more unpredictable. A log bridge collapses under the weight of a heavy tank, but the ditch is dry, thank goodness, and we soon find a way round. Still, the whole of the baggage train has to get through – and it does. In one sandpit, every vehicle has to be guided, every single motorcycle pushed through. A number of trucks have to be towed through by the heavy armoured reconnaissance cars. But we manage it. And all practically in silence. We use our sidelights, at most. No vehicle is abandoned.

Never before and seldom since have I seen what someone can do when he has to, when there is no alternative. The driver of our command tank asks me to take over from him for a while. His arms hang like logs at his sides. He cannot raise them any more. And even for a short spell I find driving the tank difficult.

We had covered 50 kilometres (36 miles) getting to Ceichanoviec. It has taken us nearly as long to get through the 15 kilometres (10 miles) of sandy desert. This is no good; we are losing valuable time. So we must get back to the main road. The scouts are re-directed. But the commander is too impatient to wait for this to be put into effect.

Then at the head of the column, which has just reached the main road, flares go up, and shots are fired. Darkness and peace then return. Shortly afterwards we hear from the leaders of the column that there are Polish troops of every kind, with many vehicles, on the move from north to south along the main road. At the same moment this news is confirmed in the strangest manner. The orderly officer of another reconnaissance detachment – accompanied by a light armoured reconnaissance car, a *Kubelwagen* and a motorcyclist – reports to our commander. He is rather pale. He had travelled for half an hour jammed into the middle of this Polish column. When he finally got to a side-road, he made himself scarce – and ran across our leading vehicles. You need luck in this world, especially soldiers!

So we push on down the side-road. For 5 kilometres (3 miles) we run parallel to the Poles. And we have our share of luck, too. The road improves, and we can get on faster. The Poles on our left are not our concern. We have a different job.

Dawn breaks. We are 10 kilometres (6.2 miles) from the bridge on the Bug. The scouts report back: bridge undamaged, no troops holding it. Here we go, then! An advance party is formed: a few armoured reconnaissance cars, motorcycle troops, engineers. Objective: take over the bridge, and defuse explosive charges if necessary. The detachment follows on immediately. We skirt round the town of Drohiczyn; why invite a 'fuss' to be made over us just yet?

After barely half an hour, the advance party reports: bridge taken intact. Fantastic! A tremendous feeling of pride and pleasure comes over us. Over 100 kilometres (62 miles) ahead of our own troops, after an almost superhuman night drive, we have firmly secured one of the most important east–west bridges between Warsaw and Brest-Litovsk!

By *Rittmeister* Freiherrn von Esebeck

Reconnaissance Patrol Cornered

– Two close encounters with death

A fter many days and nights of strenuous reconnaissance work, after hard fighting and many a brush with death, for the first time all the reconnaissance patrol units were back with the company. As daylight slowly ebbed away, patrol leaders, tank commanders, radio operators and drivers sat sociably around a few campfires and let the flames warm their cold, tired limbs. A quiet murmur of voices floated across the wide fields, and here and there a song started up, accompanied by the haunting tones of a harmonica. Schnapps bottles did the rounds, and the last remnants of chickens plucked and roasted by the men themselves disappeared into hungry mouths. Most of them sat by the fire and talked about the fighting of the past few days and nights: 'Do you remember, Hans, at Brest-Litovsk, on the Tuchola Heath, at Zabinka ...?'

Around one of the campfires sat the 'Schulz reconnaissance unit', with their leader, Colour-Sergeant Schulz, in their midst. They had all returned safely from their patrols: the driver of the second vehicle, Corporal Petschner, the two troopers Roland and Müller, the drivers Kempener and Kowalsky, and the radio operators Klare and Kreiss. They were just finishing their evening meal, and sitting in small groups close to the fire. Only one of them, Lance-Corporal Kempener, remained a little apart from the others. On his knees there was a small black note-book, and he was bringing his diary up to date for the last few days: '14 September; reconnoitring in direction of Brest-Litovsk. Fighting at Zabinka.' Once again there passed in front of Kempener's mind's eye that long, eventful day when the 'Schulz unit' had twice faced death. They had set off very early, at 04.00 hours, without breakfast. They had only had a few hours sleep since their last trip. But uncomplaining they climbed aboard their reconnaissance vehicles after Sergeant Schulz received his latest orders: 'Investigate bridge 1 kilometre (1090 yards) south of Zabinka and keep it open!' They reached the spot without encountering the enemy. It looked as though it would be a quiet day, but it did not turn out quite like that...

On the approach to Zabinka the patrol crosses a wide railway junction. The place itself is clear of the enemy. The detachment's commander is notified of this by radio. As they leave the last houses behind, the leader of the unit can see from here that the bridge 1 kilometre (1090 yards) south of Zabinka is still standing. A radio message updates the unit's orders. They are now directed to reconnoitre the second bridge, even further south. This time they are too late, however. All that is left of the bridge is the wreckage of girders and beams, lying in the narrow river-bed. Another radio report to the detachment. The new assignment is to 'secure first bridge and hold open!'

The task of holding the bridge seems to offer the men time to catch up on their missed breakfast and snatch a couple of hours of sleep. About 100 metres (109 yards) away from the bridge the tanks move into position, under cover of a few trees. Except for the gunners, who continue to man their weapons, the men leave their vehicles and start settling in and making sandwiches. Hardly have they unpacked their bread and sausage when the patrol leader calls them over for a quick briefing about the situation. The men lie on their stomachs around their leader, with the map in front of them.

Then, completely unexpected, a few bursts of machine-gun fire whistle over their heads. Everyone jumps up, races to the tanks, grabs the kit lying next to them, and disappears like the wind into their vehicles. Where is the enemy? The commander of the second tank looks all around with his binoculars, but cannot identify anything. Then the rear driver shouts out: 'Enemy tanks ahead!' 'Let's go!', orders the tank commander. The vehicle starts up and faces the opposing tanks. Every second, the men are expecting the screaming noise of a heavy anti-tank shell. It never comes.

'They're Carden-Loyd tanks' shouts Roland, the gunner, 'I've got them in my sights! Stop!' A judder goes through the vehicle. Hardly has it stopped, when the first shells are howling towards the enemy. They hit their target with pin-point accuracy. A giant jet of flame flares up from the enemy tank. A mortal blow! 'Next one', enthuses the rear driver. The reliable gunner Roland is always on his toes, and he has already taken new aim. The gun immediately spits out its deadly load in the direction of the second tank. Another jet of flame. He's out of action, too!

In the same instant there is a rattle of sustained firing from the lead vehicle, which has been held back for a moment with a jammed loading mechanism. Its gunner, Müller, also pulls off a master-stroke. His very first burst of fire penetrates the armour of the third enemy tank. Flames break out from the vehicle and spread with enormous rapidity.

Three enemy tanks destroyed in a few minutes! That's not too bad.

The unit pursues the two last, fleeing tanks at top speed into the town. The lead vehicle has just rounded a corner there when the crew are thrown off balance by a violent jolt. The armoured car has stopped.

'Back, back!', shouts the driver in horrified tones. In the middle of the railway junction, where the reconnaissance unit had crossed unhindered only about an hour ago, stands a Polish tank transport train. Tank after tank is rolling down the loading ramps at this moment, and infantry are jumping out of the train's compartments. On the last wagon Polish gunners are working rapidly to bring the massive barrel of a train-mounted gun to bear on the two German armoured vehicles.

With lightning speed, the vehicle commander grasps the surprising scene. 'Get going, Heini, reverse, quick! Come on!', he roars at the top of his voice. Only the greatest possible turn of speed can save everyone's lives now.

And as usual, it works. The two armoured cars are already moving away in reverse gear. They are too quick for the gunners on the train. The first shot from the enormous gun screams high over their heads and away into the town.

At a furious pace the two vehicles cross the small town, suddenly teeming with Poles. From all sides, rifle and machine-gun shots rattle against the armour like peas. But there is no stopping the tanks now. The Poles have not had time to put up a road block.

On the edge of the town, near one of the last houses, a burst of machine-gun fire unluckily catches the wheels of the first vehicle. Once again, minutes of extreme danger follow. The tyre comes away from the front wheel of the first vehicle, whips around a few times in the air, and lies in the road. There is a jolt to the right – will the armoured car turn over, travelling at this furious speed? It doesn't, thank God. At a crooked angle, and running only on its rims, it drives on. Anything to get out of this mess! At top speed the two Polish tanks that were knocked out earlier are passed; they are still burning. But the road is a dead end! Ahead lies the second, blown-up bridge, on the left marshy ground stretches away, and the river flows in a wide bend towards Zabinka. The patrol is cornered.

The only escape route appears to be a narrow path that runs from the right of the blown-up bridge to a hill with three houses standing on it. 'Schulz reconnaissance patrol boxed in', runs the radio report to the detachment. The order comes back from the commanding officer: 'Leave vehicles, blow them up, fight your way out!' But things are not that bad yet. Weapons are still usable, and vehicles drivable. The two machine guns are dismounted and positioned; the two commanders reach for their submachine guns; the drivers arm themselves.

Any hope that the passage of the reconnaissance unit has gone unnoticed turns out to be deluded. From the town eight groups of Polish infantry machine gunners fan out towards the hill, and tank after tank appears on the road. The situation has become hopeless.

Explosive charges are laid under the vehicles, and the most important things removed from them. In a series of short advances, the enemy infantry is moving ever closer to the hill. The two machine guns fire for all they are worth. Many an attacker will not be taking part in the next advance, but what can two machine guns do against eight! When the Poles have worked their way forward to within 500 metres (547 yards), the two gunners call for more ammunition. But the ammunition is practically finished. The last full drum is already lying next to them. Any attempt to break out towards the river now would be futile.

In this dire emergency an SOS goes out to the detachment: 'Request fire mission on hill one kilometre south-west of Zabinka.' The Poles are getting nearer and nearer. The last drum magazine is clipped to the machine gun. No more firing now except where the target is practically unmissable. The approaching enemy can be seen clearly ... 300 metres (330 yards) away ... 250 metres (275 yards) ...

The radio operator Klare is calmly going about his business, sitting at the apparatus as though it is an exercise, and sending out one SOS after another to the detachment. Just occasionally he opens the hatch to ask: 'How close are they now?'

The ammunition is running out. There can only be a few shots left in the drums now. Then, to howls of delight from the men, the first artillery shot comes droning in. Just before the hill, the shell drills into the earth and tears it apart with a deafening crash. 'Fire too long' goes the radio message to the battery. The very next shots land precisely among the Polish attackers. Secure in his sense that they are no longer abandoned, the unit leader directs the artillery fire over the radio. 'Range is good!' – 'Shift fire to right!'

When it is 200 metres (218 yards) from the hill, the Polish attack collapses under the artillery fire. For a short while they remain lying where they are, and then they slowly retreat. The engine of the tank transporter train gives a whistle, and in headlong flight the enemy returns to the town. A few minutes later the train chugs off in the direction of Brest-Litovsk.

The reconnaissance unit has been saved. The men's faces relax. But this experience, the greatest test of their military quality, affects them long afterwards, so that the motorcycle troops who soon arrive are greeted neither with shouts of joy nor with cheers, but with a brief handshake.

Lance-Corporal Kempener's diary has not survived. During a reconnaissance mission on the western front, it was destroyed by fire in the vehicle in which Colour-Sergeant Schulz, Lance-Corporal Kempener and Lance-Corporal Roland died a heroic death for the Fatherland.

By *Unteroffizier* Petschner

A Medic with the Frontline Pioneers

Outside Brest-Litovsk, 2 Company of my pioneer battalion, together with a rifle company, receives the order to launch the attack along its allotted sector and storm the citadel. As the battalion's assistant medical officer, I am sent in with the assault.

It is a lovely autumn morning as we march over the marshy ground along the banks of the River Bug towards the citadel, over which hangs a high cloud of smoke, obscuring the clear sky. The pioneers are heavily weighed down with demolition and wire-cutting charges, as well as inflatable rafts with assault ladders. Every man has hand-grenades, and we are also taking two manpack flame-throwers with us.

Behind a railway embankment the company prepares for the assault. The preliminary shelling lasts from 07.30 hours to 08.00 hours; the noise is deafening. Screaming shells fly just over our heads and strike with a clear thud beyond the embankment. Zero hour for the assault gets closer. In a long line we stand halfway up the embankment. Next to me is the medical orderly and my motorcycle driver, along with a few stretcher bearers, each carrying one half of a stretcher. One of them carries the pack with medical supplies.

The second-lieutenant checks his watch. Our hearts are in our mouths. At last the whistles blow. We rush up the few metres to the top of the embankment, jump across the railway tracks, race down the other side – and are immediately surprised: we are not received with the expected withering fire. Ahead of us lies peaceful parkland, with only a strong, sharply pointed iron fence to suggest the fortress this area belongs to. The equipment, bags and stretchers go flying over the fence, and we begin climbing frantically, with everybody helping his neighbour, until we are moving forward again. Then we find ourselves in thick undergrowth. Loud, single shots slam into the trees, and ricochets whistle through the air. A few long sheds arouse our suspicion. The first hand-grenades go flying in; they explode with a great crash, but afterwards everything is quiet again. The undergrowth comes to an end, and there is a cabbage field ahead of us, and a pond on our right. On the other side of the field there are more trees and thickets, with a road running along in front of them. Behind them we suspect the presence of the fortress ramparts.

I see the two first platoons of the company working their way forward over the field in stages, and a third follows with most of the equipment. Panting, there are six men dragging each inflatable assault boat; we have four boats with us. Now the bullets are whistling around us with a vengeance. Individual men stumble, pulling their comrades down with them, but pick themselves up again, and we reach the road without loss. Jumping across it, we come across some abandoned tennis courts surrounded by bushes. Here we catch up with our company commander, and pause for breath. Bullets are now flying at us from all directions.

'Watch out for snipers in trees!' shouts a hoarse voice. We flatten ourselves against the ground, and wish we could crawl into it. Then – some distance from me – there comes a penetrating cry petering out in an agonizing groan, and a shout of 'Medical orderly!'

It takes a second to overcome the coward that lurks in all of us, and then with a bound I am at the wounded man's side and trying to pull him into a shallow dip in the ground. But at each tug he emits a bloodcurdling moan. Oh well, we are being fired on from all sides here, there is no cover anyway. The orderly cuts open the man's trousers. His thigh is shattered, as it transpires by a shell from the gun of an armoured car hidden in a forward position. For the moment he is not bleeding too heavily, and I pack his large wound with the gauze dressings with which the pockets of my tunic are stuffed. I am only vaguely aware of the crashing of shells and the splintering of wood. Come on, get the stretcher ready! But who is going to carry it to the rear? 'Lieutenant, I need two stretcher bearers.' 'For God's sake, doctor, I need every rifle I've got at the moment!'

But there is no choice. Two pioneers hurry off with the stretcher. Now a corporal leaps towards me, holding his upper arm: a bright red stream is spurting from his elbow. The tourniquet, quick! But his arm is covered in blood, and the rubber strap is slipping off. The wounded man watches nervously; he is becoming scared. Oh God, if only the bleeding would stop. It does.

Another cry of pain from a badly wounded man. While still busy with him (shot through the neck, bullet exited through the collar bone) and bending low over my patient, I half-consciously register the order: 'Back 250 metres (275 yards) to the edge of the wood!' The wounded man has heard it too: 'Take me with you …' There are no more stretchers. Lying nearby is one of the cumbersome assault ladders, and we place the man on it. Who will help to carry it? The medical orderly and I are alone. I have to issue a harsh command to two pioneers to cut back to us in the midst of frantic gunfire. We pick up the ladder, and try to get it moving – but what's happened? The ladder is caught somehow. A damned telegraph wire wound round it! At any moment we expect to see the enemy, filled with hatred, come charging out at us with howls of triumph. Give me a knife! But the wire is too thick to cut. I lay it on a tree trunk and hit it with a spade – but the wire remains intact, buried in the wood. There's nothing else for it; we've got to put the ladder down, undo the wire, then lift the wounded man again. We carry on across the cabbage field, not stopping for anything. At the edge of the wood we collapse, pressing our faces to the cool earth, incapable of coaxing our heaving lungs to let us run even a few metres further.

The artillery has now shifted its fire back to our sector, so we gain a short respite. I go back to the embankment, check that the transfer of the wounded to the dressing station is working all right, and then run back to the front-line, by the same hellish route as before. But the going is so easy now, without any weight to carry!

The company has gained some ground; it is beyond the tennis courts. I even find my bag lying where I dropped it to deal with the telegraph wire. 'Lieutenant, they're going in!' With this joyous shout, everybody storms forward towards the ditch, just as I catch up with the company commander. The outer rampart of the fortress is ahead of us, abandoned by the fleeing Poles. Now for the assault boats. Only two are still serviceable; with a splash they go flying on to the black water. The others are riddled with bullet holes.

The ditch is being raked with fire, although thank goodness the shooting is not specifically directed. The boats paddle to and fro a number of times, in the end with the aid of a pulling rope. There is a sudden shout and a splash; a machine-gunner has lost his balance and toppled backwards into the muddy depths. His comrades' hands grab him and pull him out – but he has lost his machine gun.

A few minutes later I am utterly astonished to see a naked man lowering himself into the ditch and hunting around in the mud. All round him bullets are throwing up little spurts of water. But he goes on looking, and eventually finds his beloved weapon. It takes him half an hour to clean it, and then it is once again spraying bullets at the enemy rampart we still have in front of us.

The pioneers display heroic courage, forcing their way with explosive charges past a covered passage across the ditch, and racing with feline agility up the steep slope of the inner rampart, from which the Poles are fleeing in wild panic. Gasping for breath, they stand at the top, with the broad courtyard of the citadel in front of them, across which the defenders are fleeing; they fire at them from a standing position, and occupy their foxholes. But they cannot hold out here for long. The Poles put pressure on their flank from the part of the rampart we have not yet taken, and try to bring up a gun. One enemy gun crew after another is wiped out with the light machine gun, but more olive-green figures constantly emerge from the casemates, driven on at pistol-point by their officers. In the end, when the pioneers have fired their last bullet and thrown their last hand-grenade, they are forced to retreat.

As they pass the passage they had cleared earlier, they are met with devastating fire: the enemy has used a hidden connecting corridor to occupy it again. A number of brave men are left behind here, hot weapons in hands growing cold…

Meanwhile, on the slope of the outside rampart, I am bandaging, giving injections, and taking the wounded back across the ditch on the slowly deflating assault boat. This trip needs resolution every time: half submerged in the brackish water, we are constantly exposed to enfilading fire that gets fiercer all the time. One machine gun after another falls silent; we are running out of ammunition. Signal flares requesting help go hissing up into the sky. With amazing precision the artillery, whose battery commander and observer are with us, batters the inner rampart and pins the Poles down. All the same, we have to think about retreating across the ditch. Some large trees right next to us are blown up to serve as a makeshift bridge. During the powerful detonations, everybody hugs the ground. I am lying next to a man with a chest wound, which I had bandaged even though he was dying because, with pleading eyes, his comrade had asked me to do so. He seemed to be dead, but this colossal explosion sends a shudder through him too, and he opens his eyes with a last, questioning look.

As the sun sinks we receive the order to withdraw: our long-awaited reinforcement by an infantry battalion has arrived at last. I am covered in dirt and blood right up to my helmet, and rendered completely unrecognizable. I have long since stopped trying to count the number of wounded I have treated.

The fighting had put all sensation of thirst out of my mind, and for days afterwards I am greedily pouring every kind of liquid down my throat.

The next day the citadel surrendered, not least because of the impact of the assault I have described. In the small cemetery of the fortress, we buried 22 brave pioneers from 2 Company, alongside their comrades from the Great War. There were about 40 wounded, and only a handful of men appeared before the commanding officer for roll-call that evening.

By *Assistenzarzt* Dr Frahm

An Artillery Observation Aircraft over Brest-Litovsk

Every aircraft returning from a sortie reported heavy flak over Brest-Litovsk.

On the morning of 15 September, I was delivering a machine to our first new advanced airfield, at Vyliny-Rus, 15 kilometres (9.3 miles) north-west of Bransk. As I landed, I was immediately accosted by another observer. He had been directing artillery fire down on the citadel in Brest-Litovsk for the division. He greeted me with the words: 'That's a fine display of flak over the town. They've shot my dynamo to pieces.' I looked at his plane. There was a massive hole in the fuselage. It was amazing that neither the observer nor the pilot was hurt, and that the plane had made it safely back home. Nothing could beat our good old Henschel 126!

[The Henschel Hs 126B-1 was a high-wing monoplane tactical reconnaissance aircraft that equipped 80 per cent of Luftwaffe recconnaissance squadrons in 1939. It had a maximum speed at sea level of 310km/h (193mph) and range of 560km (348 miles). It was armed with two machine guns and could carry 150kg (331lb) of bombs.]

The town itself had been captured by this time. Only the citadel remained in Polish hands. My job was to take over directing artillery fire.

I take off about midday. The weather does not look exactly rosy. There are low-lying clouds. My approach takes a good half hour. Around Brest-Litovsk the weather clears up somewhat, but the town and the citadel are covered in a thick haze. In many places dense smoke is rising. The wall around the Central island of the citadel stands out clearly. We are soon met by thick flak bursts, but they are out of range.

The first thing to do is to locate our battery, a heavy field howitzer battery which is supposed to be sited north of the Northern Fort. I have not yet managed to make radio contact. Let's go!

It is hard to find the battery. Down below there are all sorts of guns, one battery after another. Which one is it? Why can't I make radio contact? I fire off a flare. Aha, now they're putting out a marker to identify themselves. Perhaps they're on the wrong radio frequency? I drop a message to tell them the right wave-length. And suddenly the connection is working!

Meanwhile, a good deal of time has been lost. I can only stay airborne for another 40 minutes at most. Radio reception is getting worse all the time. There are flashes of lightning on the horizon. It gets darker and darker. There's a thunderstorm on the way. Now I can see why the radio contact is so poor; it is only now and then that I can make anything out. There's the Polish flak hammering away again! This time their range is better. The enemy batteries seem to be in the region of Terespol and Blotkov-Maly, not yet reached by German troops. Among other things, I report the enemy batteries to the artillery. Hardly have I finished transmitting my reports, when the storm breaks violently over the city. No question now of directing artillery fire. In any case, I'm almost out of flying time. So home we go! – I am given no more orders for today.

Next morning in our tent, my pilot and I are awakened at 04.30 hours. It seems to be a clearer day. Take-off at 05.44 hours.

This time radio contact is made immediately. The flak greets us again, like an old friend. There are dense clouds of haze and smoke over the citadel.

I am able to start straight away directing fire onto the targets reported yesterday. The most important of these, it seems to me, is the northern perimeter wall. Our battery signals it is ready to fire. Two rounds, then. I fly ahead and find myself directly above the wall. Watch out, shell coming over! But not directly on target.

Suddenly, drifting nearby is a series of small black clouds: that damned Polish flak, so harmless to look at. These guys seem to be finding their range! My pilot banks away steeply into the clouds. We've got to steer clear for a bit, or they'll have us again.

Meanwhile, our battery is ready to fire once more. Let's have another go! They fire. Unfortunately, I overcorrected last time. But the next shell is bound to strike home. Battery ready – fire! Very good; right on target! Now the shooting starts in earnest. It is highly accurate. One direct hit after another.

By now it is 07.00 hours. We have to make way for the dive bombers, storming in to drop their heavy load. We turn back.

Shortly after landing, we take-off again at 08.35 hours. The citadel can now be identified from a distance by the black clouds of smoke hanging over it.

We cannot call down fire on the fortifications any more, since the ground assault has already begun, and we must avoid endangering them. A smaller fortification inside the perimeter wall appears to be a rewarding target.

There is no further sign of flak. The air raid has no doubt neutralized the Polish anti-aircraft guns.

Our shelling of the fortification is successful. Next in line is the south-west bridge over the Bug, which is still carrying some lively traffic. I must have miscalculated somewhat, because the first shot falls 400 metres (440 yards) to the left. A bad start! A pin-point target like this is hard to hit. After the sixth range-finding correction, I have got my eye in. Now for the serious shooting! After three salvoes the bridge is broken at the southern end. That will deny the Poles the chance of a rapid retreat. The other bridge, over the southern arm of the Muchaviec River, has already been partly destroyed. A few more quick shells for good measure! While the firing is going on I reconnoitre for new targets. It's a pity I cannot have several batteries shooting at once. Things would go much faster.

Time's up again! Back to our airstrip.

At 11.19 hours I take off once again. This time with a colleague's pilot. I have to get used to him first. But our cooperation soon works flawlessly. I notice a large shed. It could hold ammunition, since a few piles of munitions are clearly visible in the yard in front of it. Once the guns are on target a massive explosion shows that my hunch was right. A few more targets, equally worthwhile, are very effectively tackled before I have to break away and land again.

At 15.25 hours I take off again with my own pilot. There is not much left to do. A few more salvoes among the ammunition containers in the parkland on the other side of the Bug and inside the perimeter wall, and our job is finished for the day. We have done excellent work. It will continue tomorrow. We go to bed early.

A report on 17 September: 'For the moment, artillery will fire without direction from the air'. We wait ... At 08.30 hours a radio message reaches us: 'Citadel surrendered at 08.10 hours!'

By *Leutnant* Becker

Sidelights on Great Events

We become acquainted with a typical Polish village. Dirty, fairly uninviting rows of houses; uneven, poorly paved roads – that is the picture from the outside. Housewives standing in their doorways wear a sullen and baleful expression that makes caution advisable. The morning being chilly, they are wrapped in the strangest garments. A few are wearing rough fur jackets. When we look down expecting to see equally warm footwear, the contrast is a shock: for the most part they are completely barefoot.

Stormy weather brings streaming rain as the company marches upstream along the river Bug. But the men do not let it affect their good humour. An NCO hears suspicious noises coming from one house. Out with his pistol, and in he goes to tackle the enemy! This must be the room. The door is thrown open – and there, calmly standing in front of a full-length mirror, is a dispatch rider in a dusty greatcoat. He has taken a large scent spray bottle from a drawer, and is liberally applying the contents to his person.

'What are you doing there?', asks the NCO.

'Just to smell different for once, Sergeant!'

On the move or waiting, tense concentration or crippling inactivity – it's a never-ending pattern. The first hold-up is caused by the wrecked bridge at Vizna. A number of refugee carts totter past us, pulled by shaggy horses, but the refugees' faces seem to us strangely friendly and familiar, even though their troubles have etched deep lines in them. Small blond lads and lasses sitting high up on top of the small, packed wagons give us a clue. They are farmers from the scattered German villages beyond the Narev. Some had even elected to make their homes on the banks of the Bug, until driven out by the Polish terror.

The only sleep we can get comes in half-hour packets. Night is only distinguished from day by the amount of concentration it demands from the driver. After five days and four nights we arrive at a Russian-speaking village. The inhabitants stare curiously at our armoured vehicles. It is twilight. A Russian girl called Vanya shyly starts to sing. It is the kind of sad, melancholy song that belongs only to Russia. At every third line of the song, the bass voices of the men join in, and it as though a church choir is offering up its harmonies to the dark, overcast sky. We remain solemn and silent. Later, one of our number hums the tune of the Volga Boat Song, and Vanya nods her approval. The folksong about Stenka Rasin and his loyal followers is struck up. The high soprano of the girl is cradled like a gently breaking wave on the organ-tones of the men's voices. That must be the Volga that is murmuring quietly in our ears; or is it just the melody of the wind, reaching us from far away in the Russian steppe?

'A BRIDGE, A BRIDGE ...'

A Polish military vehicle is slowly approaching the bridge we are holding, with our soldiers perched on the running boards to right and left, grinning from ear to ear. A Polish driver had bought up several thousand cigarettes. The fact that they were not intended for us did nothing to diminish our enjoyment.

A couple of fat Jews from Brest-Litovsk, travelling to Warsaw, are obliged to step out of their large limousine. We don't really need them to announce our arrival in advance in Warsaw. With a thousand assurances of thanks, they swear eternal gratitude to us for taking nothing more than their car.

We continue to lurk by our bridge. Unsuspecting, a Polish officer drives up in a private luxury car. He has obviously enjoyed a pleasant evening in Warsaw, and has not yet thrown off the alcohol. The effects of his lady friend are still lying on the rear seat. No, he doesn't understand anything. He doesn't understand how we got here, nor that we are reproaching him for drunk driving. Worst of all, he can't understand that for this reason we cannot let him go on driving, but – solicitous as we are – we are going to keep him as our prisoner, to protect him from himself, so to speak.

The most comical face made by anyone crossing the bridge is that of a telegraph engineer from Warsaw, who comes tearing up in his maintenance van, absolutely furious that somebody has had the temerity to cut through his wires. He is just drawing a deep breath and opening his beard-framed mouth, no doubt to give vent to a mighty curse, when I stop the poor man's mouth in the open position by asking him kindly to step out of the vehicle in order to ascertain for himself the damage we have caused him. No doubt he was readier to believe he was seeing a mirage or black magic than to grasp that he was now surrounded by Germans.

By *Unteroffizier* Gebert and
Rittmeister Freiherrn von Esebeck

How the Hauptmann Fell

The terrain was anything but favourable. If it was not sand, it was marsh. All the same, we had to move our guns up closer. The fortress had to be captured. The Poles were still occupying the surrounding woods. So 1 Platoon was making its way forward. It waded through knee-deep sand and marshy land off the beaten track, to finish up 5 kilometres (3 miles) closer to the target. The march lasted many hours. The drivers faced enormous difficulties. The tracks threw the sand up to head height. But on we went, inexorably. When had we ever failed to get through?

We were in a large meadow near a village. The two guns were removed from their limbers. Ammunition was piled up. A little further forward a thin line of infantry advanced towards the woods. The fortress was within firing range. Two forts were to receive our iron visiting cards.

But first we had to clean up the woods. Strong, active Polish troops opposed us, holding out doggedly in every corner of the forest. The infantry had some tough fighting to do. To aid their progress, a day later 2 Platoon of the battery was also moved up to the new firing position. There was now a series of gun emplacements, side by side. All the artillery available to the division had its gun barrels trained on the Polish position. The next day was to be decisive.

By the next morning, heavy rain had set in. It was hazy, and visibility was poor. The captain [the *Hauptmann* of the title], together with the radio operators and the senior radio NCO (the latter acting as observation officer), had already driven off to meet up with the infantry, for whom the captain was liaison officer.

During the night the Poles had attacked at various points. Now it was quiet. But the calm was deceptive. At any rate, we had to get on, we had to have this area safely in our hands before we could deal the fatal blow to the fortress itself. Such were the thoughts of the captain as he approached the infantry front-line together with his radio operators. An officer directed him to the regimental battle headquarters. Great care had to be exercised. Nobody knew exactly where the Poles were that morning, and you could easily lose your way.

The vehicle pulled away again. The captain would manage to find the regiment. He would find work for himself and his battery to do.

At a crossroads the driver stopped briefly to check the direction. The railway line was straight ahead, a few hundred metres away. Over there, where there were a few houses, might be their destination. The car hurtled on again over the shell-holes.

A number of shots ring out simultaneously, whistling over their heads. My God – how is this possible? Aren't the headquarters somewhere around here? What are the Poles doing here, then?

There is no time to think about it. Out of the car, quick! The sergeant suddenly groans quietly and clutches his chest. Blood stains the front of his tunic, but he makes no further sound. There is ferocious shooting from the houses. They are also being attacked in the flank, from the edge of the wood. A ditch affords scant cover; the Poles have a good line of sight and their shooting is accurate.

Everything happens very fast. The driver of the small signals vehicle that is following at some distance just manages to turn round in the road under fire, though he is hit in the arm. He will go and fetch help. But by then all the men in the ditch will be wounded. They take cover as well as they can. But there is nothing they can do against such murderous fire. They have emptied their magazines. One of the radio operators leaps up to get to the car. It contains more ammunition. After a few steps he falls forward silently, face down. A bullet through the neck has killed him instantly. Then the captain stands up. He is very pale, his teeth biting into his lip. With iron determination, he goes to the car. Shots whistle furiously around him. He does not notice them. He is bleeding from a number of wounds. He gropes for the machine gun in the car, and calmly loads it. He places it against his hip and shoots, standing firm next to the car until he has fired the last shot, and then collapses. He just manages to drag himself over to the others …

The Poles fire continuously at the mortally wounded men.

Hardly an hour later the radio operator reaches the area, with the second-lieutenant and some volunteers. They can hear no more shots. But they must be getting close to the spot. Then it all starts up. The Poles must think there is an attack in progress, and they fire at the small group of men as though they were a whole army. Take cover! The lieutenant takes two men and crawls forward. He wants to get to the car, which is now burning. But it is an open space with no cover. He is some way ahead of the other two. The Poles realize his intention, and subject the men to merciless fire. It is impossible to get any closer. Then the lieutenant calls back to the men that he is wounded, and that they should get away. 'Without our lieutenant?' They try to reach him, to take him with them. But the Poles respond to every move with rapid fire. It's no good. They have to leave their lieutenant behind, and crawl laboriously back to the others.

Different groups move forward twice more, but without success. The Poles are too strong here.

The sergeant-major too is brought back wounded.

Next day the infantry goes in, their numbers now reinforced. The men of the battery are in support. The captain's vehicle is a wreck. Only the red pennant has escaped burning. A few metres away from the road lie the bodies of the captain, the sergeant and the radio operator. Where are the lieutenant and the driver? If they are still alive, they must be prisoners of the Poles.

When the vehicle with its sad cargo returns to the gun emplacement, the gunners silently salute their dead captain.

Next day, the lieutenant passed through our position in a field ambulance. German troops had already liberated him from the Poles!

We did not hear anything about the driver until much later. He too had been captured, and eventually taken to a field hospital, where he wrote to us.

A few days later, the fortress surrendered. The Stukas had finished it off.

As we reach that spot during our march to the rear for a spell of rest, our eyes seek out the birchwood crosses over there by the church, to salute the dead for the last time.

Soon the wooden crosses are lost to our sombre gaze – but we will never forget: The *Hauptmann* fell ...

By *Unteroffizier* **Paulussen**

The Battle Around Kobryna

– Victorious attack and 'retreat'

S kirting round Brest-Litovsk, where a fierce battle was raging, we were supposed to take over Kovel from the 2nd Battalion. But once again, things worked out differently. A powerful new enemy group was approaching from the east, and even before nightfall on 16 September, the advancing 3rd Battalion was forced to secure waterway crossings in order to progress towards Kobryn, now their next objective. The vehicles churned their way through the Polish sand during the night, often away from the highway because the crossroads were frequently destroyed. But nothing could stop our vehicles. Planks, trees and anything else lying about were thrown into the marshy watercourses, and on they went. The drivers had done it again!

Before daybreak, despite all the difficulties of the terrain and the darkness, our battalion had assembled behind the 3rd Battalion, which was already positioned to the west of Kobryn. The rest of the night was spent in haystacks or in our vehicles. The 3rd Battalion began its attack on Kobryn next morning. To our annoyance, this time we were not sent in as a front-line battalion. But there was no point in getting impatient. Our time would come.

The noise from where the 3rd Battalion is fighting ahead of us is getting louder. Our impatience grows. Then at last we receive our orders. Moving round behind the 3rd Battalion, we are told after all – in accordance with our original instructions – to take over Kovel.

Orders are issued. While the noise of the fighting to the east (involving the artillery and the 3rd Battalion) is constantly increasing, our commander is suddenly called to regimental staff headquarters.

Another new situation! The Kovel mission has been cancelled, because the enemy is considerably stronger in Kobryn than first suspected. The new assignment is to attack Kobryn from the south.

Now our trusty vehicles have another chance to show what they can do. Once again we veer off the highway, swinging round on bad country tracks to reach the main Kovel–Kobryn road. We follow it in the direction of Kobryn. Suddenly the column comes under brisk rifle and machine-gun fire from a small birch wood on the right. Dismount, deploy and engage in fire fight! This all takes a few seconds and goes like a training exercise. An infantry gun is unhitched, and as the first shells fall on the little wood, a detachment of Polish cavalry gallops furiously away from this unhealthy spot. Push on! We must make progress in order to give our hard-pressed 3rd Battalion a breathing space. But the Poles have noticed what is at stake, too. Our forward troops are unable to prevent them from torching the bridge over the Kobryn Canal.

Machine-gun fire crackles towards us. Shortly afterwards, artillery shells begin to fall on the canal near the bridge. Get those vehicles moved back!

And now to push on – forward into the infantry battle! Both 7 Company on the right and 6 Company on the left – supported by all the heavy weaponry of the battalion – reach the canal on either side of the Kovel road. Here we are held up for a few minutes. A cry goes up for boats to get us across. But the battalion's few inflatable assault boats are still far to the rear. Without hesitating, the commander and his adjutant, together with the extremely tall commanding officer of 7 Company, wade through the chest-high water of the canal. The men follow. Although as wet as drowned rats, we quickly get across.

Under fire on the main road, drivers soon bring up the pioneers' equipment truck carrying the much-needed inflatable boats. They ferry anti-tank and infantry guns across, and the attack presses on over the flat plain towards Kobryn and through gardens and copses on the eastern side of the town.

On the right, 7 Company's attack – supported by our artillery – goes forward as though on a training exercise, and they quickly reach their objective, a country house in a large park on the outskirts of Kobryn. Their losses are comfortingly few. The company makes such rapid progress that a Polish gun in an exposed forward position has no time to pull out and is captured.

The 6 Company has a much tougher fight on its hands.

From haystacks and bales of straw, from the cellars of isolated farmhouses, the Poles put up a stubborn resistance. The attack here makes slow progress, especially as the 3rd Battalion is stuck by the canal and the company is now under fire from the left flank.

Gubernya Farm, next to the Kovel road, is defended with equal tenacity. From its buildings and from positions dug in front of the farmyard, the attacking troops are met by extremely heavy machine-gun fire. The battalion commander becomes impatient. It is unthinkable that motorized Pomeranian infantry should be delayed, however tough the enemy! Throwing in the reserve platoon of 6 Company and bringing up two of 8 Company's machine guns, he manages to get close to the outlying farm. The machine guns, firing from a roadside ditch, keep the Poles pinned down, and with fixed bayonets and hand-grenades the battalion staff operational group, together with the 6 Company platoon, breach the Polish position.

There is a brief, wild melee, into the midst of which the Poles pour artillery fire. An officer, a medic selflessly attending to casualties, two NCOs and a private soldier all die a heroic death in this assault.

But it is decisive. After the loss of the farmyard, where lie the bodies of 35 Poles killed in close combat, the enemy begins to retreat. The machine guns hammer away like mad, now creating carnage among the Poles. Dispatch riders are sent tearing across the landscape with new orders; 6 Company, in extreme disarray, is to stay where it is and 5 Company will move past it into a front-line position. Everywhere there are brief skirmishes, with the enemy defending himself stubbornly. But soon the battalion is ready to advance. They have a battery allocated to them in tow. The 6 Company forms up again as a reserve unit, so far as this is possible under Polish fire in the flat terrain.

The new objective is the town of Kobryn itself. Suddenly, 10 minutes before the action is due to begin, a completely unexpected order arrives: call off the attack, because the Russians have entered the war, and Kobryn lies deep within the Russian sphere of interest. The battalion commander curses. Halting an assault 300 metres (330 yards) from the enemy is a bitter pill at any time, but there is great concern in this case that the Poles may think calling off the fighting indicates German weakness, and in their turn launch an attack on the battalion, whose right flank is not linked up to our own troops!

These fears turn to certainty when the Poles attack the right flank of the battalion, but are beaten back. However, the second wave of the attack is already under way – only to be repulsed as before. Nonetheless, the enemy have succeeded in getting closer to our lines. Simultaneously with this attack, they move out further and further to enclose the right wing of the battalion, so that the artillery has to get ready to face to the rear, and sections of the reserve company must be deployed to protect the endangered vehicles. In this situation the battalion seeks permission to withdraw behind the canal they had waded through that morning, and organize a defensive position. By the time the necessary orders have been drawn up, it is beginning to get dark. Heavy clouds hang in the sky, and as the battalion disengages from the enemy in the darkness a severe storm breaks out, at the same moment as the Poles launch their final attack. Lightning darts luridly across the sky, and flashes from rapidly firing weapons intensify the picture. But the disengagement operation is successful. Soaked through, the battalion soon re-forms behind the canal, sentries posted to the fore.

Resentful thoughts run through our heads during the night. We had attacked; we had fought through; we had been forced to stop fighting – for reasons that are surely rare in the history of warfare – and then go on to the defensive. This last requirement came particularly hard, following upon the excellent outcome of the day's fighting. Motorized infantry are in their element when attacking again and again, and not in defence.

With the dawn on 17 September we are able to see the full extent of our success. In the battalion's sector of the battleground outside Kobryn lie 250 Polish dead; they fought with the utmost courage and tenacity. The enemy have retreated during the night, and now at last we can give ourselves over completely to the happy feeling that comes from embellishing our battle honours with a victorious attack on a well-entrenched enemy of at least equal strength.

[In the Polish campaign, Guderian's XIX Panzerkorps had initially attacked east from Prussia to cut the Danzig Corridor and punch through the Pomorze (Pomeranian) Army under General Bortnowski composed of the 4th, 9th, 15th, 16th, 27th Infantry Divisions and 'Pomerania' Cavalry Brigade. It then swung south-east through the Modlin Army under General Przedrzymirski composed of the 8th and 20th Infantry Divisions and 'Mazow' and 'Nowogrod' Cavalry Brigades, crossing the Vistula and reaching the fortified city of Brest-Litovsk on the river Bug.]

By *Major* von Müller

The main German Panzer assault crossed the River Meuse at Sedan on 13 May 1940 and pushed to the coast at Boulogne. Despite some spirited French and British counterattacks, the British Expeditionary Force and French First Army were cutoff around Dunkirk.

Breakthrough to the Atlantic

The Alert Signal in the Eifel Mountains

I t is two o'clock in the afternoon of 9 May 1940, in a small village in the remote Eifel region. Suddenly – a general alert!

The alert was the command, the signal that we soldiers in the west of the Reich had been waiting for with feverish anticipation throughout the seven long frost-bound months of the 1939/1940 winter on the West Wall. Was that all it was, anticipation? No, it was burning desire. The yearning for action and fighting, the soldier's life-blood.

Alert! It ran through our ranks like the removal of a heavy weight from the shoulders of every one of us. Couldn't you hear a sigh of relief from every comrade? Wasn't there a bright gleam in their eyes? Didn't everyone have a happy song on their lips? The iron discipline, the hard military training of the past few months, all made profound sense at last.

Now was our chance to enter the decisive battle and to prove ourselves. An uncertain future lay ahead of us. Who knew what he would have to face? Who among us would have to give his life in the great struggle towards which we were marching?

Certain of victory? For us there was no other outcome but victory. We never discussed it. Confidence in our victory was too strongly anchored in our hearts for us ever to doubt it; though we never underestimated the strength and stamina of our enemy in the west. We knew that defeating him would demand great sacrifices from us and tear out many a breach in our ranks. But none of that could shake our belief in our ultimate victory.

And it was this absolute faith in victory, together with the feeling of relief from almost unbearable tension, as well as the expectation of unique military experience, that inspired in us the mood and the spirit that welded us into a determined community and rendered us as hard as steel for the coming conflict.

'Forwards', said the rhythm of our hearts, and 'forwards' was the song of our engines!

By *Unteroffizier* Keitner

Border Crossings: Three Frontiers in Two Days

Behind us lies a long, hot march right across the Eifel, on minor roads widened by the construction battalions. Over there is a signpost: 'Wallendorf 1 Kilometre' (1090 yards). We have reached our first-stage objective, the Luxembourg border! The sight of the yellow road signs has clearly perked up our tank drivers, after sitting for five hours in this terrific heat behind their gear levers, changing gear – steering uphill and downhill – stopping and starting.

The afternoon of 10 May 1940 …

Our lead vehicles are crossing the Sauer Bridge. It looks rather strange; our pioneers have laid thick planks across a block of wood barring access to the bridge, so that a small bridge has been formed on top of the larger one. Luxembourg makes an orderly impression. It seems a clean and affluent country. The inhabitants look at us with curiosity, neither friendly nor hostile. They have probably not yet got over their astonishment at watching an endless procession of German columns with artillery, armoured reconnaissance vehicles, radio cars and now tanks filing past them since early this morning. On the straight, wide, well-paved roads we keep up a good pace. Woods, waving corn-fields, streams and villages follow each other in quick succession: Reisdorf – Diekirch – the Rivers Alzette and Wark – Grossbus – the Forest of Arsdorf – Martelange, then the Belgian frontier!

The bridge across the Sauer has been blown up. There are gaping craters at bottlenecks in the road; mines, as well as road blocks made of iron stakes and mounds of stones, delay our advance. The river itself snakes between two high ranges of hills, from which narrow and partly mud-covered paths lead down.

At dusk, the regiment is ordered to push on to Witry via Gremelange and Bodange. But the advance soon comes to a halt. The terrain along the river at Bodange is marshy and has been mined. The pioneers have not yet finished their work. We've got to wait. The path is finally cleared by midnight! In total darkness, tank after tank is 'piloted' over the timber laid on the soft ground and across the narrow bridge.

At 02.00 hours the regiment tucks in close behind the forward security for a short break. We throw ourselves down on a farmer's floor. The contrast between Luxembourg and Belgium could not be more striking. Back there, obvious affluence, well-dressed, well-fed people; here, clearly, a good deal of poverty, misery and dirt. We are so tired that the clatter of newly arriving vehicles and the bustle of in-coming orders and reports can only rouse us momentarily from our sleep.

I wake up at first light. Shivering, I disentangle myself from my blanket and go outside. The village is a sad sight in daylight: tumbledown houses, dung heaps in the road, neglected paths, and careworn peasants, whose anxiety about where their daily bread is coming from is etched upon their faces.

Parked close to barns and other buildings stand our proud tanks. The stragglers from the march have nearly all caught up by now. Most of the crews are awake and shivering, trying to shrug off the cold by running around, eating breakfast and smoking. All of them ask the same question: when are we going on? All we know is that our sister regiment, the artillery, and most of the riflemen have not arrived yet. The obstacles at the frontier did succeed in slowing down the advance, after all, despite minimal enemy resistance. But we must make ground and get on; we are a young, dynamic service, eager to prove ourselves and impatient at any delay. Headquarters agrees to our regimental commander's proposal that we should at least move up immediately into the agreed assembly area.

Instantly, our men spring to life. Engines are warmed up, vehicles drawn up ready to leave, muzzle covers are removed, radio antennae slotted into place, and officers brief their platoon commanders. Over here, someone curses; over there somebody shouts a joking remark to a comrade. I clamber up into my command tank; the commander, too, is already aboard. Two minutes until we fall in. All sorts of things go through your head at that moment. Will the radio network, the nerve system of a tank regiment, function OK? When will we have our first brush with the enemy? Enemy tanks? Is it true what intelligence tells us about fortifications in our sector? What about the French artillery, for which old soldiers from the Great War have taught us so much respect?

The order comes through on the intercom: 'Move now!' The regiment moves off, initially in the direction of Neufchâteau. We are just going through Traimont, when we suddenly stop. There is a hold up! 'Mines and enemy motorbike troops ahead', comes over the radio. The lead company has opened fire, a few machine guns rattle, we can hear explosions, but the shooting does not sound familiar, not like the way our shells explode. Suddenly we have space again up ahead. What is going on? The commander of the leading platoon has had a sudden brainwave and opens fire on the mines visibly set into the road surface, blowing them sky-high.

We get to the stretches of woodland east of Namoussart, the assembly area for the attack on the stronghold of Neufchâteau. The vehicles rapidly go to ground in the woods. Armoured patrols scout cautiously beyond the low ridge ahead of us. The grey of the early morning has meanwhile given way to bright sunlight; fresh dew glistens on the grass and shrubs. It is a busy scene. There is a familiar sound of cotter-pins being driven home; fresh water is being drawn in a neighbouring farmyard; the Opel-Blitz tanker trucks are roaring up; fuel cans are clanking, and vehicles are quickly got ready. If you have time, you take a rest.

The commanding general is coming! Are we going straight into the attack? A visit by a high-up is always followed by some action! – The briefing is over. I just manage to catch the last words: 'the regiment will attack!'

We travel in two groups. Not a sound from the enemy. The tanks are getting close to the Belgian defence line. Shouldn't we be getting to the anti-tank ditches? Nothing! Shouldn't we be getting within range of the forward gun emplacement at Le Sart? Nothing. Only around Neufchâteau do we come across some minor fortifications, keeping the riflemen quite busy. We skirt around to the south of the place: we don't like towns.

The regiment is approaching the Posiere sector. The rear detachment moves forward on the left at a higher level under cover of a ridge, while the leading detachment takes to the valley floor. A brief pause in radio traffic, which has kept us busy encoding grid references in this brisk advance, gives me time for a quick look through my binoculars. Up ahead are the reconnaissance patrols; behind them, in a V-formation, the two light companies. The heavy combat vehicles lumber along behind, and above the ridge can be seen the threatening outline of the other detachment's turrets.

On the floor of the valley lies a peaceful village with whitewashed houses, baking in the sun – Petitvoir. Machine-gun and gun fire comes from the leading companies, rattling down into the village. I can make out artillery. This spot of resistance is soon overcome. Now, on our left at the edge of the woods, things become lively. You can see vehicles, and figures running about. Tracer ammunition is flying, one or two vehicles are burning, but it soon goes quiet over there, too.

High up behind the village, enemy gunners are trying to bring their guns into action. They are soon caught in machine gun and shell fire. Those not put out of action disappear at top speed. Our first group gains the slope on the other side. The woods are unoccupied by the enemy. Over there, on the road to Bertrix, a dense column is pouring westwards. The shells from our main armament just manage to catch the tail-end of them.

It is only some days later that we discover that French tanks had passed us and reached Bertrix. There the inhabitants told them that 'many German tanks' had passed by two hours earlier, travelling westwards. On hearing this, the Frenchmen had panicked and left their vehicles, so that parts of our division bringing up the rear had found them abandoned.

As a result of this sudden chase, our units had become rather disorganized. The sections re-group behind the shelter of security precautions. A quick radio message to the brigade. We ask for fuel, for artillery – to extend the range at which we can engage the enemy – and for troops to secure the flanks of the territory we have captured. After all, we are just a single regiment, all alone in open land, with nothing to right or left of us. Brigade agrees to send us troops and artillery. But when? – We can't wait that long. Better to trust to the fortunes of war and our own strength! After half an hour's rest, we press on.

'Halt!' shouts the commanding officer suddenly. Clunk – the driver pulls on the gear stick, the tank dips a bit, and we stop. 'Back!' Hello, what's happening? The others are still moving forward. I take a look. A fine state of affairs! We were inches away from plunging into a pit a good 8 metres (26 feet) deep, with rocky vertical sides. The driver could not see this treacherous hole, because the edges were overgrown with shrubs.

Like a squadron of ships in a gently undulating sea the tanks plough on at a smart pace through fields, meadows, hedgerows, rivulets and scrubland. They descend into valleys, climb up slopes. Unopposed, we cover the ground. Nevraumont, Orgeo and Saupont Bertrix heave into sight to right and left, and disappear again. South of Bertrix *dragons portés* [light armoured vehicles] offer a fight; they are scattered by the first wave of tanks.

The large wooded area further to the south-east slows us down. As a result, when we get to the village of Fay les Veneurs the lead vehicles of the rest of the division link up with us again. We had made an advance of 40 kilometres (24 miles) alone!

We receive new orders. In two groups, we are instructed to secure a crossing over the Semois. It is a steep valley; there are only a few bridges.

Initially, only the tanks are available. So forward we go to the river – perhaps we can take a bridge by surprise attack. We are covered in thick dust; roadblocks force us to make detours. Finally, shortly after sunset, we arrive in Rochehaut. But it turns out there is no suitable bridge there. We reconnoitre in the direction of Poupehan.

The road bridge at Poupehan is intact, but the opposite bank is heavily defended. By the early morning light, the commanders carry out a joint exploration of the terrain. Positioned high up on the steep banks, the enemy responds to every movement with machine-gun fire from out of the mist. We try sending in our medium-weight tanks, but to no avail. So at about 06.00 hours there is a new decision: 'Group B will cross with all sections at Mouzaive!'

The re-routing to Mouzaive is not without problems. Many vehicles, narrow roads, and constant French artillery fire!

We arrive at the ford. Our flak guns are very busy chasing away a few French planes that are not too happy with what we are up to here. The motorcycle troops cross by a narrow bridge, while the tanks churn through the Semois. Near this footbridge the river is easily forded; with a stony bed, it is about 40 metres (43 yards) wide and 70 centimetres (27 inches) deep. Only a few vehicles need towing. Then we go swiftly on over the Alle to the crossroads at Ban d'Alle.

We are in the middle of a dense forest, the Ardennes. Our lead tanks sometimes catch a glimpse of shadowy enemy reconnaissance cars flitting round corners, but they can never catch up with them, however hard they try. Otherwise, the only signs that we are facing an enemy are the immobilized vehicles and the jettisoned equipment. The enemy troops have disappeared into the thick undergrowth to left and right of our route.

We have reached the crossroads, with its few houses. Everything is deserted and quiet as the grave. The French frontier is only a few hundred metres away. Suddenly the lead tank, which has forged on so rapidly until now, begins to falter. The head of the column even comes to a complete standstill. The commander is annoyed. What's that sergeant doing up there? A massive explosion interrupts his chain of thought. A thick cloud of smoke rolls across the road. When the commander hurries forward to the leading tank, he is soon enlightened. 'The blighters have blown up the road. I didn't drive on, because I could see movement, and the whole thing seemed suspicious to me'. Nothing like the instincts of an old soldier!

We skirt round the enormous crater, and on we go. Our first few companies are directed southwards. On a winding road they drive uphill, through woods with fresh green leaves dappled by the sun. Abandoned weapons and equipment litter the road. The tanks have clocked up 220 kilometres (137 miles) since we left our last base in the Reich. Hello! Just ahead gleam the red, white and blue stripes of the frontier post! Another 1000 metres (1090 yards) to the edge of the forest, and we will have reached our first objective. But already a signpost reminds us of our next assignment: 'Sedan 11 km [7 miles]'. We are about to be put to a tough test, but one which we will pass.

By *Hauptmann* Carganico

The Advance

The sun beats down mercilessly upon the bare roads of France. The waiting for action is over. Battle is close at hand, has become a living reality. We feel that we have broken free from all that surrounded us before, and from what we possessed. Now we are living entirely the life of comradeship, fulfilment of our duty, and the sacred struggle for Germany!

The tanks roar ahead of us. It is a massive show of military might. They have smashed through all resistance, so that until now we have driven unopposed through enemy towns and villages. We have been on the move for five days and five nights. How long since we had any sleep? Our eyes are burning and stinging. It is as though the eyelids were inflamed.

The drivers are the silent heroes of this march. They clench their teeth. Stay awake at all costs! Roads, roads, roads – always the same. The men at their side talk to them, telling them anything that comes into their heads. Anything to stay awake!

It has been dark for some time. Suddenly, we stop. Four hours of rest. We wrap ourselves in blankets and lie down somewhere on the grass or in a field. We can stretch our legs out properly at last. How marvellous it is to shut your eyes. We don't need to fight the tiredness any more. We sleep ... sleep ...

Dawn breaks. It is cold. We pull our knees right up to our chins. The command to 'mount!' We roll onwards, devouring the kilometres. Tanks roar past us again, an endless chain. The roads are clear. We are driving in two columns now, close to the edge of the road. The sun burns relentlessly down.

We have wound cloths around our necks, a new fashion. Someone started it, now everyone is doing it. It's a marvellous feeling to have a soft cloth nestling around your raw, painful neck.

We advance – on and on. Past endless ditches by the roadside. For us there is a kind of 'mystery' in roadside ditches. They characterize the nature of the advance! Abandoned vehicles, broken weapons, discarded ammunition of all kinds, helmets, uniform items. And everywhere the bodies of fallen enemies. We can see from the ditches exactly what happened here.

Advancing, on and on! The first POWs. Their uniforms are pathetically poor, their boots even worse. They shuffle along lethargically, with grey, vacant faces. A miserable 'march on Berlin'.

Lifeless towns, houses to left and right. All abandoned; silent but for the cattle lowing. We roll on. When will we be in action? It could come at any time. We are ready, prepared for battle at any moment.

In a field, a few metres back from the road, a narrow cross surmounted by a helmet. A soldier's grave. Fresh flowers on the small mound. A comrade who will never again march with us, who has made the ultimate sacrifice for his nation.

We drive round a bend in the road, and the cross disappears. New images appear. The fellow soldier beside me has let his head sink. His helmet jerks upwards occasionally. A nap, just for a few minutes, and then my neighbour pulls himself together again.

We can hear heavy artillery fire to the left of the road. We will soon be taking up our position. The sun sinks slowly below the horizon. It is evening once more. A house is burning somewhere. The flames leap into the sky. We are in the midst of war, in the midst of an advance. And we keep moving, onwards, forwards … forwards …!

By *Gefreiter* Möllmann

Point 247

– An infantry regiment attacks

———————————

It is 13 May 1940. Whit Monday. We have yet another long night march behind us. Now, around noon, the sun beats down relentlessly. Along the narrow track through the Bois de Sedan, the companies of the 2nd Battalion of the infantry regiment are lying beside their vehicles, driven into the woods for cover, sleeping and gathering strength for the impending battle. Letters home are being written, dispatch riders are darting to and fro on their motorcycles, heavy weapons are being brought forward, the field kitchens are steaming, and but for the low rumble we can hear in the distance, everything is so calm and matter-of-fact that we might be on manoeuvres. Up ahead, on the southern edge of the forest, pioneers and infantry are repairing a bridge blown up by the French, and clearing away mines and wire barriers. The French have no idea that their 'great hope' [the Maginot Line] is about to be consigned to history by German infantrymen in a few hours time. Now and again they aimlessly send over a few shells, without doing any damage, into our assembly area.

It is 13.00 hours. Dispatch riders rush up and down the battalion shouting: 'Company leaders to the fore!' Rations are being handed out to the companies; canteens are being filled with coffee again; machine guns and rifles checked.

The battalion command post is set up at the junction of two tracks. The commander is sitting on a rock, surrounded by his officers and the commanders of the support weapons units. Orders have just arrived from the regiment. 'The 2nd Battalion will spearhead the regiment's crossing of the Meuse, break through the Maginot Line, and secure Point 247.' The commander's voice sounds steely. Officers mark the route of the battalion to its crossing point on their maps. 'The battalion will leave its assembly point at 14.00 hours. 7 Company supported by the assault pioneers will cross the Meuse near this factory at the western end of Sedan, followed by 6 Company.' The orders are repeated, and shortly afterwards the companies are on the march to cover the 10 kilometres (6.5 miles) of no-man's-land to the Meuse in the two hours available. All the equipment, ammunition, the heavy machine guns and mortars have to be carried across fields, over hills and through deep ravines. But these soldiers will get there, despite the great heat, though there will be plenty of sweating and much cursing at the weight of the machine gun, the mortar and the ammunition boxes.

The terrain gets more and more difficult, until at last we are looking down on the valley of the Meuse: on our left, the town of Sedan, which is on fire; directly ahead of us the completely destroyed Floing; and to the south, beyond the Meuse, our objective. Smoke everywhere you look, bursting shells and bombs. No sign of the French; there is something uncanny about the enemy's silence. Has he been hit so hard, or is he simply waiting for us to try to cross the river? In all the smoke, you cannot make out his fortifications at all, as squadron after squadron of Stukas approaches to drop its deadly load.

We haven't got to our objective yet, though; we will have to push ourselves to get there at the appointed time. We tramp through Floing, keeping a watchful eye to right and left; not a shot is fired. The inhabitants have all fled; dogs and cats roam the streets, whose shattered houses bear witness to the violence of war. Down on the high street we turn off to the left, and soon arrive at our factory. Only now do the French become aware of the threat; they begin to fight back, ignoring the falling bombs. Pioneers bring up their assault boats, but they cannot reach the river. Despite the decent cover we have, our opponents can spot all our movements from their bunkers. We have to call in assistance. Assault guns are brought up, but their shells are ineffective against concrete and iron. Valuable time is lost, until heavy anti-aircraft artillery silences the enemy.

The assault boats are brought up again, but once more the attempt has to be broken off under heavy defensive fire. A young second-lieutenant from 7 Company and two pioneers pay the price of courage with their lives, and the wounded are trickling back. Our flak intervenes again, and under their protection the foremost sections of the leading company cross the Meuse in the assault boats. Rapidly, just as we practised it during the winter, the first few men of 6 Company follow, headed by the first platoon, with its lieutenant leading the way. Behind them is the company section with part of the second platoon and a machine-gun team. The rest of the company is positioned down by the Meuse covering the assault boats.

Four kilometres (2.5 miles) ahead of us we can clearly see Point 247, whose eastern slope is the company's objective. We set the pace of the march, and for this under-strength company there commences an attack that has earned it a glorious place in the battalion's war diary.

The first platoon has hardly moved away from the bank of the Meuse when it is met by concentrated machine-gun and rifle fire from positions that were previously invisible. As on a training exercise, the units work their way up to within charging distance, hurl in hand-grenades, and then with a shout of 'Hurrah!' go in to storm the enemy position. The first few Frenchmen, their hands up, start the trek to the rear, abandoning their weapons, equipment and personal kit, happy to have escaped the raging inferno of the day with their lives. The grenadiers of 6 Company surge onwards, forgetting the exertions of the day before and that afternoon, with only one goal in mind: Point 247. Those in front have already disappeared into the suburban estate that lies athwart the line of attack; there is house-to-house fighting, and prisoners are taken. On, on, keep moving forward, we haven't got to the bunkers yet. The blue-painted window-panes of a large factory stare out at us eerily. It once served France; today it lies destroyed, flames and acrid smoke pouring from its windows. Shots ring out. Are the Frenchmen putting up resistance here, too? It is quickly overcome. More and more prisoners make their way to the rear. To get them moving, all they need is a forceful command of 'Allez!' and an indication of which way to go.

Having crossed the Sedan-Mézières railway line, the company reaches the Sedan-Donchéry highway. Old memories resurface. Where exactly is the small house in which the collapse of the Second French Empire reached its dénouement 70 years ago?

A glance to the left reveals that the big road-bridge has been blown up; on the right, sections of 7 Company can be seen. Brief contact between the two company leaders yields the information that several bunkers are keeping the 7th pinned down by the roadside. Action is required, and there is no time to lose, for the French artillery is beginning to take part in the defence. 6 Company quickly reaches its decision, the only one possible, even if they are only half a company and have no heavy weapons at their disposal – attack! A quick look round shows that there is a large six-gun bunker 200 metres (218 yards) south of the road, at the edge of an orchard which will provide good cover for an approach, and another one – somewhat smaller – 250 metres (273 yards) away from it and set back on its right at about two o'clock. Platoon and section commanders are briefed, and get their orders: 'Company will first secure the large bunker. 1 Platoon will attack from the orchard, 2 Platoon will move out to the left and work its way forward from the clump of trees there.'

What seemed impossible at first sight is achieved quite quickly. The surprise is complete; after a short struggle an NCO and two men reach the bunker, and the enemy are smoked out with hand-grenades. They emerge in a state of utter collapse. The Frenchmen stand with their backs to their bunker and put their hands up. 'Tirez! – Schiesst!' When the company commander asks in astonishment what this means, they reply that they have been told the Germans shoot every *poilu* they capture in a bunker!

In the midst of this exchange there are bursts of fire from French machine guns, which are now in the hands of German troops firing at the positions on Point 247.

The enemy artillery fire becomes heavier all the time. We are completely alone; there are no German troops to be seen on either side of us. Fierce machine-gun fire is coming from the park and chateau of Frénois. An anti-tank gun is firing continuously, though its position cannot be established. The first wounded men shout for medical orderlies. One of them asks his platoon leader to pass on a last message for his mother, and closes his eyes forever.

But there is no time to linger; our objective must be reached by daylight, because if we can take Point 247 a route will be opened up for our comrades of the tank corps into the hinterland behind the Maginot Line. The enemy must be allowed no respite that would allow him to throw his reserves into the breach we have prised open. Inexorably, the attack goes on. The second bunker falls, and it is now possible to spot the position of the anti-tank gun. Halfway up the slope, on the edge of a park, stands a barn resting on a suspicious-looking green base, which is now clearly recognizable as a gun emplacement. The shock troops attack again, while the machine-gun crew takes on infantry posts further to the left, allowing the company to move forward unhindered. When this bunker is taken too, we are overjoyed – especially because we discover it contains 10, 20, 30 bottles of mineral water, finally allowing us to slake our unspeakable thirst. Our canteens were emptied long ago, and it is now 18.00 hours.

During our short, well-earned rest we succeed in connecting with the rifle regiment that has been advancing on our right. Our contact is only with a single machine-gun crew, who report that their regiment is about 500 metres (546 yards) to our right, level with us. So no linking up just yet, but the two machine guns are a welcome support as we enter the last phase of the attack. The grenadiers go forward again, uphill past deep bomb craters and wide barbed-wire defences, until the French suddenly open up with furious defensive fire from a strong reverse-slope position. Two or three comrades fall to the ground; the light mortars begin firing at short range, with incredible accuracy, while machine guns and submachine guns pump their deadly projectiles at the enemy. Hand-grenades cartwheel through the air, exploding with a crash; enemy fire is ignored. Now we have attained our goal, there is no holding us. The first few men have reached the position, close combat, hand-to-hand fighting, we are all pulled forward in one great surge.

Point 247 is in our hands!

The way to the south lies open! Twilight slowly descends on the war-torn landscape. The enemy cannot grasp the enormity of what has happened: his artillery is silent, only a few bursts of machine-gun fire come our way. We are still alone on the hill from which Moltke conducted the battle that destroyed the French imperial army 70 years ago. It is two hours before the rest of the battalion catches up with us. The company leader's report to the commander combines rejoicing in victory with thanks to the comrades who gave their lives as grenadiers for Greater Germany.

The song that the company so often sang in peacetime has now acquired a profound significance for them: 'By far Sedan, upon that hill ...'

By *Oberleutnant* von Coubière

Tanks Protect Pioneers

A solitary signpost bearing the direction '5 kilometres [3 miles] to Sedan' is all that is left of the crossroads. The rest of it consists of rubbish scattered across the fields. A precision job by the German Stukas! The walls of the houses around have been blown in, the roofs ripped off. No reason to stop here. The tanks continue across country, always following the command vehicle. They have their radio masts extended, swaying to and fro with the rolling motion. An order comes through: 'Prepare for action!' At last! For days the company has been expecting to make contact with the enemy, and now it has. Just time for a shouted remark from one tank to another: 'D'you know what today is? Whit Monday!'

With hatches closed, the tanks travel at speed across a completely flat meadow towards the Meuse; the river itself is not yet in sight. A high railway embankment obscures the view. But there are things that can be seen very clearly indeed; the hills of the Meuse and the French bunkers they contain, staring down malevolently under their grey humps at the approaching tanks. The company has spread out and reached the embankment. On its slope there are riflemen and pioneers detailed to cross the river using their inflatable assault boats. The distance from the embankment to the river is about 600 metres (655 yards). Six hundred metres without any cover! Along a broad front, the company begins to target the bunker embrasures. Up and down the line, tongues of fire flash from gun barrels, and black clouds of smoke are thrown up on the other side. The enemy has not yet fired a shot. A pioneer hurries over to us across the wide field and asks for our support. A unit of shock-troops is stuck in a village on the right, and cannot move forward. In the meantime, however, an order comes in from the commander for 1 Platoon to take its tanks into Donchery, and from there give covering fire for the pioneers' efforts to cross the Meuse. Hardly have the vehicles turned round when there is a whistling sound from beyond the river, and one explosion after another conjures up spouts of earth, steel and fire from the peaceful meadow. The hissing and screeching of the shells rises to a hellish chorus, and everywhere men can be seen hastily looking for cover. As calmly, confidently, and clearly as though on a training exercise, the platoon commander, experiencing his own baptism of fire today, issues his orders. His calmness is transmitted to each man in turn, and every one of them makes a silent vow to go through the fiercest fire for the boss.

The 3 Platoon has orders to get the pioneers down to the Meuse with their boats. Their command tank stands in an orchard on the edge of the village, facing the Meuse, and keeps the French bunkers under continuous shell fire. The lead tank of the patrol takes off, tearing across the open space to the river bank. There are pioneers clinging for dear life to its hull, so as not to be thrown off the vehicle. For the moment, not a shot is fired. They seem to have pulled it off. The tank has covered three quarters of the way unscathed. But now the French open up: salvo after salvo is hurled at the lone vehicle, aggravated by fire from an anti-tank gun shooting from a superbly camouflaged position. The pioneers jump down and try to get the boat to the Meuse under a hail of fire. They are separated only by a few metres from the bank, but every step is hell.

The tank is using main and secondary armament, trying to give covering fire to the doggedly working pioneers. The boat is on the water and the paddles plunging deep. The machine guns in the bunker spray the lone boat with bullets. The water is kicked up in spurts all around, and a number of the audacious pioneers die a hero's death. Hopeless! – Back! They return to the bank and try to find cover in the long grass. Other men and boats are brought over to this lethal river by three more tanks, but they suffer the same fate.

Meanwhile, the lead tank has returned. But out there the wounded are groaning with pain, and are still under machine-gun fire. The French artillery, whose observers have an overview of every inch of ground, is shooting continuously and accurately. In the village their shells are tearing up the road 1 metre (3 feet) ahead of, to the side of, and behind the tanks. Once again the command to 3 Platoon is: 'Out of there!' The wounded are laid on the tank hulls and taken back to the aid stations. And then the platoon leader, who on this torrid day was the first of our company to win an Iron Cross, has to venture out for a third time with a boat across the ruinous meadow. This time the courage of the pioneers brings success. The first boat is across, the objective achieved.

In the meantime, the persistent and accurate fire of the lead tank's gunner has put one of the bunkers out of action, and forced its surrender. They are waving a white flag over there.

Meanwhile 1 Platoon, after its entry into Donchery, has moved on down to the Meuse and is trying to give the pioneers cover while they cross. One or two well-placed salvoes from the platoon leader's tank put a machine gun out of operation. It is a good position, but it has to be abandoned after a while. The French are directing very heavy fire on the 1 Platoon tanks. The fire is so accurate that it would be suicide to stay there any longer. The bursting shells demolish whole rows of houses in the area where they stand, and throw whole truck-loads of debris against the tanks' armour. After a change of position, the same thing happens again. The shots get closer and closer. The shells churn into the ground ahead of the tanks and with a blinding flash rip out deep craters. The air is full of dust and whirling clouds of smoke from the exploding shells. Move further back still! But not before the infantry have established a footing on the other bank, and the pioneers have finished off the bunkers with flame-throwers.

At dusk the company assembles behind the village. Nobody is missing. Even as they pull back, the Frenchman cannot resist sending over a few more shells in our direction. But the company only laughs; it is the last pleasure he is going to have!

[The Junkers Ju 87, universally known as the Stuka from the German acronym for Sturzkampfflugzeug *– 'diving warplane' – would take an important role in the campaigns in Poland and France. The scream of the diving aircraft was terrifying to men attacked on the ground. Some aircraft were fitted with sirens called* Jericho-Trompeten *– the 'Trumpets of Jericho' – fitted to the spatted undercarriage to enhance the psychological shock. The Ju 87 was armed with two fixed forward-firing 7.92mm (0.31in) MG 17 in the wings, one flexible-mount MG15 on the rear cockpit, and had a maximum bomb load of 500kg (1102lb).]*

By *Grefreiter* Frömmel

Capturing the Bunkers at Sedan

– How Sergeant Rubarth won his Knight's Cross

———————

The air is full of roaring, screaming, hissing and whirring. Thunderbolt after thunderbolt smashes into the ground, a black wall of smoke obscures the view ahead, the vivid flash of explosions flares out of this darkness that envelops the early afternoon of 13 May. It is no longer possible to make out how far away the bombs are falling; the uproar in the atmosphere paralyses the senses; there is a turmoil of thunder, steel and fire. The ground is trembling; it is like the end of the world, as though the pillars holding up the sky are being shattered, and the earth is being buried beneath their debris.

The 3 Platoon of 2 Company of Panzer Pioneers is moving into position for the assault. They have thrown themselves to the ground in a park on the southern edge of Sedan. They are used to all kinds of things, these pioneers who overcame the line of bunkers along the banks of the Narev in September 1939 – assault pioneers, broad-shouldered fellows, not easily scared … But they have never seen anything like what is happening here.

A German Stuka attack. Wave after wave breaks without a pause and with monstrous force over the concrete walls along the Meuse west of Sedan; the extension of the Maginot Line. Although the pioneers lying there in the grass of the parkland know it is intended for 'them over there', all the same the hurricane strength of this attack rages so fiercely that you can only lie there helpless – a few hundred metres away from the Meuse. It was near Bazeilles that 1 Pioneer Company made their first attempt. It was shot to pieces. Of their 52 inflatable assault boats, only two remained serviceable. On the heights south of Sedan the enemy has dug in hundreds of guns that deliver a murderous pinpoint fire upon the assault troops. At last the French artillery falls silent. It is shortly before 16.00 hours.

While the pioneers remain under cover, only one person moves freely in the open, as though it were nothing at all; he probes, scouts around and ponders: Sergeant Rubarth. Open meadows ahead. The puffs of smoke now reveal where the enemy bunkers are. On the far bank – what a place to attack! Hell, practically no cover, nothing – nothing at all. Two minutes to 16.00 hours. The last of our Stuka bombs hits the embankment on the other side with a crash. The moment has arrived for the Rubarth assault commando to successfully carry out the job assigned to it: 'Close combat assault on the bunkers and fortifications on the south bank of the Meuse and penetration of the extended Maginot Line.'

Everything now depends on the audacity and superior quality of this handful of men; the progress of a whole armoured division of the Tank Corps Guderian depends upon them. At this moment, the steel tracks of the division are carrying it over the mountain road through the Ardennes, past countless enormous craters on the road via Cugnon, to La Chapelle, to Sedan …

Rubarth knows his 3 Platoon. They are a band of brothers, bound by life and death – ever since Poland. He knows the worth of every one of them and how much he can rely on them. 1 and 2 Platoons will stay behind for the moment. '3 Platoon, forward, march!' The men have now reached the Sedan stadium. The enemy has shaken off his paralysis – he is firing at the assault troops who have taken cover in the stadium. How can they get clear of the building again? Luckily, enemy artillery or AA fire has battered a hole in the high wall – 3 Platoon emerges through it with good cover and gets to the river bank. Lance-Corporal Podszus, an East Prussian who is platoon leader Rubarth's driver, should really stay behind, but volunteers to go with the shock troops; he and Rubarth are inseparable.

Death stares across from the bunkers on the other side of the river. The machine guns are shaving the flat terrain. 'Even if I have to go across by myself – we've got to do something …!' mutters the platoon leader through his teeth. The Meuse is 80 metres (87 yards) wide at this point – that means covering 80 metres while offering target practice for the enemy … The two rubber boats are prepared; they only carry three men each, but one will have to take four: Rubarth, Corporal Theophel, and Lance-Corporals Bräutigam and Podszus. The other seven members of the platoon will follow at a distance. Will the three-man boat take the extra weight? 'Throw away everything that isn't essential!' Rubarth orders his pioneers; the Bangalore torpedo above all is unnecessary ballast. 'What about the spades, sergeant?' – 'Rubbish, we aren't going to have a chance to dig ourselves in – either we get through, or it all comes to nothing', replies Sergeant Rubarth.

Here goes! The boats are launched into the water, and the men fall rather than climb into the narrow rubber dinghy. There is only a hand's-breadth of clearance above the water; if it spilled in over the rim of the boat, the men with their heavy equipment would sink to the bottom like stones. An assault pioneer's pack is no joke: wire-cutters, hand-grenades, iron rations, steel helmet, gasmask.

And now, when every second counts, this blasted tub starts to spin, turning three times on its axis. The four assault pioneers aren't moving from the spot, until Rubarth takes the rudder himself. 'Shoot, Podszus, shoot!' he roars into his comrade's ear; it is important above all to hold down the fire from the bunker nearest to the bank.

And the driver Podszus, now a volunteer assault pioneer, shoots from the swaying boat, over the shoulder of his neighbour – not exactly well-aimed shooting, how could it be, but the best he can do – and the earth kicks up around the embrasure, which is then closed ...

One jump – and they are on the bank, without loss! Maintaining the momentum of his leap ashore, Rubarth makes for the first bunker. Podszus jumps up on top of the bunker. Rubarth hurls his explosive charge into the embrasure – Podszus lurks above the reinforced rear door, hand-grenades at the ready. There is an explosion that makes your ears ring. The occupants open the door, Podszus throws in a hand-grenade – they all come out with their hands up.

Onwards – Rubarth is up ahead already! All fear of death has been lost – how could you be afraid when following such a leader, calmness itself and ice-cool in his calculations even in the most nerve-racking moments; there is no surprise he is not equal to.

The enemy, having got his breath back, is pouring artillery fire into the Meuse, exactly at the crossing point – he can observe it in every detail from the heights south of Sedan. One of the anti-tank gun bunkers is now barking out its sharply exploding shells at the attackers. The next bunker is approached from the rear; the group creep up in the blind spot created by the gun barrels. Rubarth goes first, as usual. Low wire entanglements block the way, but once again the explosive charge is placed in the embrasure – Rubarth takes cover. But nothing happens. The fuse has failed. So up again, new fuse – explosion. Part of the bunker wall lies in ruins. Hand-grenades encourage the occupants to move, and they come crawling out, numbed by the powder smoke – crying, whimpering, completely finished.

'Oh – camerade!' they stutter, waving a white flag. The Stuka attack has shattered their nerves, and Rubarth's concentrated charge has reduced them to a jelly.

Over their heads an aerial battle is going on. French and British fighters are attacking German planes. The rest of 3 Platoon and the infantry units standing by on the north bank to make the river crossing whoop with joy – encouraging shouts reach the Rubarth shock troops in between explosions. They look back, and see the rest of the Commando crossing – they have just reached the middle of the river. But what's going on? Obviously hit amidships, the boat is folding up, and the men – they've been plunged into the water, and do not reappear.

The six men left on the enemy bank of the river leap as coolly at the bunker walls as though they had a battalion on their side. Only a small group of infantry covers their right flank. They have already broken through the first line of bunkers, extending for 300 metres (330 yards). But what now? They have run out of demolition charges and hand-grenades.

Rubarth tries to get back to the south bank, from where the commander of 2 Company is watching the progress of the battle. They must have reinforcements, or it will all have been for nothing.

Theophel, Bräutigam, Podszus and Monk stay behind in the cover of a shallow dip with their prisoners. They are pretty exhausted, hungry and thirsty – above all thirsty. With his school certificate French, Bräutigam conveys to one of the prisoners – with whom the pioneers are already sharing their cigarettes – that he should take off his shirt, wave it over his head and go back to the bunker to fetch something to drink. Instead of running away, the prisoner does what he's told, coming back with an enormous bottle of red wine …

They cannot enjoy their drink, though – however much you flatten your nose to the ground, the bullets come whistling over dangerously close to your steel helmet. The shots are coming from the railway embankment over there, from the linesman's cabin, 40 metres (44 yards) away – no doubt a camouflaged bunker. Yes, there's the flash of a rifle coming from its roof. Monk shouts: 'Help! I've been hit!' He has gone very white; one bullet has caught him in the hand, another in the elbow. Podszus and Theophel bandage him and place him in the deepest part of the hollow; the prisoners sit all round. If we stay here, they're going to polish us off, one by one, it's a dead cert. We've got to get out – out of this trap. Such are their thoughts. 'I'm going to hop back over – something's happened to Rubarth, I've got to find out what's going on', says Bräutigam feverishly, 'there's something wrong down there.' With one move, he's out of the hollow – then a shout: 'They've got me in the leg!' – 'Is it bad?' – 'It's OK', comes the weary reply. 'Hans, Hans', shout the others after a while, 'what's up with you, Hans?'

Lance-Corporal Hans Bräutigam is no longer answering.

Podszus is about to check on him, turns round – there's a blow to his left shoulder, his sleeve is ripped, a Frenchman has to apply the emergency dressing. The wounded Monk will have to stay in the hollow. 'We're going back – whatever happens', says Corporal Theophel. Like a shot from a cannon, Theophel and Podszus dash up the embankment and tumble down the other side. They get through, meet Sergeant Rubarth by the bank bringing up reinforcements, and deliver their report: 'Bräutigam dead, Monk wounded ...'

Across a 150-metre (164 yards) stretch of terrain completely exposed to enemy observation, Rubarth pushes on in short stages with the infantry towards the second line of bunkers. The enemy artillery follows the shock troop like a shadow. 'To go through fire for somebody' is a [German] expression that is often used lightly. But here the word becomes deed, and a moving reality. Everybody is determined to keep up with his platoon leader. Enthusiastically they 'go through fire' for him, for Rubarth.

A bunker with a double embrasure is attacked from both sides at once. A Frenchman who has just left the bunker aims his rifle at Rubarth ... a split-second quicker, Rubarth rips out the pin from his hand-grenade. Lance-Corporal Hose attaches a charge to the fortification, and pulls on the fuse to activate it. Take cover! Keep your mouth open – cover your ears ... Job done.

Rubarth makes a prisoner from the bunker's crew prepare a French machine gun for firing, and with it Rubarth obliges the anti-tank bunker on the left to shut-up shop ... Another bunker surrenders without putting up a fight.

So the second line of bunkers has been penetrated, and the enemy barrage comes too late. The Rubarth shock troop takes cover in the captured French trenches, and at dusk stands shoulder to shoulder with the infantry to defend the hill south of Sedan.

Objective achieved.

Exhausted, uniforms in tatters and covered from head to foot in mud, the assault pioneers try to snatch a few hours of sleep in the trench. Enemy reconnaissance planes vividly light up the terrain with floating magnesium flares. Then there is a gas alarm. It is a wearing night. But as dawn appears over the Meuse valley, Lance-Corporal Hebeler looks over the parapet of the trench. He alerts his dozing comrades with an exultant shout: 'There they are!' The battering ram that is the German tank corps rumbles up to the memorable heights of Sedan and breaks into the enemy battery positions, crushing everything beneath it.

It was us who started the breach that our tanks are now forcing wide open with their V-formation – us! That is what the men of Rubarth's platoon are entitled to think, and it lifts them up with a pride to which no other pleasure in the world can be compared. And with clenched teeth they also see a loyal comrade, left lying silent somewhere or drowned yesterday.

One of these comrades was found, riddled with machine-gun bullets – in his right hand a pencil, and on the ground next to him his back-pack reading, *For Right and Freedom*, open at the picture of the Führer. His comrades picked up this soldier's breviary to read the barely decipherable last words, written in a failing hand, of Lance-Corporal Hans Bräutigam: 'Dear parents – it wasn't recklessness – Hans.'

Even as he lay dying, he was apologizing to his parents, who had probably warned him not to be rash: '…it wasn't recklessness'.

No, it was the quiet heroism of the assault pioneer, whose penultimate thought in this world was concern for his missing comrade. 'Something's happened to Rubarth!' – With this worry on his mind he broke from cover, and went to his death.

Your parents, assault pioneer, will have to forgive you, in view of the faithfulness that drove you, and your platoon leader will always keep you in his heart, Hans Bräutigam; but your nation will always remember you with reverence, and all those who died as you did …

By *Sonderführer* Dr Leixner

The 'Black Hussars' at Bulson

During the night of 13–14 May, most of the division crosses the Meuse. The first armour the tank brigade send over, with the job of protecting the infantry, are the main battle tanks of 4 Company from my own tank regiment. The lively attention paid to the bridge by enemy planes forces the tanks to cross singly and at long intervals.

We reach the highway from Frenois to Chehery without loss. At a bend in the road 1 kilometre (1090 yards) north of Cheveuge, the company commander halts the column to give us his briefing. 'Infantry attacking Chehery, a regiment attacking Bulson. What progress they've made is not known. 4 Company's objective: advance via Bulson and Chemery to secure the canal crossing at Malmy.'

An advance guard is sent ahead, and off we go. At the crossroads 500 metres (546 yards) from Cheveuge, we turn off the highway, in the direction of Bulson. Half way to Bulson, our tanks overtake the regiment mounting an attack on the town. You can see small groups of enemy infantry making their way to the rear. Cautiously we drive through Bulson, now clear of enemy troops, and gradually, driving in columns, we approach the hill 100 metres (109 yards) south-west of the town. As soon as the first vehicles reach the hill, fierce artillery and AA fire opens up. Our two lead tanks take direct hits from anti-tank guns, and catch fire. We manage to get their crews back under cover, and even to put out one of the fires. In the meantime, I have driven up to the hill, and am stationary about 20 metres (22 yards) behind the burning tank, whose exploding shells are whizzing around all over the place. Despite concentrating very hard on the terrain, I cannot make out the position of the enemy. The artillery fire increases, punctuated by that of anti-tank guns and the enemy infantry.

Having reported briefly to the regiment, we now hear from them that a strong enemy tank force is attacking our right flank. The thoughts race wildly through my mind. Two of my tanks have already been knocked out. Under these circumstances, the idea of breaking through this enemy position is no more feasible than to carry out our original objective, securing the crossing at Malmy. Shall I go back to the unit, so that we can launch an attack in full strength? But the supporting infantry are following us, and if we pull out that will leave them exposed, facing the enemy tanks alone. Decision: hold on to the hill!

I cannot pass this on to the company because my radio antenna has been shot away. I walk towards my company, gesturing with arms spread wide in the direction of the hill. The men understand immediately what is wanted, and in the midst of heavy enemy fire they deploy to the right of the track. There is a steep bank to climb first. The first enemy tanks now appear beside the hill. Battle is joined at a distance of some 300–400 metres (328–437 yards). I rush back to my own tank. I have hardly mounted and given the order to fire, when a direct hit destroys the turret traverse and firing mechanisms. The battle becomes more unevenly matched all the time. I get down and run to the tank nearest me. But he has received a direct hit, too, and is out of action. Our nearest tank is now 400 metres (437 yards) away. I can't reach it, so I take cover behind a grassy mound, and watch the battle now being maintained by only three tanks on our side against overwhelming odds.

However, by adroit manoeuvring along the edge of the forest to the right of the track, and by constantly changing their firing position, the courageous crews of the three tanks manage to knock out one enemy tank after another. But these few remaining battle-worthy vehicles will not be able to hold off the enemy for long; his strength is increasing all the time. My men must be running out of ammunition. To my horror, I see that two more tanks have been hit. We only have a single vehicle left in the battle! But he is fighting so well that we are still holding on to the hill. No enemy tank has yet succeeded in breaking through. About 40 minutes have elapsed since we arrived. The crew of our last remaining tank, at the edge of the wood, are working with exemplary sang-froid. The enemy suffers further losses. He shows no vigour in attacking, but crawls around slowly on the hill.

It can only be a matter of minutes before our brave men run out of firepower. At this critical moment things, take a turn for the better. From my vantage point, I can suddenly see a number of tank shells striking the turrets of the enemy tanks. Some penetrate their armour, while others bounce off. Where is this last-minute help coming from? I look round carefully and see a German tank hull-down behind a ditch, with only the upper part of its turret and gun showing. I breathe a sigh of relief. Other sections of 1 Detachment of my regiment have appeared on the battlefield at precisely the right moment.

I signal to them to show my presence. They close smartly on the hill and put the remaining enemy tanks to flight. Only a few actually manage to get away.

The company commander has arrived with the first tanks, and I put him in the picture. The battle for the hill is not quite over yet. The enemy launches a new counterattack. The infantry troops that had been advancing towards the hill stop, and pull back somewhat. The tanks that have been put out of action are placed under cover.

And then our counterattack begins. The infantry follow behind, and the enemy retreats headlong. At this moment sections of our artillery appear – the armoured assault gun detachment and the assault battery – and open direct fire from the hill. Any further signs of the French are obliterated.

With his remaining tanks the commander of 1 Detachment follows through, closely followed by the infantry. The hill south-west of Bulson is in our hands at last! Its capture, along with the equally tough and successful battle fought by our 2 Detachment at Chemery, represents a decisive contribution to the breakthrough at Sedan. Later experience serves to confirm this fact.

By *Oberleutnant* Heinrich Krajewski

Midnight in Defeated Sedan

It is a moonlit and starlit night. The vehicles are travelling without lights. A red line appears on the nocturnal horizon, and slowly but ever more distinctly a glow of fire emerges from the darkness, reddening the sky over a wide arc. It is the burning city of Sedan, which we reach at around midnight.

The houses on the edge of the town are plunged in profound darkness, and the sound of our engines echoes loudly from their walls. The streets are littered with a desolate waste of shattered window glass, broken wires, overturned cars and trucks, fallen masonry, and household goods abandoned by the fleeing population. We are the only people in a dead-looking city, picking our way laboriously through the darkness towards the city centre in the echoing streets, in which every step reverberates. Close to the centre we scent fresh fires.

We are met by a terrible sight. The big town square is bathed in the light of crackling flames coming from nearby houses. It is one furious sea of fire, beyond all control. Red and white flames shoot upwards as though reaching for the sky itself, amidst thick smoke and constant showers of sparks; every gust of wind sends smoke and sparks flying across the square and into the streets.

This giant conflagration radiates a colossal heat, illuminating in spectral fashion the empty window apertures of the large buildings, and penetrating to their deepest recesses. The remains of incendiary bombs burn and glow on the ground, and the tarmac is soft, sticking to our boot soles. The heat is so fierce that window panes are cracking some distance away.

We stand silent in the face of this tremendous expression of destructive fury. Here roofs are crashing in, great slabs of masonry collapsing and sending up showers of sparks in their fall; while over there the flames are licking at untouched roofs, or establishing a hold – just with tiny flames at first – on doors and window-frames. Suddenly, as though at the climax of a fireworks display, the whole front of a large house moves towards us out of the fire, fragmenting into many pieces as it falls, collapsing in upon itself with a loud cracking noise, and hurling glowing debris far across the square.

We go back to our vehicles. Ahead of us is the red of the burning town, above us the starry sky, streaked with white smoke, and next to us the rippling Meuse standing out brightly in the moonlight from the darkness. Around the town the artillery rumbles, and salvoes of flak flare up. Our thoughts are with our fighting comrades.

By *Oberarzt* **Dr Ahle**
Medical Corps Leutnant

Members of a Danzig-based SS Polizei unit advance behind an Austro-Daimler ADGZ armoured car during the early days of fighting near the border, 2 September 1939.

PzKpfw I tanks pass through a burning Polish village. The two-man PzKpfw I was intended to be a training vehicle but saw considerable action in the early stages of the war.

A Panzer grenadier pitches a Stielhandgranate *24 stick grenade into a Polish position. The Poles fought hard against the invaders but were defeated by fast-moving* blitzkrieg *tactics.*

A PzKpfw I commander wearing his distinctive black uniform sits high in the turret of his tank as German armoured units head towards the Polish border, 1 September 1939.

Using a crowbar, lightly armed German soldiers prize open the shutters of a locked and deserted house as they search a town for hidden Polish troops and snipers.

Stakes mark the shallowest areas for German tank crews to follow as with a bridge demolished they ford one of the many rivers in western Poland.

Wrecked bridges in Poland, either demolished by Polish Army engineers or hit early in the campaign in attacks against communications by Luftwaffe *bombers.*

A column of PzKpfw II tanks move along a dusty track. Poor roads did not restrict the mobility of these tanks in the late summer of 1939 in Poland.

A German MG34 machine gun crew provide covering fire from a captured road block improvised by retreating Polish forces on the outskirts of Warsaw.

Carefully spread out to present a limited target against artillery fire, German soldiers move through standing crops past a blazing farmhouse in the Champagne region, May 1940.

In a very exposed position German soldiers hug the ground as French mortar or artillery fire explodes uncomfortably close.

One of the new PzKpfw IV tanks that served with Guderian's Panzergruppe emerges from a wrecked French farmhouse. Guderian was keen to test the PzKpfw IVs in action.

Heavier armour moves forward to the ridge as PzKpfw I tanks wait with dispatch riders ready to take orders to forward positions.

French troops emerge from farm buildings to surrender. Some French units fought fierce rearguard actions, but many were too frightened and demoralised to resist.

An Obergefreiter *tries out a captured French bugle. He has a wallet containing a gas cap slung across his chest since chemical warfare was seen as a real threat in 1940.*

A young German machine gunner with 50-round belts of ammunition over his shoulders wears a rag to soak up sweat and reduce chafing in the heat and dust of the French summer.

The power of the Panzerwaffe: *a mass of German armour, including the Czech-built PzKpfw 38(t), PzKpfw II and some of the rare PzKpfw IVs that fought in France.*

A PzKpfw III blasts a British position in France, seen from the viewing hatch of a PzKpfw 38(t). In the foreground is the muzzle of a 7.92mm (.303in) Czech CZ 38 machine gun.

Forced to abandon their vehicles on a wooded track, British tank crews have poured fuel over their Matilda II tanks and set fire to them during the hasty retreat to Dunkirk.

In what is probably a posed picture, PzKpfw 38(t) tanks are used to collect captured French colonial troops. The Czech tanks were a crucial addition to the Panzer divisions.

A PzKpfw I commander, immaculate in his black uniform and Schutzmütze *beret that covered a padded crash helmet, scans the horizon through 6 x 30* Dienstglas *binoculars.*

The embodiment of the power and menace of the blitzkrieg, *a PzKpfw III rumbles through the narrow streets of a battered and burning town in northern France.*

An infantry platoon laden with boxed ammunition for their MG34 machine gun plods past a PzKpfw II and PzKpfw 35(t) as German forces close up to the Somme River.

Pioneers carry a large inflatable assault boat across open ground in the Dunkirk area. With good equipment and training, rivers proved no obstacle to the Wehrmacht.

An infantry squad are ferried across a canal near Dunkirk. These inflatable boats could also be linked together with decking to make floating bridges.

Moments after he was shot a wounded French soldier pleads for help as a German patrol moves hesitantly down the street of a deserted northern French town.

The heavy calibre guns at the port of Boulogne now in German hands. French coastal defences like this would later be incorporated in Hitler's defensive Atlantic Wall after 1942.

The architect of victory – Generaloberst *Guderian in his SdKfz 251/6 half-track command post watches as a message is drafted to be transmitted over the Enigma encoder.*

A Great Day for the Flak Guns

O n 13th of May the French defences on the Meuse were crushed by a continuous eight-hour attack by concentrated Luftwaffe forces. Bridgeheads had been established at Donchery, Sedan and Thelonne.

My flak regiment had been given the task of protecting the Guderian Panzer Corps while it secured crossings over the river, and then during the actual transit, for which purpose our forces were to be deployed very far forward. We were also to defend the bridgehead itself from high- and low-level attacks, and from threats on the ground.

The flak detachments of the regiment had crossed the Meuse with the first troops of the Panzer divisions, and taken up firing positions.

The afternoon of 15 May was to show what a sensible measure this was.

The enemy, stunned by the aerial attacks of 13 May, had managed to re-group his air power by 14 May, and by throwing everything into the counter-attack was attempting to destroy the Meuse bridges used by Guderian's Panzer Corps, make the approach roads at Bouillon impassable for the troops moving up, and prevent a breakthrough at Sedan.

One French squadron attacked after another. Flying in low, planes tried to hit our bridges; as though on a pheasant shoot, they were picked off by the batteries – and not a single bomb hit a bridge!

The 14th of May turns out to be a great day of fighting for the flak regiment.

The flak units attached to Guderian's Panzer Corps succeed in shooting down 112 aircraft on this day.

While our fighter pilots aloft were dispatching one reconnaissance and fighter plane after another, the job of the flak batteries was to set their sights on the 'hedge-hopping' planes that utilized every slight rise in the landscape to approach the bridges at low level and tear across them at great speed. In peacetime we had been taught that 'hedge-hoppers' are hard to shoot down. Fortunately, this turned out to be untrue. Of the 112 aircraft brought down by the von Hippel flak regiment, 80 were destroyed by light flak artillery, a number of them within just a few minutes. All our batteries had had ample opportunity to shoot down planes the day before in the Semois sector, but most still suffered from 'first night nerves'. However, the men became more confident after their early successes, which confirmed their faith in the guns. Cooperation between air sentries, fire-control predictors and guns functioned outstandingly well everywhere. Every plane shot down was greeted with a veritable Red Indian war-whoop, and the dreadful yet beautiful sight of burning aircraft plunging to earth raised the excitement of all participants to fever pitch.

We could not help admiring the guts displayed by our opponents, attacking the bridges again and again despite all their losses and the fierce flak fire, and even shooting from planes already on fire, wounding some of our artillerymen. It was particularly gratifying for the batteries that their activities were being watched closely by their tank corps comrades as they passed over the bridges, loudly applauding every hit. The scene was more like a drama played out against the broad backdrop of the Meuse landscape than a battle in the normal sense. Because by the afternoon all enemy activity on the ground had ceased, in the hot sunshine our gun crews dressed in a motley collection of outfits, some of them in bathing trunks.

Apart from these successes in the air, on the ground machine-gun positions were eliminated, and in the bridgehead south of Bulson tanks were knocked out. The 3 Battery of the Pickert flak detachment alone on this day demolished nine bunkers and five machine guns, some of them at the first shot. The Bauer light flak battery, which had gone forward in the bridgeheads near Malmy and Chemery, made an outstanding contribution in fighting off strong enemy tank units, accounting for four armoured cars. The light batteries also successfully took part in the street fighting in Sedan.

These flak regiment successes in the air war, and its rapid and accurate intervention in ground warfare, not only consolidated its reputation with the tank troops, but also gave it unlimited confidence in the value of its own weapon. Once the battle for Flanders and Artois was over, the flak guns accompanied the fast-moving advanced troops via Amiens and St Just towards the Oise, and then via the Marne in the direction of Lyon. Fighting in the very front-line, the guns achieved further successes in smashing the enemy's armoured forces and his planes, achievements of which every artilleryman can be justly proud.

By *Oberst* von Hippel

The Infantry are Across!

– Crossing the Meuse and breaking through the Maginot Line

It is early on Whit Sunday morning. We are lying in the sun on deck chairs on the terrace of a small hotel on the Semois River. All that is needed to complete the idyll of this peaceful valley scene is church bells. Have we really crossed Belgium, to finish up just a few kilometres from the French border? Through Luxembourg and Belgium in just 24 hours times two? We drove right through the previous night on bad minor roads, through woods and small villages, often having to stop while our advance troops dealt with the enemy rearguard, or pushed aside hastily constructed road blocks. We had a few skirmishes with the Belgians behind us, and many blown-up bridges and large craters at crossings which constantly held us up, but never for long.

Near Libramont the first Frenchmen begin to appear among the PoWs. By chance I happen to spot on one prisoner's helmet the insignia of the Republic, the letters 'R.F', belonging to a cavalry unit from Sedan sent out to fight us on horseback!

Now we are sitting by the Semois – whose bridges have naturally also been blown up – waiting for our bridge to be built. We might have a long wait, because the Panzer Pioneers' bridge-building vehicles made heavy weather of the bad roads during the night, lagging far behind. The Semois valley is deep and lovely. With both banks covered in the fresh green of beech trees, the valley with its winding course reminds me of the Neckar above Heidelberg; a little gentler, perhaps, the hills not quite so high. My riflemen have dismounted from their vehicles, which have been placed under cover, one company with heavy weapons forming a bridgehead above the river, with the battalion placed in the woods north of Membre, a small town whose population were undoubtedly more astonished by the blowing up of its bridge than we are. The division is building its bridge further east, near Vresse, where sections of the two other rifle battalions are advancing southwards towards Sugny. From the other side of the river we hear the short, harsh bark of our machine guns, which have encountered the enemy and are dispersing them. It will soon be noon, but there are still no orders to continue the march.

I drive over to brigade and see that it is going to take a long time to get our bridge in place: there are marshy banks on either side. The sequence in which we cross the bridge is long established: motorcycle troops, riflemen, artillery. Far behind us, the tanks are labouring to catch up with us along those narrow, long, poor-quality roads that it cost us so much effort to negotiate last night. It is dark by the time the regiment moves off at last, and in the pale moonlight, on a good, winding and dusty road, it slowly approaches the heights of Sugny. The roads to the west, south and north have been secured. A short pause. Orders are issued.

At 06.45 hours we cross the French frontier on our southward march. The forest tracks are terrible: very narrow, badly churned up, wet and boggy – there was still snow lying here a short while ago. But our eyes light up when we see on the map that we are now in the Forest of Donchery. Donchery? Surely that is the small place near Sedan? I recall an old coloured print: 'Bismarck accompanies the Emperor Napoleon on the road from Donchery.' I can see this little picture distinctly in my mind's eye, the sleek brown horses with unnaturally small heads and large eyes pulling Napoleon's coach. The lacquer of the coach is glittering, the red and gold of Napoleon's *kepi* gleaming, and next to the coach on a large heavy horse trots the chancellor in his dark-blue greatcoat with its yellow collar.

There are road blocks everywhere in the forest, but they are not manned by the enemy. It takes a long time for the infantry to find suitable detours or to saw through trees laid across the path. A battery takes up its position in a small clearing near us. We cannot see anything at all ahead of us except tall pines and dense beech undergrowth. It is very warm, and the flies are already becoming a nuisance. From time to time a vehicle gets bogged down and has to be pulled out by the infantry, or we are hampered by a tree-stump or a stream. The struggle to progress along these poor tracks lasts hours. Reconnaissance patrols report that the next French village, Bosseval, is clear of the enemy, but we encounter heavy artillery fire there, as we do in the eastern part of Vrigne aux Bois. At the edge of the woods west of Vrigne enemy strongpoints are identified. By now it is noon, and we are still driving southwards through the forest, hoarse from the heat, dust and cursing. A dispatch rider struggles up to me at the front and hands over 'Divisional orders for crossing the Meuse at 16.00 hours on 13.5.' – On 13.5.? – What? – Good grief, that's today, in just two hours time! And we're still stuck in this damned forest! The 3rd Battalion, behind us on a different track to our right, is not faring any better. The outlook is great. And those swine over there are still keeping up their artillery fire on Vrigne, which we have to get through. A dispatch rider from the 1st Battalion brings over a handful of dum-dum bullets that have been found.

I turn off to the right from the track into the bushes and read the divisional order. From 08.00 hours to 12.00 hours disruptive attacks by the Luftwaffe on the south bank of the Meuse – 12.00 hours to 16.00 hours, Stuka attacks. Immediately after the air raids the infantry regiment will attack on either side of Donchery, and secure the hills on the other side of the Meuse. After gaining these heights, the attack is to be continued immediately, turning towards the west to take the Ardennes Canal in the Hannogne-Omicourt sector. The commander of our light artillery detachment now tells me, moreover, that the regiment's heavy detachment has been allocated to the neighbouring division, on our left – since Poland, nothing surprises us any more. My adjutant gives appropriate expression to our thoughts, and then comments: 'Nice work'. So we get on with it. Orders are quickly issued to the battalions. The question remains whether the dispatch riders will be able to find their way in this labyrinth of blocked forest tracks. The direction of our march is clear; towards the south, the direction of the sun, where our bomber squadrons are heading at this minute.

Finally we are out of the forest, and we emerge into the open at Château du Rossignol. We can see that Vigne is still under fire from enemy artillery, but I am encouraged by the news that a company of the 1st Battalion had already entered Donchery at 15.45 hours. At 16.00 hours, the regiment is certainly not ready to attack. But far away, against the steep wooded slopes above the Meuse, we can see the Stukas diving in, and where they go in, enormous round clouds rise from the earth. We pass right through Vigne; the church on the left of the road is burning to the ground. Strange how ghostly the red glow looks in the sunlight, and how the outlines of the red-hot gothic portals shiver like delicate filigree-work. At the southern edge of Vigne I transfer to a motorcycle combination, and seated in the sidecar I race over to the 1st Battalion. At a curve in the road cut rather deeply into the hillside, I find the commander under cover. He reports that one of his companies is in Donchery, and coming under fierce fire there from artillery and machine guns on the opposite bank. By daylight it was impossible to bring up the battalion, and particularly the inflatable assault boats, to get across the river. Meanwhile, the 3rd Battalion has arrived in Vigne and is securing the terrain to its right. I drive to the brigade to find out about the progress of the 2nd Battalion, which belongs to the group marching up on the left and approaching the eastern side of Donchery along the other road.

The brigade and division commanders are on Point 203, at the edge of the forest between the two roads, from where they have an excellent view of the terrain right down to the Meuse. The battalion on the left, like the one on the right, has tried a number of times to cross the Meuse in assault boats, but all their efforts have been beaten back with heavy losses. It is only on the right, with the 1st Battalion, that a lieutenant with a few volunteers has succeeded in swimming over to the other bank. After some time, he returns with excellent intelligence, but with only a couple of his brave men. The division's light artillery – the heavy detachment having been re-allocated – does not quite manage to disable the bunkers on the other side, particularly west of Donchery. A platoon of heavy tanks, sheltered by houses in Donchery and firing at close quarters, does not succeed in silencing all of them, either. There is still fierce enemy artillery fire landing in Donchery and on the railway line that both prongs of our attack must cross.

It is now slowly getting dark, and I am back with the 1st Battalion. How old the commander suddenly looks; there are two deep furrows framing his mouth, and his eyes beneath his helmet are deep-set. We walk behind each other along the roadside ditch, followed by our adjutants and the dispatch riders. An infantry pioneer troop drags slowly along ahead of us; they are carrying a pneumatic assault boat, inflated ready for the crossing, and camouflaged with a few branches. What an effort it is for the men to move, hardly lifting their feet off the ground.

We too plod along wearily. After all the sleepless nights our feet are heavy, and feel like swollen clumps of wood in our boots. On the right there are a few bushes, from which another inflatable boat emerges to be carried forward; on the left, one or two houses, and then the road rises and crosses the railway cutting via an iron bridge. The bridge is under fire. We go to the right through a farmyard, through gardens and a park, and see the railway station in front of us. How hard it is making your way over the sharp ballast between the many lines. We have hardly passed the shed on the right of the station, when a barrage of shells whistles over our heads, forcing us to take cover. They hit the garden we have just passed through. We go, still in single file, past the rows of houses. The place is burning, and all the streets are brightly lit by fire. You have to feel your way forward from one block of houses to the next, because all the roads leading to the river are as bright as day, open to view, and raked by machine-gun fire. We clump along the main street that runs parallel to the Meuse, close to the market place. This square too is lit up like daylight by the burning houses; you can read the map out here on the road. The house where we have paused has a little front garden that sets it back a few metres from the other houses.

The dispatch riders of two companies are here, and a doctor is treating the wounded that have just been brought up from the river bank. The rear of this house faces on to the Meuse. I walk the few steps to the nearest corner and sit on the ledge of a shop window. The road on the right leads down to the river. It is impossible to cross the street without making yourself a target silhouetted against the brightly lit market place. I want to get across to the 2nd Battalion. The dispatch riders we have sent out, who have to make a big detour via the station, have not yet managed to make contact with the 2nd Battalion. Contact seems impossible …

I jump into the light armoured reconnaissance vehicle and drive fast, back over the railway bridge. The surface of the road has taken a direct hit, but it isn't too bad. On one side the parapet has been shot away, too. As soon as we get to the bridge, a couple of shells explode behind us. My dispatch rider is still obediently standing where I left him. I drive with him at speed to brigade, and report that with the means at our disposal it is impossible to cross the river in the western part of Donchery, or further west. And now I learn that my 2nd Battalion – although with heavy losses – succeeded some time ago in crossing the Meuse to the east of Donchery, with one company at first, and then with all the others; and that the battalion's heavy weapons are being taken across on rafts at this minute. The two battalions on the right receive orders to strike north, after leaving security measures in place, and to cross the river as soon as possible, either behind the 2nd Battalion or at some point further east.

That's wonderful – the 2nd Battalion has got across! How quickly I throw off the mood of depression that was weighing me down a few minutes earlier. Orders are quickly drafted for the two battalions on the right, and sweeping round to the north the regimental staff now drives through Vrigne once more. The burning church has collapsed in the meantime, and is now just a glowing heap.

We take the road along the bend in the Meuse to the 2nd Battalion's crossing point, east of Donchery. The battalion has crossed by now, along with its lighter combat vehicles, and so has the motorcycle battalion. A raft having just become available, I go across on it with my adjutant, taking my 'mount' over, too: the dispatch rider with his heavy motorbike and sidecar. The other vehicles stay behind on the bank, because it will be some time before the construction of a ferry and a bridge can be started.

When we are already standing on the raft, a dispatch rider appears and shouts out after me that the 3rd Battalion is arriving! And now we are on the Meuse. The current is stronger than I would have guessed, considering the breadth of the river, which also seems to be quite deep. On the other bank our combined efforts succeed in pulling the motorbike out, and since there is only one seat in the sidecar, I have to leave my adjutant behind, and carry on alone down the highway towards Sedan, soon turning off on to the road that runs south in the direction of Chehery and Malmy. I note with astonishment the heavy damage to all the strong bunkers along the Meuse. Almost all their apertures have been smashed to pieces. The roof of one bunker has been torn off completely and pushed upwards, so that it is now sitting at an angle like a beret on top of the bunker. The Stuka bombs have created masses of enormous craters; rifles are lying by the roadside, along with a smashed anti-tank gun and some big branches blown off the trees by the bombing. The road runs alongside the river, separated from it only by a 50-metre-wide meadow. On the other side of the road, there is a strip, barely 100 metres (109 yards) wide, of gently rising meadows and fields with a few fruit trees. Between them, every 100 metres (109 yards) or so, stands a bunker. Some of these bunkers are still unfinished. The wooden shuttering is in place, but the concrete not yet poured into the foundations. Amazing, these Frenchmen! They have been working on their line of fortresses for 20 years and have created special elite fortress troops, who wear a special badge bearing the motto: 'Here none shall pass.' And yet here they are with their bunkers on the Meuse still unfinished, more than six months after the beginning of the war!

Behind the field of fire left open for the bunkers, dense deciduous woods rise steeply up to Point 325. The rise in altitude from the river to the top of the ridge is nearly 200 metres (218 yards). I overtake tanks from our neighbouring division, brought across the river by assault craft and now heading south, and I take the first forest track off to the right and up towards the heights. The hill is criss-crossed by a tangle of paths, all as carefully maintained as in a park. I think to myself that there must be something like a monument here. The battalion has now turned towards the west; I cannot afford the time to look for its commander, but drive straight on over the hill looking for map reference Point 237, on the edge of the forest, which must offer a clear view to the west. It is not at all easy to find the spot, because there are far more tracks through the woods than are marked on the map. From the edge of the forest, I can see the River Bar far below, and just beyond it the Ardennes Canal. There is no sign of the enemy. The motorbike gets caught up in a telegraph wire, which of course winds itself several times around the axle. While the driver is disentangling it, the commander of the anti-tank detachment arrives along the same path looking for Point 237, where we are expecting to receive new orders from the brigade commander. We drive back together and find the place at last; it offers an excellent view. A few metres outside the wood two holes have been dug, 5 metres (16 feet) deep and 5 metres (16 feet) square, with vertical walls. Corrugated iron for roofing lies nearby. It is a mystery what kind of 'fortifications' these are meant to be! We hear machine-gun fire some distance away, getting gradually nearer. It is completely quiet around us, neither friend nor foe to be seen. Aren't those tanks, clattering through the woods? They are shooting, and getting closer. From the rapidity of their firing we can tell that they are ours. French machine-guns fire much more slowly, almost sluggishly, so that at first we thought they were artillery. We exchange a laugh, and agree that it would be best to take cover, after all, because if we are spotted from a distance through the tanks' narrow slits while they are under way they might mistake us for Frenchmen! So with our dispatch riders we disappear down the ladder into the uncovered dugout to wait until the tanks, accompanied by infantry, break out of the woods quite near us. They are firing at French troops who are retreating downhill towards the Ardennes Canal.

I now drive back up to Point 325, where my adjutant has arrived in the meantime, as well as the artillery observer. The French pilots seem to have noticed at last that we are here. They come over singly, and sometimes in pairs, towards the Meuse and our crossing-points, which we cannot see from here. We can hear fairly intense fire from our flak guns, though, and occasionally see a plane going down in flames. They mostly fly very low, so that we have a superb view of the pearl necklaces of bullets flying up from our light flak, and can observe the hits perfectly without binoculars. A plane approaching from due south flies vertically into the tracer path of the flak; we see the shells crash into the big bird, and see it explode in mid-air into a brilliant ball of flame – presumably its bombs have been hit. Above the fireball a dense black cloud instantly forms, and out of it all plummet like large drops, easily distinguished, the two engines and the two crew members. Then a few fragments plunge more slowly to earth, and finally the aluminium parts flutter down very slowly like burnt pieces of paper. In these few hours alone we saw 12 enemy aircraft brought down, and our view was limited to the south and west: we could not see northwards to where the real target of these planes lay – our bridges – and how many were shot down there.

The 3rd Battalion has now crossed over, too, and immediately behind Donchery swings round towards Pont à Bar and in the direction of Flize. I place the 1st Battalion as a rearguard and reserve on the western slope of the hill. On our left, the neighbouring division is advancing southwards. That morning the enemy attacked them with tanks, but was beaten off with heavy losses. The majority of our artillery is still on the other side of the Meuse. The bridge is not finished yet, its construction having been continually hampered by bombers and by fire from artillery in the region of Flize. A battery commander reports that individual batteries are moving across our neighbouring division's bridge, which is beyond the bend in the Meuse and has been completed without disruption by artillery fire. A few of our tank companies have also crossed there. We now receive an order from brigade for the infantry to advance to the west and establish a bridgehead across the Ardennes Canal on a line running from Flize to Hannogne and St Aignan. Attack to begin at 12:30 hours.

On our hill we are excellently placed, as though in an aircraft, to view the terrain for the attack, lying clear and open beneath us. We can see the infantry reconnaissance troops moving off first, to be overtaken by the tanks; we can see enemy fire coming from the edge of Hannogne, and the rapid response to it guided in by our artillery observer; we can see our shells landing in Hannogne along with the tracer shells from our tank gun. More tanks are now beginning to appear on the meadow-land outside Hannogne. You can clearly distinguish the different platoons, driving as though demonstrating manoeuvres on the training ground; their formation is perfect, and the whole thing looks unreal, like the little counters representing troops in a sand-table exercise. The files of riflemen advance behind them. From here you can see from the organization of the infantry where the heavy weapons are distributed among them. It is a wonderful attack, perfect for showing as a demonstration in peacetime.

Then suddenly we can clearly see the track-marks left on the green of the meadow by one tank platoon. They are getting close to the river, and the marks are becoming darker, and then completely black. They must have reached marshy land, and sure enough one of the platoons stops; fortunately, it is well sited to support the infantry's attack across the River Bar. Many tanks now concentrate their fire on the access road to Hannogne, while the artillery's shells are landing in the village itself and the road out on the other side, where with the binoculars you can clearly see enemy units retreating. There is only a footbridge across the River Bar at this point, but the bridge over the Ardennes Canal, just beyond the Bar, is undamaged. The tanks turn off to the right when the infantry reach the beginning of Hannogne; driving fast, they find a bridge over the river at the nearby Viller sur Bar. After a moment they can be seen approaching the village of Hannogne, which is burning in places, from the east.

The division commander arrives just in time to see the last sections of the battalion crossing the canal, and its foremost units pushing forward with the lead tanks on the other side of the village. I am in radio contact with all battalions, and they report that the enemy is retreating; so we will have formed the required bridgehead very soon! The bridge over the Meuse is not yet ready, and will probably take some time yet. The many air attacks have only disrupted the work; none of the bombs has hit the bridge itself. A plane is brought down into the water only metres away from our bridge. The enemy increases his artillery fire on the right flank, so that work on the bridge has to stop from time to time. The regiment's vehicles are still back on the other side of the Meuse, but we need our combat vehicles, and we need ammunition and, above all, field kitchens. The brigade commander, too, is still on the other side of the Meuse, in charge of the division's transit over the river. I inform the divisional commander that I am going to drive quickly down to the bridge to find out when I can expect our vehicles to appear.

By the Meuse I meet the brigade adjutant, who holds out very little hope of our bridge being serviceable before midnight. To get back to my command post, I take the little country track that leads directly from the shattered Meuse bridge at Donchery to Point 325. By doing so, I obtain my first view of the town from the other side, and also take a look at the demolished bridge, and the many bunkers opposite Donchery that gave us so much trouble last night. Some are shot to pieces, some are completely intact. From one bunker, west of the bridge, the barrel of a French field artillery piece is still protruding, although badly damaged by a hit, and jammed. In one bunker, the twisted end of a railway line, forming the inner frame of the aperture, is poking out from the dead eye of an embrasure; the metre-thick concrete around it has been pushed outwards, and the inside of the aperture and the bunker are completely blackened – probably the result of a direct hit on the aperture, exploding the ammunition inside. If so, our tank and artillery gunners did some good shooting last night, in spite of the darkness!

The track up the hillside is very steep; on both sides of it there are abandoned machine-gun posts, and discarded rifles lying near them. Next to a transverse path, I see a fabulous artillery observation post. From the front the flattened, thickly reinforced dome is barely visible; the observation slit is even more strongly reinforced, and hardly bigger than the peak of a cap; the whole thing is difficult to spot from 30 metres (100 feet). Reached by a trench from behind, however, this little post is very well arranged to take two men, with seats, telephone connections, and everything necessary. Looking at the thing again from the outside, I am astonished. Running out on both sides from the post is a little channel, 30 centimetres (12 inches) wide and 15 centimetres (6 inches) deep. This was presumably meant to be the trench for the telephone cables, but these cables for conveying firing orders from the armoured observation post have not even been laid in the small channel, but hang at knee height above the ground from laths of wood nailed to little posts. The cables are nicely variegated: red, green, yellow and blue, six of them on each side, neatly divided.

This is really amazing! These people have built a wonderfully reinforced armoured observation post which, to judge by the grass growing around it, must have stood there for at least a year – and then, what do they do but suspend the cables in the open air, nice and low and designed so that, if they are not ripped apart by our shells, at least their own poilus will trip over them in the darkness. It is not hard to imagine how proudly this armoured observation post was shown off to superior officers, before the trip wires were hastily strung up at the last minute. Still further up the slope, with a good field of fire, machine-gun posts have been dug in everywhere and well camouflaged. I later establish that they surround the hill completely, making it heavily fortified on all sides.

I drive on, and on the hilltop I emerge without any obvious transition from the forest into a beautifully maintained park. Among a group of tall old trees stands a wonderful little château, modern and elegant, in light red brick with white relief features, behind lawns and flowerbeds. Very elegant stables and heated garages stand opposite. Entering the house through the lobby, I walk into a superb hall with high arched windows rising from the floor, with magnificent armchairs, a fireplace, and a massive oak table with lovely candelabra, and I think to myself what wonderful quarters this would make for the night, if we don't have to move on! It's not impossible, because the vehicles are hardly likely to arrive before the morning.

Returning to my command post, I send my orderly officer with a few men up to the château to secure it in case we are lucky enough to snatch a few hours sleep here. Hardly have I given out the order, when the division commander asks me whether I know anywhere around here where we can spend the night.

– What can I do? I've lost my château already! But no, the general is extremely kind; his staff are not with him, and he only wants us to share the place with him and his adjutant for the night.

I drive with the general up to the little château. By now it is 18:30 hours. After a wash and brush up, we go out on to the terrace, which offers a wonderful view to the north. Immediately below us is Donchery, with Sedan on the right. From here the course of the Meuse can be clearly seen, with its great bend between Sedan and Donchery; you can see the canal that cuts off this bend, and every man, every inflatable raft on the bank; you can also see where our bridge is being built, and the many bunkers; and you can see far to the west where the river fades away into the dusk. In front of the hills opposite, from which we descended, lies the burning village of Vrigne. You can see the two roads on which my battalions advanced yesterday, and you can see for kilometres along our approach road, and every man and every motorcycle on these roads; the light shell damage to my bridge over the railway can be made out very clearly. I am silent, gazing out over this wonderful landscape. It is incredible that we were so completely over-looked, and yet managed to get up here! What were the French actually doing? From here, they must have been watching every one of us from noon yesterday onwards, when we left that forest over there. After all, on this whole long stretch we only had cover for a few minutes, from the houses in Vrigne or from a few trees. The general must have been thinking similar thoughts. We look at each other and cannot express our feelings. Now we are through, though! Down below lies the Meuse, and all these bunkers comprise the famed Maginot Line. France's fate was decided once before in this same place. I calculate that that was 70 years ago. In between there has been the victorious summer of 1914, as well as 1918, the bitter years after the war, and the national revival. I am profoundly happy to have experienced this. Victory is a glorious feeling!

The evening news is on the portable radio. We hear about successes in Holland and Belgium, and are deeply disappointed that there is nothing about us. Damn it all, we've crossed the Meuse and broken through the Maginot Line, doesn't that count for something? Berlin must have known about it for ages. We got up here last night, and now it's evening again. It takes a while to dawn on us that the people in Berlin want to let our opponent go on thinking that we have not fully realized how much we have achieved, so that he takes as long as possible to become aware that the thrust of our tank corps into his hinterland is in fact the terminal grip of the iron fist on his jugular. My driver twiddles the knob of the radio, and faintly it picks up the interval signal of a broadcasting station: 'Deutschland, Deutschland über alles'. We have always sung 'From the Meuse to the Memel' [river forming the border of the old East Prussia] – and it occurs to me that today we really are on the Meuse! And it is just a year since the Führer won back the Memel for us.

A little later we sit in deep, heavy chairs by the fireside in the hall of the château; flushed with victory, red wine and the flickering glow of the fire.

[The events described above cover the attack across the Meuse at Sedan by the XIX Panzer Corps composed of the 1st, 2nd and 10th Panzer Divisions on 13 May 1940. At this point the river is about 60 metres (65 yards) wide, fairly fast flowing and unfordable – if it is covered by fire it is an effective obstacle. The French had constructed concrete bunkers about 457 metres (500 yards) apart and 274m (300 yards) from the river and reinforced them with field defences. Guderian knew that once they were committed to the attack it was essential to keep the pressure on the French. Though his tanks were still reaching the river, he launched his attack, supported by no less than 1500 bombers of Generalleutnant Bruno Loerzer's I Fliegerkorps and General Wolfram von Richthofen's VIII Fliegerkorps, a force he called 'the whole of the Luftwaffe' when briefing his commanders. The men who made this vital assault were the 1st Rifle Regiment commanded by the energetic Oberst Herman Balck. Balck had trained his regiment hard for war and would go on to command XLVIII Panzer Corps in Russia and Army Group G later in the war. Protected by artillery and fire and air attacks, using inflatable assault boats, the riflemen not only crossed the river at 15.00 hours but by the evening had pushed 5 kilometres (3 miles) in the dark and seized the dominating high ground on the left bank. Opposite them was the French 2nd Army under General Huntziger. From Monthermé to Sedan the front was held by the 61st, 51st and 71st Infantry Divisions, formations that had a high proportion of older reservists, many of whom were badly trained and led, and which broke after the intense dive-bomber and artillery attacks. Some, however, fought until the Germans were actually in their positions.

During 14 May the French and British air forces attempted to destroy the bridgeheads at Sedan. Their light bombers – Fairey Battles, Bréguets, Amiots and LeOs – braved the German fighter and flak screen, but when the survivors broke through their light bombs did little damage. By the end of the day, the Allies had lost 90 aircraft. The RAF official history stated that 'no higher rate of loss in an operation of comparable size had ever been experienced by the Royal Air Force.']

By *Oberst* Koelitz

The Main Aid Station at Floing

It happened surprisingly quickly: at one moment we were on the march over the Ardennes, part of a double column, and the next, having just crossed the French border, we could only move a metre at a time. We had plenty of time to look around us. The enemy had obviously been overwhelmed by a shock attack. On and near the road lay dead horses, already beginning to smell quite badly in the heat, as well as shattered vehicles and tanks.

The frequent aerial battles quite reasonably made us keen that the enemy should not drop his bombs accurately, hemmed in as we were between the forest and a column of pioneers carrying large charges which no doubt would have blown us several hundred metres over the trees if there had been an explosion. Then – at about 16.00 hours – a dispatch rider arrives from the head of the column with an urgent demand for surgeons to help in the forward aid station at Floing, a small suburb of Sedan. Admittedly, it will be difficult to get through to the front.

A case of instruments is quickly collected, and a medical corps second-lieutenant, a surgeon, rushed off by motorbike to the front. He is in luck, because an air attack has forced most of the columns off the road. In the burning village of St Menge, shortly before their destination, there is no space for even a motorbike to slip through. Here in the crush he meets another dispatch rider sent to fetch further medical assistance. The doctor sends him to the rear, and partly on foot, partly with lifts from other motorcycle riders, he reaches the aid station in Floing. It is impossible to get 3 Platoon through. The only response our company commander can make to the new plea for help is to send just his other surgeon, a captain, to the front by car with a supply of instruments and a couple of orderlies.

It is a journey that few of the participants will forget in a hurry. The little Mercedes ambulance demonstrates fabulous manoeuvrability. Where there are two columns on the road, it slips in between them, and where three columns block the whole of the highway, it negotiates the ditch at the side of the road, and gets past that way. The military police holding up their 'stop' signs drop them on seeing the Red Cross, and the breakneck trip continues over open country and close to the edge of massive craters. But just as it was difficult to overtake the stream of troops, it is suddenly equally difficult to escape from the pull of the stream of traffic just before the military bridge. It takes a leap from the swaying car in the choking dust and smoke from the burning houses of Floing to reach the entrance to the little château that has been designated as an aid station, only 300 metres (328 yards) away from the pontoon bridge.

Things looked bad in the château, however. On the left, in the largest ground-floor room, on stretchers and on straw lay man after man, friend and foe mixed together, a scene it was impossible to take in at first sight. There was no question at this point of checking the casualties in an orderly procedure. The corridors, the rooms on the upper floor, the kitchen area, were all full of wounded men. The first thing to do is to create space and order. It is understandable that the medical officer in charge, having been diverted here from the advance, and working without the rest of his unit, could not cope alone. There were dressings to be checked, pain-killer injections to be administered, and patients to be moved with the aid of French stretcher bearers. Cloth is brought over in great bales from a nearby textile factory and cut up to make blankets; and the room selected as an operating theatre has to be cleared and cleaned. The onset of night with its fireworks from the flak all around, fighting off the constant air-raids on the bridge, brings further problems with it. The blackout must be enforced; you step on people's feet, and get caught up in straw and stretchers. The pocket torch is a blessing. You hold it with your teeth to keep your hands free. Water has to be brought across the road from a farmyard. We are really overwhelmed at first by the sheer volume of work, especially as more wounded are being brought in all the time. Individual patients fall silent for ever, and make way for others.

By the kitchen stove, hidden behind curtains they have rigged up, a few stragglers have been discovered waiting to re-join their units, and are busy cooking just for themselves. The hearth has to be released for tea-making and for sterilizing instruments. The way our wounded men put up with their pain and discomfort is truly courageous! Not one of them screams for attention, every one of them is considerate towards his even more seriously wounded comrades, and even helps as far as he can to lighten our heavy load. Hats off to the French soldier, too, who suffers the pain of his wounds in quiet dignity and goes about his Good Samaritan duties without letting up!

Finally, at 04.00 hours, 15 May, the company arrives. On the choked roads they had only been able to move at a snail's pace the whole night long. And now in an instant everything is as it should be in a main aid station. The surgeons work at two extremely well-lit operating tables, and one wounded man after another passes rapidly through their hands. Anaesthetics, treatment of wounds, splint dressings – all bring the longed-for relief from pain. The less serious cases are treated in the open air by the company commander and a junior doctor.

The mass of casualties can no longer be accommodated in the building itself. The wide lawns of the park fill up. Tents for the wounded and for dressing stations are set up; there is practically no chance of cover from air-raids. Around noon, the medical officers of a Luftwaffe squadron arrive to help out. In view of the colossal task we face, help is certainly needed, and gratefully accepted. Again and again the bales of cloth from the nearby factory serve to provide more blankets for the wounded, who begin to feel freezing cold as soon as the sun goes down. Operations continue throughout the night, with everybody making a supreme effort to overcome sleep and physical exhaustion. However, at least the stream of wounded has decreased since the late afternoon and stopped altogether from time to time, so that we have a chance to catch up with our work.

With the radiant sunrise of 16 May we are able to say with pride: 'We've done it, we've passed the greatest possible test of action our company can face!' Dead tired, everybody who can be spared stretches out, limbs as heavy as lead, to take a short rest. After a refreshing wash, the sunny day tempts us to relax under the huge trees as the ambulance crews busily transfer the wounded.

During this short period of activity, our company tended 650 casualties. The best reward for our work is our proud knowledge that nobody failed the test, and that each can rely on the other, today as ever.

By *Stabarzt* Dr Eisler
Medical Corps Hauptmann

You Need Luck!

My detachment has taken up positions in a French artillery emplacement, part of the fortifications around Sedan. A few hours earlier the sudden appearance of German tanks had left no time for an orderly retreat, and head over heels the enemy crews abandoned their carefully sited guns, their teams of horses, baggage trains and convoys. They ran for the nearest cover, leaving their ready-loaded guns and making for the woods.

The night passes quietly. Towards morning we are woken up by the commander of the regiment personally. He is looking for our command post, and only locates it by our loud snoring. We are utterly exhausted; even cigarettes are no help any more. It is not surprising that we do not wake up of our own accord at 06.00 hours. But the regimental commander is not happy in the role of orderly NCO. He gives clear voice to his displeasure – but it passes, and has already passed when I get orders to move forward via Chemery and Malmy to check out artillery sites around Vendresse and observation posts near Omont. Suddenly, I'm wide awake! Get the motorbike driver ready, and off! I am on my way.

It is a lovely clear morning. There is no sound except for our engine. 'Keep below 30kph [20mph].' The driver reduces his speed. I am able to follow our route perfectly on the map without it flapping around too much in the wind.

The peaceful country scene in this glorious morning sunlight is undisturbed as I turn north just before Vendresse, to check the potential of a gorge for artillery positions, as commanded. 'Oh, there's a war on.' I had almost forgotten, thinking I was going it alone, since I had not met another soul on my roughly 12-kilometre (7-mile) trip. Ahead of me and to the right of the country road stand French tanks. Around them lie their crews, just where they fell last night, attempting to escape from their knocked-out vehicles.

The gorge in question turns out to be excellent for a battery, so it's back to Vendresse. I take a different route back, and in a copse I stumble across some perfectly camouflaged units of a Panzer regiment from our division. Enquiring about the situation from the regimental adjutant, I notice that a third cross is being set up next to two that are already in place on a small hill. The adjutant says: 'Yesterday. An old classmate of mine and two of his men, for heaven's sake!' He is choked. I look away quickly and run through the situation report again. It is only then that I realize that our advance guard has only got as far as the west side of Vendresse. But I am supposed to be reconnoitring for possible observation posts at Omont! When I tell the others what is on my mind, they reply: 'Just wait till this afternoon. We're going to be attacking in an hour's time, and we'll have reached Omont by about noon.' I am not listening, for I have just noticed a pair of boots sticking out from under a dirty piece of canvas stained with oily marks. Someone is grimly digging nearby. Somebody else is tying up a small parcel. I am not quite concentrating: two boots under that dirty canvas! But the information I have picked up is 'infantry spearhead outside Vendresse!'

I drive through Vendresse; my motorbike driver takes a look around. 'Lieutenant, they can't have got this far yet!' But maybe they are even further ahead. We are bound to meet up with the forward infantry units on this road. Damn it, what's that? Small brown boxes lie like a crude necklace strung along the carriageway. Mines! No, they can't be – our infantry is still ahead of us, and they would have cleared them away well before this. But drive carefully between these things! There is a couple of centimetres leeway on either side.

There's somebody over there in the field: at last we can find out what's going on. On closer inspection, this turns out to be a little old Frenchman, almost totally deaf. I have to yell to make him understand my question: has he seen any German troops? No, no Germans yet, but 'Vive l'Angleterre!' So that's the way the wind is blowing! I am puzzled. Maybe the infantry are ahead of us, after all? How else could the old man mistake me for an Englishman? Back on the highway, I observe the stretch of road ahead. There is nothing suspicious to be seen. Some way off there is a roadblock. Horses are running around loose. Vehicles straddle the road. It does not look like the site of a battle, more like a hasty retreat. So those were mines earlier on! I shudder: two centimetres leeway on either side! I lower my binoculars, borrow the motorcyclist's rifle, put the map away, and take off the safety catch. Slowly and cautiously we drive on. It looks as though the enemy cleared out of here some four or five hours ago. There are none of our people up ahead. So be careful, very careful! We travel in shadow, close to the edge of the wood on our left hand side. We have to get round the roadblock: we get off, push, and get on again. I stop on the next rise. The round hill ahead might be Omont. About 3 kilometres (2 miles) away, by my estimate. The road itself is clear. There is no movement to be seen through the glasses. Although I am now completely calm, I do not relax my concentration for one second. The observation posts near Omont and on the next hill are unusable. Somewhat disappointed, I drive down again, round the tight bend below the top of the hill. It does not improve my mood to discover that south of Omont, too, there is only continuous wooded terrain. But perhaps there will be a clear view from somewhere around Chagny, 3 kilometres (2 miles) to the south-west.

I get through Omont without incident. The village is as quiet as the grave, and somewhat sinister. The motorbike engine is far too loud. I would rather have crept through Omont. But we have no choice but to fly through at top speed, and down the road to Chagny. Whinnying horses scatter. I am struck by their strange stirrups. My driver, Desoye, roars at breakneck speed between cars, bits of equipment and animals. Finally the road ahead is clear. Below us, cut off by the bend, I see the edge of Chagny village.

From the roadside ditch, in the dark shadow of the trees, I scrutinize the hill opposite, behind Chagny. People are walking around peacefully over there. I can't make out any details. I wonder whether they are our own infantry that I've been looking for. If so, that would mean they have advanced 10 kilometres (6.5 miles) beyond Vendresse …?

'Lieutenant, French troops up ahead.' 'Where?' I shout without thinking, because I have already spotted a Moroccan horseman trotting cautiously around the bend in the road 70 metres (75 yards) away. He pulls his short rifle up sharply to fire from the hip. But my shot is quicker.

He gives a jerk, the horse rears up, turns – and disappears around the bend, its rider sliding from the saddle.

The locality gets rather lively. My driver has already started up his machine and got going. I make a mess of leaping on to the passenger seat –

we nearly finish up in the drainage ditch. Full speed ahead! Above the thunder of the bike there are thin, singing noises. We tear at breakneck speed back up the hill to Omont.

Suddenly I see German armoured reconnaissance cars ahead. I wave my arms desperately, because I can see the roofs of the four-wheel vehicles shutting, the machine guns taking aim. They haven't recognized us. We are coming out of the shadow of the woods. The sun is behind the trees to our rear, blinding the gunners. I want to yell and shout, but I can't – there's a lump in my throat. There's no point, anyway: if they pull the trigger now …

It is only when we stop close to the cars to wipe the sweat from our brows that they open their roofs again. 'By a hair's breadth,' says the lieutenant to me. He even acts as though I should be grateful to him for not opening fire on us. I am furious, even bursting with rage. I inform the tank men in detail about my observations. Our leave-taking is not exactly friendly on my part.

As I look back, I cannot see anything along the edge of the woods. There is just a shimmering in the air. If we had not bolted up the hill like the wind, the machine gunners would have had time to crook their fingers! It doesn't bear thinking about.

We drive slowly back through Omont. It all keeps going through my mind – the sudden appearance of the Spahi, the upward jolt of the gun at his hip, the closing roofs of our own armoured cars, the machine guns taking aim … You need luck in this world.

And at this minute, too. For I spot a Frenchman in one of the houses, who suddenly takes a convenient tumble through the window on to the road, straight into my arms. He is not altogether willing to follow my invitation to squat on the bike in front of me and behind the driver, on the handgrip of my seat. But he has no choice; he's got to climb on. My previous bad mood has gone, and so has my anger. My first prisoner! Off we go, Monsieur! We have already been standing around for 30 seconds. Who knows what else is lurking in these houses, or who is taking aim at us? The next thing is to get out of Omont.

The good old machine, expertly steered by my demon driver, makes heavy weather of the trip back with its unusual load. The Frenchman in front of me howls. This form of transport, on top of his sudden plunge from 'freedom' into this predicament, does not seem to be to his liking. I don't care. I pat him on the shoulder in a rather familiar fashion as the wind whistles sharply past our ears: 'La guerre est finie.' He nods nervously. He has turned white with fear at this hellish journey, shutting his eyes and clinging on desperately to Desoye. I have to laugh about my first prisoner. He behaved like a rabbit when he felt my hand on his neck and saw my little pistol as he was pulled out of the window.

Suddenly I spot our forward sentry post. The sentries take cover when they see us careering towards them, but leave us alone when I signal with my arms. Astonished, they watch us go past, and then burst out laughing. I am still feeling annoyed with them for not putting in an appearance earlier as we set out so innocently, when there is a bang. The Frenchman slides to and fro on his handgrip as though being shaken; his eyes roll, and he thinks he's done for. The machine goes into a skid, but Desoye corrects it flawlessly. Before he can bring the bike to a halt, there is another thump, and we are thrown up into the air. In masterly fashion my driver maintains control of his machine, despite the fact that three people are struggling to regain their balance. My prisoner is a broken man. His head is drooping, and he just wants to shut the world out.

What happened? A few metres in front of us, one of the mines we so fortunately survived on the way out went off. Immediately after the explosion, we zoomed into the hole it had made. Once again, for the umpteenth time today, I can only shake my head in surprise.

In the course of the night, my surprise reaches new heights when I lose my way and wander into a group of Frenchmen I do not recognize as such. In fact I am quite pleased to come across somebody to give me directions. I call out and go over to them. I only become aware of the true state of affairs when several rifle muzzles point in my direction and I recognize the outlines of the French helmets. Never have I felt smaller than at this moment when I am looking down the barrels of three rifles 5 metres (16 feet) away. With one jump I reach the ditch at the side of the road. The Frenchmen are startled, and throw themselves to the ground. I slowly crawl back to the waiting motorbike driver and wipe my brow. It was my pistol against three cocked and aimed rifles, while my pistol was in its holster on my belt! I was too agitated to pull it out.

I go forward again, armed with the motorcyclist's rifle. The Frenchmen must be totally confused. They have retreated. But I still catch up with them. As I have taken cover, they cannot see me. But I can see their helmets. I call on them to surrender. They recognize their untenable position and come over, to march willingly into captivity. With a feeling of being truly born lucky, I can go to sleep with an easy mind … touch wood!

By *Leutnant* Deparade

Thirteen Men and Four Tanks

N ear Monthermé we are formed into an armoured pursuit group. Consisting of 13 men with four reconnaissance tanks, we are sent out as a reconnaissance patrol. As we trundle across the newly assembled pontoon bridge over the Meuse, three French bombers attack the bridge. The bombs hit the water and the banks. We step up our speed to get out of danger. Soon afterwards, just seconds after German fighters have put in an appearance in the sky, we can see all three enemy planes plunging earthwards, flaming like torches.

There is no time for thoughts or feelings! *Pursuit* is what our orders say! Every one of us is inspired by the same thought: 'Forwards!' 'Forwards' has always been the entire meaning and content of our education, training and preparation for this struggle. 'Forwards' is the name of our commander's tank. And 'forwards' is the message drummed out by our recce group rolling along the devastated roads that were so recently the target of German bombs and shells.

Shattered vehicles, tanks and artillery litter the countryside, the smoking ruins of a strong position. Some stragglers even loose off pointless shots at our armour. We do not return fire, because our objective is much further away, and we need to conserve our ammunition.

There is increasing movement in the forest. In places we overtake small groups of French and Negro troops, all in a terrible state. We drive past vehicles full to overflowing with fleeing soldiers. The numbers of retreating troops become ever greater. In larger groups, sometimes up to platoon size, they move westwards, shaken and demoralized. We meet no resistance anywhere; most do not even realize we are Germans. At all costs we must avoid getting held up here, anyway. Our goal lies 80 kilometres (50 miles) ahead of us.

That is why we leave the highway, and continue on side roads. We have a constant view of the enemy's lines of retreat. The radio operator works feverishly to relay all that we have seen.

As a reconnaissance troop, we are supposed to avoid fighting as far as possible, and we often find it difficult to pass by the most tempting targets without firing a shot. However, we make rapid progress. Suddenly, we cannot avoid crossing the enemy's main retreat route. Densely packed, his horse-drawn and motorized columns are travelling towards the west. We watch for a while. There are no gaps through which we could slip across unimpeded. There is only one solution: a sudden push through! A short command to the tank commanders. We drive under cover through the woods up to the road. The unit commander gives the signal, and then we are blazing from all barrels. The road is raked in both directions by our shells and machine-gun fire.

Orders, shouting, vehicles turning over, teams of horse bolting, a chaotic tangle of men, animals and equipment – hopeless confusion. Apart from a few shots, no sign of resistance – and our four tanks continue on their way, leaving the bloody scene on the road behind them.

After a short drive a village looms up in front of us. When we are about 700 metres (765 yards) away from it when the enemy appears on the road! An infantry company is marching towards us, with horse-drawn vehicles to its rear. We drive towards them. They have not recognized us yet. Nobody expects German tanks here. We are now just 20 metres (65 feet) from them. Perhaps we can spare the Frenchmen bloodshed and loss of life? The recce leader jumps down from his tank. Pistol in hand, he goes up to them. 'A bas les armes, haut les mains!' he yells at the crowd. – 'Allemands!' The cry of terror goes up on all sides, and they scatter in all directions, looking for cover in ditches and gardens.

The driver of the first tank sees a Frenchman at the back aiming his rifle at the recce commander as he stands alone. In a split second, the enemy soldier is brought down by a shot aimed through the tank's vision slit. That is the first shot. It sets off a mad frenzy of shooting from houses, gardens and hedges. But then our weapons deliver their deadly reply. The road, on which an ever-longer tailback of vehicles and soldiers has been forming, is a scene of panic. There is no escape for the vehicles. They are torn to shreds by our guns, some of them set on fire. Our machine guns and main armament hammer away for minutes at a time. This bloody work comes hard, but is unavoidable. We must get through here. Two anti-tank guns at the rear of the column are destroyed before they can aim their dangerous maws at us. The enemy begins to flee, if he still can. The Frenchmen leap from house to house, over gardens and fields, pursued by a hail of shots from us, and discarding everything on the road and in the village.

'March!' orders the recce leader, and slowly the heavy grey vehicles force their way unstoppably through inextricable tangles, over the gruesome remains of everything that a moment ago was striving to bring German tanks to a standstill. Repeatedly we have to dismount from our tanks and tear down the heaps that are blocking our progress. At last we fight our way clear. The journey goes on, towards our objective.

In the course of the next few hours we frequently encounter oncoming enemy troops, and every time the earlier scene is repeated. The clashes and skirmishes become ever more numerous. In the end, we have to fight for nearly every kilometre of road. Slowly, night falls. All our senses are doubly strained. It is a situation of the utmost tension, driving through enemy territory alone, far ahead of all our other troops. But it is a proud sensation to belong to the spearhead of the German assault.

Our pace becomes slower with encroaching darkness. We cannot risk driving into an ambush. From earlier battles, we are also very familiar with French mines. A glance at the map tells us that we must be just outside the small town of Brunehamel. We proceed cautiously, and then we roll through the streets of a dead town. In front of us is a large market place, with many streets emptying into it. In the middle of the square stand two French trucks; there is no-one to be seen.

As a reconnaissance man you develop over time a certain sixth sense that tells you when the enemy is in the offing. That is why the situation seems suspicious to us, despite or precisely because of the silence. We send one tank back a bit to cover our rear, because an ambush in a built-up area can be a very serious matter.

Then the recce commander takes his tank across the market square, while the rest of us stand by to give covering fire. When our vehicle is roughly in the middle of the square, a tank emerges out of a side-street in the semi-darkness. His gun is already flashing, but the shell passes over us. The gun of the tank we have positioned at the rear barks three times. The gunner was at his post. Three shells tear open the body of the tank from the side. The duel is over. The noise of tracks from the side-street reveals to us that more enemy tanks are there, but they are pulling out. We are about to set off after them, when the commander of the second tank, which has now rejoined us, yells out: 'Enemy to the rear!'

You can hear the roar of engines, and a column of vehicles emerges from a side-street. As far as we can make out, it is headed by a tank, followed by troop carriers. They are received with a hail of fire on our part. Badly hit, the tank is just able to veer away and disappear, and our shots slam into the long row of lorries. Jets of flame flare up eerily from their engines; the vehicles, having in many cases lost their drivers, pile into each other. Soldiers jump out, shoot, take cover in houses, or flee. We drive along the column, which consists of 40 vehicles, including four tanks. About 100 men surrender. Their weapons are destroyed, and the Frenchmen meekly set off on their journey into captivity. We send them east, towards our own troops. Perhaps they will run into other French columns and avoid their fate for the time being. But we cannot take them with us. At least we have destroyed their weapons.

In the darkness we look for the right exit from the town. Then the tank commanders report that the ammunition is running low. It is a painful message. We have used up practically everything; but we had no choice. We are still 20 kilometres (12.5 miles) away from our objective, Vervins. We'll see how much further we can get. Over the radio we ask the detachment for more ammunition.

About 500 metres (547 yards) from Vervins, we come across two enemy motorized columns, side by side and stationary. Our path is blocked. In the pitch-black darkness, nobody recognizes us. The terrain and the map tell us that a detour is out of the question. Despite our shortage of ammunition there is only one possible decision. Fight and push through under cover of darkness and the resulting chaos! Our weapons flash vividly as we slam short bursts of fire into the ranks of the enemy. A dreadful noise accompanies the ensuing panic.

'March!' orders the reconnaissance commander. But our leading tank has already got stuck among the vehicles left abandoned all over the road by the enemy. We cannot get through.

The road goes over an embankment at this point; it is not possible to make a detour around it. Our vehicle lights come on and play eerily upon the chaos. The rear sections of the column are trying to turn round. Our machine-gun salvoes answer the shots coming from that direction. The recce leader and his NCO jump down and race along the road firing their pistols.

The confusion becomes greater still; enemy troops are gunning each other down. After about 100 metres (109 yards) the two men see the rear part of the column speeding away. They bar the road to stop anybody else from escaping. The NCO goes back to the reconnaissance unit and gets the crews to dismount, apart from the gunners. And now we tidy up. We drag the terrified figures out from all their hiding places in and around the remaining 60 or so vehicles. The wounded are recovered, weapons removed. We find a small turn-off from the road into a meadow, and make the Frenchmen drive their undamaged vehicles on to it. The wrecked ones are pushed aside. Having done all this, we count 130 men and 75 vehicles. But our weapons are down to their last magazine. In this position, apparently surrounded by the enemy, we cannot go on. We will have to stay here.

The situation is critical; the French are very well aware of our presence by now.

How long will it be before we have to fight again? Will we be getting any ammunition in the meantime? Naturally, the detachment has been fully informed by radio about what has gone on so far, and about the enemy's position. But will the others succeed in getting through with the ammunition?

The noise of numerous engines reaches us from Brunehamel. Two of our tanks drive the short distance back to the town. The place is full of enemy troops. There are a vast number of vehicles in the market place. New columns are still arriving from all directions. Frenchmen are looting the houses. Carefully, without being recognized, the two tanks withdraw.

Once more we use the radio to update the detachment about developments. From beyond our position – not far from us there is a road crossing, according to the map – we hear the sound of heavy traffic. Our scouts report that the enemy is on the road in force, and stationary. We cannot escape from here in any direction without a fight. So we construct roadblocks behind and ahead of us out of wrecked vehicles. It all has to be done very quietly. Behind each roadblock stand two tanks, weapons aiming at the road. Only the gunners stay in the vehicles. The other men occupy both barriers, armed with pistols, hand-grenades, flare pistols, and torches with coloured filters, to create a firework display concealing our true strength from potential attackers.

After only about 10 minutes, the French set out from Brunehamel. The noise of their engines comes closer. Our orders are given in a whisper. The enemy is about 20 metres (22 yards) from the roadblock. The first vehicle seems to spot the obstacle, and stops. Then we switch on our headlights and fire a burst of machine-gun fire into the vehicle. From behind and to the side of the barrier, we fire off every weapon. Three men go along the column loosing off pistols and hand-grenades.

General confusion. After a short exchange of fire, the Frenchmen surrender. Some have fled, abandoning their vehicles. Five officers and about a hundred men are disarmed and led off to join the other prisoners on the meadow. There they sit, kept in order by a borrowed French machine gun. But strangely, it does not occur to them to run away or resist. They obviously do not realize they are dealing with such a small but determined group of Germans, because the darkness covers up our weakness.

Our situation has been much improved by the rich haul of weapons. French machine guns and rifles are incorporated into our 'defence system'. All the same, we are uneasy about our ammunition supply. Repeatedly, lone vehicles or small groups of vehicles reach our roadblock, only to be shot up. The number of prisoners is constantly increasing, but the detachment radios that reconnaissance troops are on their way to us.

It is long past midnight. 'Engine noise!' hisses a voice from the other roadblock, on the western side. It is still quite far away, but clearly heading towards us. With our ears to the surface of the road, we can detect a dull, heavy clattering. – Could that be tanks? – The question hovers apprehensively in the hushed silence. – The prisoners become restless. They are only just kept under control by the threatening pistols. Three men are needed to maintain a close watch.

The others take up their positions at the ready on either side of our roadblock. Our only salvation now lies in surprising and deceiving the enemy. At night, hand-grenade explosions look very similar to gunfire. We are going to use them to simulate artillery.

The noise gets closer. Slowly, terribly slowly, it crawls towards us out of the impenetrable night. The silhouette of the first vehicle looms up. Another 50 metres (55 yards), 40 (44 yards) ... 30 (33 yards) ... the flash of our recce commander's submachine gun is the signal to engage. Our hail of fire rips through the silence and darkness of the night. On both sides of the road we leap towards the enemy. Rifle shots and hand-grenades accompany our move.

On the enemy's part, there is no answering fire from any tank gun; there is only weak resistance, in the form of isolated shots. These aren't tanks! – We recognize long gun barrels pulled by tracklaying tractors. The work of disarming and taking prisoners takes only a few minutes. We have captured a heavy artillery battery! The number of prisoners has again increased considerably.

There is still no sight or sound of the reconnaissance troops who are meant to be coming to our assistance. We inform the detachment by radio. Then at long last we hear the sound of German guns and machine guns hammering away! A wonderful sound! They're on their way – we are no longer alone! On two sides flares shoot up, about a kilometre (1090 yards) away. We reply in kind. There is the sound of an outbreak of fighting, but it does not get any closer. Two reconnaissance units have rushed to our aid. In the meantime, the detachment commander has been able to form a clear picture from all the reports we have sent back. You can't get any further here with reconnaissance troops! … 'Detachment coming', says his radio message! To our ears, two glorious words! And it is not long before the lead tanks are stopping in front of our roadblock.

Our reconnaissance mission has been completed. Even though we could not reach our objective, Vervins, at least we have established beyond doubt that the town is still in enemy hands. We were 13 men, and the 'incidental' outcome of our scouting trip was the capture of four tanks, 500 prisoners, 400 vehicles and a heavy artillery battery.

A handshake between the commander and our reconnaissance troop leader says in an instant everything a front-line soldier does not put into words.

By *Oberleutnant* Bäumen

The Masters of the 'Black Art' in Action

Not many soldiers are familiar with the function and purposes of an observation detachment in combat. Its 'secret' activities are often referred to as 'the black art'.

The way we are deployed depends upon all sorts of conditions and assumptions, and makes high demands on the commander and unit leaders. It is our job to site widely differing types of battery for the important purpose of supporting other arms by combating the enemy's artillery and locating its positions. In this way, we can prevent the enemy's enormous firepower from breaking the attacking strength of our tanks, infantry and pioneers.

Observation detachments developed out of the sound-ranging and flash-spotting units of the Great War. In static warfare, unseen artillery firing from hidden positions played a decisive role, claiming unprecedented numbers of lives. Who has not heard the veterans' stories about the nerve-racking and paralysing effect of artillery?

Spotter planes had only limited effectiveness in combating this destructive weapon, thanks to camouflage and constantly evolving anti-aircraft measures. For these reasons, artillery reconnaissance units became an indispensable weapon for our new *Wehrmacht*.

Let us take just one typical example, to stand for many, of the successful applications of our detachment during the campaign in the west. We have formed a defensive front along the River Aisne near Rethel. Together with other arms, our mission is to prevent any attempt by our opponent to drive in the flank of the tank divisions attacking St Quentin. The artillery commander draws our attention to a hostile heavy battery south of Rethel, which is giving our infantry a good deal of trouble and causing many casualties. It does not take long for the sound-ranging unit to locate the enemy guns. Even the lowliest gunner is happy to be able to show the infantry what powerful support we can deliver. Contact with our battery is quickly established, and the guns soon find the range of target 701; 20 rounds then drop on the French position.

This works wonders. The French artillery becomes much more cautious, shooting more infrequently, and without first establishing the range, which naturally diminishes their accuracy. Target 701, however, does not fire another shot.

A few hours later the French seem to have noticed where the threat to their batteries is coming from. How they discovered the plotting station of our sound-ranging unit we do not know. At any rate, they send over a burst of fire from two 15cm (6 inches) batteries that blinds and deafens us. Sitting high up in their plotting-station truck, the gunners have no protection from the devastating shrapnel as shells burst around them. Imperturbably, they go on working with their sound-ranging equipment and man-portable radio sets. Only when the wires are severed to the ranging equipment do they take cover. Marvellous soldiers, whose composure one can only admire. It is extremely fortunate that the concentrated fire of the enemy batteries does not result in a direct hit. Shortly afterwards, both targets are located, and the enemy loses his inclination to send over any more fire.

Next morning, we are allocated new positions. There are even more important sections of the front where an observation detachment is needed. Enemy troop concentrations have been reported south of St. Quentin, in the region of La Fère. The batteries are repositioned without a hitch, and the usual scene is repeated. The French artillery, initially so brash, receives a dose of shelling from the batteries under our direction; it withdraws, and anything we have not destroyed then tries to continue firing from positions far to the rear. Approach marches, the bringing up of replacement troops, and the relief of front-line troops can all be carried out unimpeded. We avoid many losses.

Where an observation detachment is deployed, the French do not dare to move their artillery up close behind the infantry and so fire at maximum range. They are scared of the sound- and flash-ranging units, and they know that our shooting is deadly accurate. Many a soldier, particularly on rear-echelon duties, may well have wondered why the enemy batteries in this war have so rarely bombarded our hinterland. Twelve enemy batteries are located by sound-ranging techniques alone in this section of the front, and three more targets are added to this score by flash-spotting during the night. Fifteen enemy batteries therefore become acquainted with the effectiveness of our detachment.

We stay only two days near St Quentin. The artillery is reluctant to lose our services; we have collaborated brilliantly with them. The bridgehead over the Somme near Amiens is threatened by French counter-attacks. A new operation beckons that is exactly after our own heart!

By *Oberleutnant* Bethge

Not Just Any
Old Truck

O ur Magirus was not just any old truck, not an anonymous limb of the grey worm that was our column, inexorably eating its way into enemy territory. He had something individual about him, and his life and death were that of an old warrior.

He had been issued to us, over and above our standard transport allocation, to carry our medical equipment. He bore his hard fate of ageing and being relegated with the same sense of duty and loyalty which may have inspired him in better days on the training grounds of the Reich, and then in a place of honour on the marches into Austria, the Sudetenland, Bohemia and Poland.

On 9 May we got the cue for action. The quiet Eifel villages were suddenly turned into beehives of activity. We had to be out of our local sick-bay within three hours, with everything packed and loaded, and on the starting line with the battalion headquarters staff. The old Magirus swallowed box after box. Medicines, dressings, instruments, bottles, dishes, stretchers, blankets, in short, everything useful that conscientious concern for wounded comrades could think of and stow in the 'vehicular combat equipment, supplementary issue', and more besides.

We were ready at last. A final check, a few more instructions, and I pulled myself up into my command car, and off we went. Two ambulances behind me, and the Magirus bringing up the rear. Big, four-square and rattling, as befits an old hero.

After the first kilometre I glanced behind me, and could not believe my eyes. Only the ambulances were following; the Magirus had disappeared. This was a good start! Going into action without the medical supplies we needed! We could not go back, because time was pressing, and my people reassured me that he would turn up eventually. I reported it to the commander at headquarters staff. He smiled; the Magirus would turn up. I didn't understand this blind optimism, and cursed the old heap.

And he didn't turn up. We had crossed Luxembourg and Belgium, and were at the French border. My worries about getting hold of the missing supplies became more acute all the time. Then, one evening, enveloped in a cloud of warm oil fumes, our Magirus came wheezing along. The fuel pipe had broken. Brittle ducts, the fate of old-timers! But he had overcome it. I could have hugged him. All our troubles were behind us, and next morning we four set off intrepidly into the great unknown.

Our companies crossed the Meuse in inflatable assault boats. We had to follow as fast as we could. But the officer operating the ferry turned our good old Magirus away: 'With that monster you'll have to cross by the temporary bridge at Floing!' It was not a big detour, he said. After a long wait, enlivened at times by air raids, we finally crossed the Meuse at nightfall.

The stars twinkled, planes and flak spat tracer at each other, and the red glow where fires had broken out showed the route of our advance, far out into the plain. As we climbed up the steep hills beyond the river-bank, across the river the anti-aircraft searchlights came on. Obviously they thought that the labouring sound of old Magirus was the whirr of a plane.

Without further mishap, we continued until we reached the sea. Sometimes he stayed behind, exhausted, but never for long, and he passed many a younger and more attractive comrade lying in a ditch, mortally sick and abandoned by his carers. He willingly accepted extra loads: crates of the best champagne, large tins of fine ham, and boxes with all kinds of confectionery. And in other ways, too, he proved himself a loyal friend. During midday halts his massive body provided shade for 20 men, and at night he offered my men a good, weatherproof shelter.

Then we turned towards the south. He struggled through the desert-like dust of the Aisne, and thundered along the smooth chaussées towards the Marne. Chalons lay ahead of us. From the wheat-fields by the side of the road there came a buzzing like that of wild bees. In the town we were surrounded by dancing women who had escaped from the lunatic asylum. Not far from the barracks in which we had set up our aid station there was a burning oil depot. The French fought back stubbornly. They were hoping for a second miracle on the Marne. There was plenty to do, on behalf of both friend and foe. Shells whistled over from the other side of the river and landed among streets and houses.

Suddenly, outside in the courtyard where our vehicles were standing, there was a heavy thump. We dashed outside to find the bonnet and cylinder block of our Magirus riddled with pieces of shrapnel. Water and oil were trickling from his wounds into the sand.

In the evening we sat in a good, vaulted cellar, putting up with the racket of screaming shells and explosions with the agreeable feeling of a wanderer secure from the storm in the hut he has come across. A large tin of ham was doing the rounds, and sparkling wine was bubbling in army mugs. Then somebody said as he chewed: 'Shame about our Magirus, but I'm glad he came to an honourable end.' That was his obituary, pronounced from a German soldier's heart as if in memory of a good comrade.

By *Oberstabsarzt* **Dr Sommerer**
Medical Corps Major

A Panzer Division Strikes at Abbéville and Boulogne

Dawn slowly breaks on 20 May 1940. Deep silence engulfs the little French village of Sorell. The doors and windows of abandoned dwellings creak in the light wind. The men who are destined to fight, make sacrifices and gain the victory are enjoying the brief peace of sleep – soldiers' dreams range far and wide. The tanks, carefully camouflaged, stand in sheds or under trees, the ardour of their steel torsos now cooled by the gentle wind playing around them.

Outside, in one of the last houses in the village, a sentry walks up and down, his legs stiff, his collar turned up high, rifle on shoulder. His look is dreamy – but the noise of an engine wrenches him out of his reverie. A motorcycle stops in front of him, and an officer jumps out of the sidecar. He knows him; it is the division's orderly officer.

'Is this brigade staff?'

'Yes sir, the door is over there.'

The second-lieutnant disappears into the house. He pauses in the first, low room; it smells of sweat, leather and cold food. Rifles and belts hang from the walls, a dim oil lamp is still burning on a table in the corner, its light painful to the eyes in the grey of the morning. Dispatch riders and orderlies are sleeping with their knees drawn up on a thin layer of straw.

He steps into the next room through the half-open door. The orderly officer is asleep on a mattress on the floor. He shakes his arm gently.

'Morning, Günther, where's the general sleeping?'

133

Two half-open eyes regard him.

'What are you doing here so early again?'

'Well, it's a long trip today – by this evening you'll be able to bathe your dirty old bones in the ocean, come on, take me to the general.'

'You and your stupid jokes – give it a rest.'

Ten minutes later the headquarters turns into a beehive of activity. The orderly officer and dispatch riders race off, higher-ranking officers appear, to disappear again after a few minutes. From barns and sheds, steel monsters emerge on to the road and form long columns. By 05.00 hours – in 15 minutes, that is – the whole battle group must be ready to move off: the tank brigade, two infantry battalions, tank destroyers, armoured pioneers and flak. Today's objective – Abbéville.

Precisely at 05.00 hours the long body of the steel snake winding through Sorell starts to move. The soft-skinned vehicles of the battle group follow, or weave their way in to the column. Charging forward tirelessly, the group all advance on the same road, past Hedeauville. All resistance – and there is not much here – is crushed. Mine barriers near Doullens are avoided, the troops are in their element. Let's just crack on!

The sun is at its zenith; with the exception of a few short stops, there have been no breaks so far. The battlegroup commander is travelling behind the lead tanks. His expression is grave. There must be something in his calculations that is not quite right. Every now and again he measures with his thumb the distance travelled, against what is still to be covered.

The Panzer regiments have reported that their fuel will last just as far as Abbéville. – What then? – What could he do with immobilized tanks outside a heavily fortified town? It would take hours for the supply columns to arrive. It was not their fault. The columns had achieved practically superhuman feats of non-stop driving for days on end, again and again bringing up fuel from far in the rear for the front-line fighting troops, who often covered 100 kilometres (65 miles) a day as they sped inexorably forward.

Was he supposed to report that the day's objective could not be reached because of fuel shortages? Damn it!

A radio message from division relieves him of all doubt. '15.30 hours – secure Somme section. No vehicles or heavy weapons on south bank of river. Bridgehead near Abbéville.' A new glance at the map shows him that it is high time he brought the tanks to a halt – 20 kilometres (12.5 miles) from Abbéville.

After a few minutes the giant snake lies in the blazing sun amidst countless refugee carts and cars. They have been passing the column for hours, dragging their few possessions with them in the most unlikely conveyances, the horrors of war and the pain of their tribulations showing in their eyes. For the most part, they are Belgians forced into exile by the French and then left to their fate.

Radio message to a rifle battalion: 'Battalion to accelerate, overtake tanks and advance on Abbéville.'

Out of their grimy, dusty faces the red eyes of the tank men look with envy upon their grey-uniformed comrades roaring past them at breakneck speed in their wheeled vehicles. They cannot forgive their 'coffins' for letting them down precisely at this moment. The riflemen, on the other hand, strained to breaking point by driving relatively slowly all day behind the track-laying vehicles, shoot off to the front like an arrow finally released from the bow. – Poor Abbéville! Charging forward at an incredible pace, the leading riflemen soon see the port town lying ahead of them, under the final bombardment of their own artillery. Defences on the western edge of the town, where weak defending forces have only just moved into position, are captured, and the assault moves on to the first few houses of the town. The communications vehicle of the battlegroup commander can be seen among the leading vehicles. Whenever there is a decision to be made, the general is to be found in the heat of the battle, maintaining personal contact with the foremost battalions and detachments.

No infantry fire from the houses and no artillery fire can hold the riflemen back now; machine-gun nests are taken out, and after some brief but tough house-to-house fighting, with a few of the pioneers' AFVs [armoured fighting vehicles] providing outstanding assistance, the burning town of Abbéville is in German hands.

In staff headquarters, if this small room containing only a cupboard, a little table, and a few chairs can be graced with that description, peace has descended. Orders have been given to secure the bridges, and the orderly officers have been told where to find quarters for the remaining tank units, which are still rolling in.

By the meagre light of a candle, after placating their rumbling stomachs with a few tins of tasty English food, the staff officers are smoking a last 'Gold Flake' before turning in for three or four hours of well-earned rest after this hot day. The general's lean, resolute features betray profound satisfaction; you can see from the way he draws so deeply upon his cigarette that he is pleased with the day's achievements.

'Have we signed off the last message to the division?'

'I'll go and find out straight away, General!'

While the signals officer hurries off to the communications centre, a sleeping bag and blankets are got ready.

'Has the last signal gone through to the division?'

'Yes, lieutenant, but an urgent message has just come through from division.'

'Damn … what's up now, in the middle of the night?'

The radio operator hands him the newly decoded message.

What's this about? The signals officer holds his torch closer to the paper to read it again.

'00.21 hours – Luftwaffe will launch all-out attack on Abbéville Bridge. Do not occupy bridge.'

After a few minutes, he holds the reply in his hand. 'Message passed on to corps. If there is reply, brigade will be informed.' All thought of sleep is gone; so are the cheerful faces. The initial heated debate is followed by an icy silence. Pondering deeply, the general sits hunched over his map, and none of his officers dares to say a word, including the unit commanders and their adjutants, who have arrived in the meantime. At the cost of some losses, all the bridges had been occupied in the darkness, and narrow but solid bridgeheads established. There are constant reports of enemy counter-attacks. Give up bridges – impossible! Stuka attacks – how often we have longed for our Luftwaffe comrades to come, and how often have we seen the devastating effect of their bombs on our opponents. But Stuka attacks on the Abbéville bridges – unthinkable.

There are only two possibilities: give up the bridge, and so give up the enormously important bridgehead – nobody dares contemplate the consequences, or stay in place and sacrifice the brave men who have still not even had a chance to get some sleep, after their great march and all the heavy fighting. Minutes pass, then hours. The waiting becomes painful. In the small room the air becomes thicker; you might imagine that all the officers here were pathological chain smokers – Nerves! Finally, at 03.13 hours the signals officer, who has not moved from the radio station all this time, arrives with a small, ominous piece of paper, bearing only four words. 'Planes now on their way.'

'Quiet, gentleman.' The steely voice of the general cuts through the 'crowd noises' that have broken out.

'All units within the town will withdraw again to several kilometres outside Abbéville and spend the night in the open. The bridges will remain occupied; I will be staying here with my staff. We can only hope the enemy do not notice.'

Having only just fallen quiet, apart from the crash of collapsing roof-beams and house walls and the crackling of hungrily advancing flames, the town springs to life again. Orderly officers and dispatch riders race through the dark streets, shouting orders to galvanize tired black- and grey-uniformed men, hardly asleep yet, back on to their feet. Engines howl into life; the echo from house walls intensifies the sound of clattering tank tracks tenfold. Where? Back again? – Nobody can understand it, but orders are orders. Their arms are tired, and the hands that reach out for control sticks are swollen. During their dynamic advance during the day with only one objective in mind – 'the Channel!' – none of these men, their faces rendered almost the colour of their uniforms by sweat and dust, would have had any thought of tiredness. But now it sits on their limbs like a ton weight.

Yes, that's what the boys in black are like – having pushed the enemy back for a 1000 kilometres (620 miles), ignoring hardships, content with little food and practically no sleep, they are ready to charge another thousand or so, but they take it hard when they have to retreat 5 kilometres (3 miles)!

In staff headquarters the candle has burnt down to a little stump.

'Good night, gentlemen; I'll be informed about any significant messages; otherwise, reveille at 05.30 hours.' Slowly the general makes his way into his room to stretch out for the remaining couple of hours on his hard bed on the floor.

Well may the Stukas' visit have been the last thought of each one before falling asleep, but sleep wrapped all the tired men in his merciful embrace under canvas and greatcoats.

It is 05.30 hours – without apologizing or announcing a cancellation, the Stukas have called off their visit. Nobody sitting wide awake – despite their short sleep – over a mug of hot coffee holds this little act of thoughtlessness against them. On the contrary. The small room, so cheerless three hours earlier, seems friendly to the officers.

By about 07.00 hours all previous positions have been occupied again.

In the course of the day a few thousand prisoners, mostly British, are assembled and taken to the rear. A French colonel is prepared to believe anything – that we came by sea, perhaps, or from the air – but cannot get it into his head that we marched overland. In the course of the afternoon the bridge at Noyelle sur Mer is blocked off, and by evening the northern exit from Abbéville is sealed off against enemy incursions from around Nouvion. The area between the Somme and the River Authie is cleaned up and made secure. In an Abbéville side-street, a pathetic scene silently accuses France of the most terrible atrocity. The blazing midday sun burns down, with an intensity that seems to want to direct all eyes to the spot, on 30 lifeless bodies, including those of a woman and a priest, lying at the foot of a wall. According to the closely cross-examined and confirmed evidence of the Dane Winter, they are hostages of varying nationality who were shot after being subjected to inhuman treatment.

On 22 May, at 05.00 hours, the tanks are on the move again.

There is no pause for rest: forwards – surprise attack – breakthrough – pursue, destroy and throw everything into it without keeping back even the very last reserves! Those are the mottoes in this war of fast-moving troops. The men's achievements are superhuman. Fearless and dogged in battle, they devote every spare minute to the care and upkeep of their steel comrades, to whom their crews are bound unto death and destruction. One can count on the fingers of one hand the number of hours when the gentle hand of friendly sleep closes the eyes swollen by dust and glaring sunlight.

Via Rue, Waben and Etaples the advance goes on, towards the day's objective, Boulogne. There can be no question of repeating yesterday's surprise, for enemy reconnaissance and fighter planes are continuously circling over the area, and enemy bombs continually dropping their deadly gifts on the rear columns, tearing painful gaps in them. Above the town itself float numerous barrage balloons. The demand for protection from our own fighters cannot be met. The weak enemy on the ground is defeated everywhere, and there are endless, unbroken columns of prisoners streaming unsupervised along choked roads towards the south. After a two-hour battle a stronger enemy force near Etaples, equipped with anti-tank guns and artillery, is crushed; and then it's onwards, until completely blocked roads in St Etienne bring the tank assault to a halt. The momentum of the attack is threatened.

'Overtake, drive on ahead.'

Erect in his command car, the brigade commander overtakes the leading tanks. A short instruction to the platoon leader of the company spearheading the column starts the work of clearing a path. The brigade commander himself cannot drive on, either, and jumps down to join 1 Company in finding a way through the deliberate jumble of military and civilian vehicles, past exploding and burning ammunition trucks. The blown-up bridge at Pont de Priques makes further progress completely impossible. At the same time, the first volleys of machine-gun fire rip across from the other side, claiming some casualties. They are avenged by the first tanks, which arrive within a few minutes, smashing through the enemy's cover with their shells, and sweeping away whole rows of houses.

Once again house-to-house fighting flares up. Once again, there is a demonstration of the wonderful cooperation between comrades of the infantry and the tank corps. One street after another is taken, thanks to mutual support. The enemy resists stubbornly, until nightfall ends the tough contest for friend and foe alike.

Shortly before 02.00 hours the general returns to Pont de Briques from the command post of the foremost infantry battalion. Radio message to division: 'Tanks and rifles securing area very close to the south of Outreau.' The early morning of 23 May sees the doughty tank men and infantry, for whom the night was shorter than short, again engaged in stubborn house-to-house fighting. Command is aware of the difficulty of the undertaking. A lightning attack by the neighbouring battle group on the right on Fort de la Creche succeeds only at the second attempt; enemy bombing near Mont Laibert claims casualties. From the port, cruisers, destroyers and torpedo boats, eight warships in all, lay down constant accurate fire on the attackers. According to reconnaissance aircraft, British troops have disembarked at Wimmereux, le Portél and the airfield south of Boulogne. Enemy tanks are reported to be advancing from Calais to Boulogne, and troop columns are marching up from Bazinghem. More and more of our units have to be detached to confront them. The artillery tries in vain to deal with the destroyers out at sea. Their range is too short. We miss the 3rd Battalion of our rifle regiment more all the time; it is still waiting on the Somme to be relieved. At about 16.00 hours the attack peters out under the well-directed fire of the destroyers ...

Last night we were glad to do without you, but now is the time to come in, comrades of the Luftwaffe ...!

Radio message to corps: 'Request Stuka attack on ships in Boulogne harbour.' For hours the officers have had their binoculars trained on the warships' manoeuvres. Their glasses have been constantly switched to sweep the horizon. In vain.

There – a glance at the time, 19.30 hours – a faint howling of sirens swelling within minutes into a deafening roar. Hardly noticed, they are already hovering above the ships, a dark, death- and destruction-dealing cloud.

The first, second, third – the eye can no longer follow them as they swoop down through the bursts of flak towards their victims. Explosions, jets of flame, enormous plumes of water, the howl of engines, and then they are off. Only one is still circling. There – he's diving down – is he hit? No, he's still got a little explosive in his belly for the Tommies down there.

Thirty minutes later the sea in front of us is clear. The corps reports next day that three destroyers and five troop transports were sunk, and one cruiser badly damaged.

While the impression made by the great spectacle is still very vivid in our minds, and conversation full of praise for our Luftwaffe comrades, there is a report from air reconnaissance: 'Five more enemy destroyers arrived in the harbour.' Once again the ships' guns spew heavy projectiles into the ranks of detachments and battalions going in to attack. We are thrown back on our own devices. One first-lieutenant sets a destroyer alight with his tank gun at 300 metres (328 yards), despite intense shelling from the enemy ships. Heavy anti-aircraft guns sink another destroyer at 800 metres (875 yards), while lighter flak brings down an enemy plane. In the town, house-to-house fighting rages. The battalion commander's request to grant his exhausted men a few hours rest cannot be met, because various reports indicate that the British have stopped landing troops, and are planning to pull out of Boulogne.

By around midnight, an iron ring has been formed around the town. The battle group on the right is holding the line from north Boulogne to Fort de la Creche and Wimille. To avoid further casualties, the troops have been withdrawn from Boulogne for the night. The group on the left has a tight grip on the south of Boulogne, the port area, and the station.

The morning of 24 May is used mainly for reconnaissance and for building-up strength. The division's plan is to attack at 13.00 hours. It has no further reserves. The divisional commander himself has joined the battlegroup on the right. From 11.00 hours onwards the British destroyers shell the whole town. Stukas are not available.

13.00 hours. Like a wild tiger the division springs at the enemy, who puts up a desperate defence. With exemplary collaboration between tanks and infantry, the eastern part of Boulogne is taken. The divisional commander himself leads the assault, and his officers attack at the head of their men. The heights around the cathedral bid to hold up the advance. The enemy has dug himself in extremely well behind a continuous wall, from 10–12 metres (11–13 yards) high, dating from medieval times. Artillery and anti-aircraft guns are brought up to pour direct fire into the wall – in vain; the attack still falters in front of the cathedral. Even a half-hour bombardment by the heavy mortar detachment, followed by a ferocious onslaught, does not produce a breakthrough. But the men go in to the assault time and time again. The battle rages up and down. Hours pass.

In the staff headquarters of the battlegroup on the left an oppressive silence reigns. The general saw for himself at close quarters the courage and self-sacrifice of his front-line troops in the battle – no human being could have done more than these fine men – before he called off the costly night-time house-to-house fighting.

The silence is broken by the shrill ringing of the telephone. The adjutant answers it.

'The division commander wants to speak to the general person to person.'

'Speaking … Yes … Yes sir.'

Slowly he replaces the receiver, and sits down. Four pairs of eyes are fixed upon his grave features.

'We must take Boulogne today, gentlemen. The men are to be informed'.

An anxious silence – everybody senses the struggle in the general's mind. The men have hardly had a wink of sleep for three days – house-to-house fighting in pitch darkness – their strength is exhausted, and there have already been heavy losses.

'Write this down: Attack orders …'

The officers sit motionless. For them, this is an awesome moment. At this minute they are more alive than ever before to the significance of those two small words: 'Yes, sir.' They believe they will succeed; duty has called, and there can be no compromise.

The general takes up his map, and the way he does so tells the officers to keep their distance.

Once again, battle strikes up the first notes of his grim melody in the silence of the night. From the south-east the battlegroup on the left smashes against the citadel, and the right-hand group from the north-east. No more thought of sleep and tired, aching limbs. All of them, officers and men, tank men, riflemen or pioneers, are aflame once more with the old wild eagerness for battle. Those taking part in the attack, from the youngest soldier to the general, are no longer soldiers ranked according to regulations – they are the *Volk*. Tanks, riflemen, pioneers, artillery, howitzers and flak guns storm the citadel. At point-blank range direct fire breaches the wall. Ladders are rushed up, and in an instant the first shock troops, with flame-throwers and hand-grenades, are pouring over the wall – one battlegroup has already penetrated the north-east side of the citadel. Not long afterwards, the enemy's desperate defence can no longer hold back the onslaught of the other battlegroup.

Boulogne has fallen; 5000 men and two generals have been taken prisoner.

The Führer's reward, the Knight's Cross of the Iron Cross, is worn with pride by the conquerors of Abbéville and Boulogne and five other officers of the division. They wear it for their comrades who fell by the shores of France, keeping faith with the saying:

*'It is not necessary for you to return,
only for you to do your duty.'*

And they wear it for the comrades who are always ready to answer the *Führer's* call to fight for Germany.

[Boulogne was attacked by tanks of the 2nd Panzer Division and was defended by an improvised French force and men of the 2nd Battalions the Irish and Welsh Guards, part of the 20th Guards Brigade, who only two days earlier had been training in Surrey.]

By *Oberleutnant* Dietz

... And Then for Us the Tank Becomes an Iron Grave

The advance continues, as inexorably as ever. A glance at the map tells me that we are approaching a small town, Nesles-Neufchâtel. We have already reached the first houses. A long street is just opening up in front of us, when we see the flash of fire from a gun barrel. In a split second we are ready to fire. The tank stops, our shot is fired, and the shell hits home, tearing a hole in the protective shield of a French 7.5cm (3 in) howitzer. Movement is still visible around the gun. A second shot falls among the crew. The third shell is a glorious direct hit to the muzzle of the gun. The barrel is split, and the howitzer is out of action.

We are getting close to the town centre, a fairly large open space where five streets converge. There seems to be something going on up ahead! There are vehicle roadblocks , Frenchmen running around, and some firing from street openings. While our lead tank, *Jochen II*, maintains all-round protective fire, I target another French 7.5cm (3in) howitzer. I can only wonder once again at the effectiveness of our explosive shells. If well aimed, the first or at most the second will achieve the desired effect completely.

The lead tank has now advanced into the open space, and is halted there firing; my tank is about 10 metres (11 yards) behind him and ranged a little to one side in order to keep its own field of fire clear. My gunner has just managed to set two small armoured Renault tractors on fire, when suddenly all hell breaks out on the crossing. There is shooting from the left, puffs of smoke on the right and gun muzzles flashing straight ahead. Where to fire

143

first? Where are they hiding, those little well-camouflaged French anti-tank guns? There is no time for thought. While I am feverishly searching out the enemy guns, I see a small cloud of dust and smoke breaking out on the tank ahead. That was a hit! A second later the hatches open. The tank commander struggles out, falls across the hull on to the tarmac, and lies there. Two other crew members leap out and run behind my tank. The tank commander, apparently wounded, drags himself to a house to seek cover. The next instant, a hard metallic blow strikes my tank, and in the crew compartment there is a display of sparks like a fireworks rocket. The driver is sitting below with his head falling forward. In the half-light, still blinded, I can see that there is blood running down his face. There is nothing for it but to get out. The gunner, who is also wounded, has the presence of mind to traverse the turret to one side, so that the hatches are facing away from the enemy. I shout something to the driver, but he does not move; he's probably dead.

We jump down, into enemy machine-gun fire – get in behind the tank! In bounds, using all possible cover, we run towards the rear. Into a shed! Then we see five Frenchmen very close to us, hiding behind barrels and washing-troughs. We are unarmed. They see that, and one of them takes aim with his rifle and shoots – but misses. I duck down, run at the washing-trough and pin the Frenchman to the wall. He is stunned, which gives me time to escape from the shed.

A few hundred metres to the rear I come across the detachment commander. I report the resistance we have encountered on the crossing and the damage to our two tanks. He takes over control. My first job is to apply a field dressing to my gunner's knee, which has been hit by a number of splinters. Then I borrow a pistol and dash forward again. It is impossible to get to the crossing. Enemy fire has it completely covered. My wounded men are still lying there. We must be patient and use a different tack to deal with the enemy.

That is already in progress. The rear companies are fully deployed, taking more than an hour to beat down the stubborn resistance. As soon as our tanks have passed over the crossing, I go to our shot-up vehicles. There's nothing to be done in my tank. My fine driver, a corporal, the best and most dashing driver of the company, is sitting where we left him. A head wound! In the lead tank lies the gunner, a lance-corporal, dead, and the radio operator with his foot shot off, as well as other serious leg injuries. And the vehicle is burning. At any moment the ammunition and the fuel tank could go sky high. A corporal achieves what is practically impossible. Wearing a gasmask, he makes his way into the crew compartment and pulls the radio operator, a private, out of the tank.

The vehicle itself is beyond saving. All attempts to put the fire out fail. With a tremendous crackling from the exploding ammunition, the tank is burnt out. And with it burns the dead gunner, whom we were not able to retrieve. His tank became for him truly an iron grave. In the meantime, our medic has taken care of the other wounded, applying first-aid dressings. We bury our dead in a garden, a few metres from where they fell.

The detachment's march goes on. With two vehicles of my platoon knocked out, the third tank naturally takes over the lead. A few kilometres further on, in Manihen, a suburb of Boulogne, it too suffers the fate of the rest of the platoon. As the tank pulls out of a bend on to a straight stretch of road, there is a flash of fire, and a blow! An anti-tank gun hit! The tank commander, a corporal, has only just located the almost completely concealed anti-tank gun, and he orders the driver to stop so that he can fire. But the tank drives on, without a human hand on the controls. For the driver is dead through a wound to the head from the first shell. His foot is still on the accelerator. A wall at the side of the road collapses under the impact of the tank as it drives into it, but the vehicle is brought to a halt. More shells hit the tank's armour, and some penetrate it and enter the crew compartment. Time to get out! Despite receiving a few wounds, the men succeed in getting away from the vehicle. The radio operator becomes a casualty, however. When he has almost reached safety he is hit by a machine-gun bullet. A shot to the head! He too is dead.

On this afternoon of 22 May, the cost to my platoon is four dead, and three seriously, one lightly wounded. A painful total. But pride goes along with our grieving. Pride in the victory for which our comrades gave their lives.

A few days later, my platoon has been re-formed. The crews, together with the fitters, have worked tirelessly to make the tanks serviceable once more, with welding repairs to the holes. With quiet self-confidence they sit there in the grey steel giants, where their comrades died just days ago.

Situation normal.

Except that where there are signs of welding to repair the holes made by enemy fire, white circles have been painted on to the dark armour plating, and within them small white figures, the date 22.V.40. It is a day of honour for my platoon, but also an obligation for all crews. As boldly and proudly as our fallen comrades we will drive out ahead once more when so ordered. 'Lead platoon!'

By *Oberleutnant* Rudolf Behr

German Tanks against English Destroyers

Boulogne. A hot day of fighting is coming to an end. Haze and smoke hang heavily, streaking the blood-red sky above the Channel coast. The sun bids us farewell with its last golden rays. A machine gun is still firing here and there, and a monster shell from the gun of a British ship occasionally whistles over our heads; it all sounds like a song faintly heard, the iron melody of a day of battle. You feel that rest and relaxation beckon. To be able to open the hatches of the turret properly at last, to be out of that thick, stifling atmosphere for a few hours! It is a gift from God to be able to enjoy such a moment; some respond with a whoop of joy, some with a deeply thankful look, some just with a harmless, hearty curse. But all are deeply grateful that their soldier's luck has served them well today.

These thoughts are soon chased away, for hunger and thirst are hammering with both fists at the door. A meal that is – by our standards – a truly gourmet feast is soon prepared, and served up on the tank turret. Good heavens, Oskar the driver has just uncorked a bottle of champagne. While he drinks, the others look on expectantly.

Then, from a distance, I hear the sound of the company commander's voice. I turn towards a block of houses and listen intently. With my last bite still in my mouth, I hold my breath and freeze. What am I hearing? Destroyers? In the port? Slowly approaching? Tanks? – What is this all about? – And now I can make out every word distinctly: 'Take the tank immediately to the port; we are going to spoil a destroyer's entry into harbour.' Like

146

lightning we take our allotted places, the engine is already howling into life, and elegantly, as though turning on its heel, our 'Heinz' spins round and roars off at amazing speed behind the company commander's tank.

Not a word passes the lips of my four men; no-one dares say anything. They know what is ahead of us. I study their faces. Fredi, our loader, a boy from Vienna; Leo, the gunner; our driver, up front behind the control levers, covered in dust and oil, one of the silent heroes of the tank company; Sichel, the radio operator, smiling as ever. Determination and the will to succeed shine from their eyes.

I give my first orders. We are already preparing for the fire-fight. Our first target will be the bridge and the forward gun turrets; the second the engine room. The loader lays out the selected ammunition on the floor of the tank. Woe to you, destroyer, you will soon be getting to know German tanks! But we're not there yet. Where is the leading tank? Wait, it's over there driving through a lovely vegetable garden. OK, we'll drive through the one next to it. We soon reach our objective. We now have a view right over the heights down to the port. We need to find a good firing position, with cover, as quickly as we can. I see our company commander jumping down from the leading tank and waving both arms energetically towards the harbour, to let me know where the destroyer is. The other tank is already opening fire. As we drive past we feel inside our vehicle the percussive pressure of his shell leaving the barrel. But keep cool! We want to have the whole of this impudent intruder in view. We can already see his smoke-stack and the tip of his mast, this Englishman. A bit further forward, then.

Right out on the slope, without any cover at all, we come to a halt. Now for it! Now we must keep our nerve and cold-bloodedly finish off this monster. There is no need to give the order to fire. Range 450 metres (490 yards). The first shell thunders out of the muzzle. Four pairs of eyes follow its trajectory keenly. Will it be a direct hit? What is its impact on the target? The shell's flight seems to take for ever. There – a flash, a blue-grey jet of flame shoots up the mast. Direct hit on the bridge. A jubilant shout fills the crew compartment. The loader works feverishly; three, four shells leave the barrel; we've got to make the most of the advantage of surprise. There are about 150 to 200 British infantrymen on the forecastle, looking for cover, probably demolition squads. Too late – anyone not swept off the deck by the devastating effect of our shelling is jumping into the water, arms waving wildly. We are operating on rapid fire. The loader demonstrates unexpected talents. Gun smoke and hot gases caused by overheating are hitting him in the face, but with teeth clenched he goes on single-mindedly doing his job.

Wham, there goes another shell into the breech, and off it goes, smoothly penetrating the thick armour of the ship's gun turret. The turning movement of the turret is abruptly halted, and scraps of iron and steel go flying through the air. Done it.

What's this, suddenly? The tank shivers and quakes from end to end. Shrapnel clatters against its right-hand wall. Are we being fired upon? We certainly are – there it is again! A massive shell lands just 2 metres (6 feet) away from the front of the tank. A column of sand shoots up, momentarily obscuring our view. Our opponent is firing!

I am in the grip of an icy calm. It is becoming a life and death struggle. There are two, three more yellowish green flashes at tank height right in front of us. Once again our steel colossus shivers. I have become aware that we are taking a terrific pounding from large-calibre anti-aircraft and naval guns. Just keep it up, gunner! The forecastle is already burning. Thick black smoke from burning oil is drifting slowly up into the evening sky and blotting out our view.

Switch targets. 'Engine room!' I try to shout at the two men – to no avail, as grey, acrid smoke fills the crew compartment. It burns and irritates my throat and eyes. The radio operator and the driver sit together, holding their hands and forearms tight over their mouth and eyes. I hold my breath. Tears run continually down my dirty face. We've got to hold on!

The next volley of shells is already hissing through the air and disappearing into the ship's interior. An incredible sight. Yes, Tommy [British], we'll show you who's going to walk away victorious here. You're shooting too, but always just very slightly missing! Relentlessly our shells batter the ship's internal structure. Engine parts, planks and bodies fly overboard in a motley assortment.

It takes some 10 or 12 shells to end this unusual contest, a battle lasting only a few minutes. Reversing at a furious pace, pursued by salvoes of shells and shrapnel from a few enemy cruisers and destroyers lying further out to sea and only just now waking up to the situation, we race for the nearest cover. Here we can open the hatches a little. Fresh, cool air rushes in. I shake my crew's hands. Our hearts are jubilant: 'We've done it!'

Two hours later our destroyer, completely burnt out, is consigned to the bottom of the sea for ever.

By *Leutnant* Langhammer

Brinkforth Mans the Telescopic Sight

First light on 27 May in the Abbéville bridgehead. Wreaths of mist swirl across the road to Huppy. Staring into them are five pairs of eyes belonging to the crew serving an anti-tank gun lying in wait at an outpost by the road. Brinkforth is sitting at the telescopic sight, his hand on the firing mechanism. With a shell ready in the breech, he is waiting with icy calm for the first victim to appear.

'This damned mist!' Somewhere an early riser among the bird population is serenading the arrival of morning. The anti-tank men do not hear it, all they hear is a muffled clattering and droning. They know what that is – tanks! To the ears of a tank destroyer, it is better music than the dawn chorus. Every nerve is stretched. They will soon be here, the enemy's steel monsters, the terror of the infantry. But we have anti-tank shells. The No 2 on the gun runs his hands lovingly over them.

The mist slowly clears. There! They are working their way along, some heavy, some light, all Tommies [British]. They look for cover behind hedges and bushes.

One, three, five, ten, twenty, thirty! 'Damn it, a bit too much for breakfast!' Their faces are deadly serious, but determination and untamed eagerness for battle shine out of the eyes of the men behind the well-camouflaged gun. Nerves are practically at breaking point. But the enemy must be allowed to get closer. 800 metres (875 yards), 600 metres (655 yards)! The muzzle of the gun follows them menacingly. This is a battle of wills! Out here, 6 kilometres (4 miles) ahead of the main front-line running for several kilometres around Abbéville, we must emerge victorious in order to protect our infantry comrades from this surprise attack. Thirty tanks and just one German anti-tank gun – an unequal contest! We can already make out their red, white and blue pennants.

But what are they doing now? They are all turning left and moving at right angles on to the road. 'Blast it! D'you think the beggars have spotted us?' But that's impossible! They're all heading straight towards us. With teeth clenched, the crew sit hidden behind their camouflaged, solitary gun, with no protection except for a single machine gun. We can only win here by keeping stronger nerves and a cooler head. We let them come on.

Then it's time. Calmly, as though on a training exercise, Brinkforth operates his range finder. '200 metres (218 yards), fire at will!' The order to fire sounds razor-sharp, and the shell roars out of the muzzle, to bore into the armour of a tank turret. The gun becomes a ferocious animal. Its roaring makes the earth shake. Where there was a tank before, there is now just smoke and fire. The tank battle near Abbéville is under way. Our machine gun joins in. A hellish racket! Shell after shell screams out of the barrel.

But the enemy has identified our position by the gun-flashes. Twenty tanks aim their large- and small-calibre guns. It is raining hot steel. The projectiles strike the road to the left of us, the hedge to the right of us, the trees above us, the air is filled with crackling, hissing, humming and whistling. Branches fall. The road is pitted. But we bite our lips, as shell after shell flies towards the tanks. Brinkforth fires with icy calm. 'Next one, Hubert, then another one, easy does it!' We've got to pull it off.

Only four shells are left next to the gun. Ammunition, ammunition! Number 4 on the gun and the driver are already struggling over with the heavy boxes. They risked heavy fire to get the ammunition from the tractor to the gun when it was needed. Every man here is doing his duty.

Our gun barrel is hot from firing. Number 2 is lying among a pile of hot shell cases that fall on to his helmet and face when he tears open the breech block. But who is aware of such things? There is only one thought in the men's minds:

We must win here!

One or two tanks have succeeded in crossing the road. We can no longer see them. The hedge on our right blocks our view. That is worrying. The first one appears, at 70 metres (77 yards), firing wildly into our flank. Thanks to the hole we cut in the hedge yesterday on the chief's orders, we can see him. That is our salvation. The gun traverses, and the beggar is immediately burning like a torch.

We have halted the attack, but we are still being fired upon. 'Damn! Where's that coming from?' There – on the right behind the hedge! 'Fire at the hedge!' yells the leading gunner. It is the other tanks who escaped across the road. They daren't get as close as the first one. Our shells tear towards the gun-flashes from the hedge, and rip into the tanks. Here, too, the machine guns fall silent.

We have done it. They beat a frantic retreat, pursued by our shells. Our gun was spewing out death and destruction for 20 minutes, and 10 tanks lie in front of it, knocked out, burnt, and destroyed. The crew sit exhausted for a moment, and then have to go back on to the alert, and take prisoners. A British captain who is among them refuses to give any information. All he will say is: 'You can be proud of your tank destroyers. We have learnt respect for them.'

Brinkforth, the hero of the hour, was mentioned in despatches next day for his feat of knocking out 10 tanks in 20 minutes. Today he is proud to wear the Knight's Cross of the Iron Cross, and he and the whole company are proud that their young branch of the army, the tank destroyers, has won these laurels. He is the first soldier of non-commissioned rank to receive such a high honour.

By *Gefreiter* Wilhelm Krawzek

Pomeranian Mans the Anti-tank Gun

O n the left flank, about 1000 metres (1090 yards) from the village of Teufles, the Number 1 on the gun – a corporal in a Pomeranian armoured unit gets into position with his anti-tank gun near the road. While he can hear an ever-increasing noise of fighting coming from his left, all is quiet in his sector. He is beginning to envy his comrades on the left, and his men look disappointed. But from the direction of the enemy positions, behind a hill, there comes a sound of engines, and then a heavy tank appears, churning its way along the road. The gun layer immediately has it in his sights, keeping it in the graticule. The colossus moves closer and closer; 200 metres (218 yards) ... 150 metres (165 yards) ... 100 metres (109 yards) ... 'Fire at will!' – Hooray, a direct hit. The monster stops in its tracks, mortally wounded, while its crew are taken prisoner.

After a while, all unsuspecting, a British armoured reconnaissance car appears over the rise. Calm and collected, the gun layer lets him approach to within 100 metres (109 yards), then he aims at the middle, under the turret, and lets loose. The car briefly rears up, then stops abruptly. That's number two done for!

There is silence for a few minutes. But it seems as though something is being planned behind the rise. Sure enough! A long drawn-out horn signal from over there heralds the appearance, half-right and beyond the road, of four enemy tanks, followed by four more, moving out in a wide arc. The men on the gun know at once that the British are trying to surround them. Eight heavy and medium tanks against one anti-tank gun! Now it is important to keep your nerve, hold your fire, and wait until the terrain and the range permit every shell to hit home, surely and effectively.

The British tanks roll steadily closer. Suddenly the four black tanks stop, far beyond our range, and open fire with their main armament. Their fire is inaccurate as yet. In the meantime, the four leading tanks have approached to within 150 metres (165 yards). 'Fire at will!' To the men's astonishment the leading Tommy immediately turns away and goes back in the direction he came from. Right behind him appears a main battle tank, presenting a welcome target. He gets the next shell, and stops moving. Immediately, the Number 1 on the gun has the gun trained on the next tank. The gun layer aims, fires – and it's another direct hit!

Meanwhile, a hellish racket has broken out around the gun. It is clearly identified by its gun-flash, and the still undamaged tanks are firing at it with all they've got. Shells and bullets are striking all around the gun. The machine gunner of the last tank in the front-line in particular has got his eye in. His salvoes smash against the gun's shield. Thank God, it holds out. But the tanks' guns, too, are shooting better and better, and now suddenly a tank shell lands 2 metres (6 feet) in front of the gun and explodes. A clump of debris hits the Number 1 gunner's helmet; he falls to the ground unconscious, but comes to again straight away. He wipes the blood from his face. 'Only a few scratches – that was lucky!' He looks up to find that two of his gunners have been wounded as well, and are out of action for the moment. Only the third one can still be counted on. He sends him a few metres to the rear to fetch the ammunition stacked up there.

The utmost speed is essential. At this moment an infantry lieutenant comes crawling over. He has registered the critical situation, and in the midst of the British bombardment he shouts to the chief gunner: 'Show me quickly how to load this thing!' 'Just pull this open, lieutenant, and the shell-case will fall out; then shove the new shell in, the cap closes automatically! These here...' – pointing to the ammunition the Number 3 on the gun has now brought up – 'are anti-tank rounds, and those are HE.' 'Then just get on with firing', replies the lieutenant, 'and I'll keep the thing loaded!' This gives the Number 3 on the gun time to put a dressing on his comrades' wounds, while the NCO and the infantry officer carry on firing together. Their first target is the last surviving tank in the front-line. It is only 80 metres (88 yards) away. The first hit explodes its ammunition. A great jet of flame shoots up. They've had it! But then the pair notice that two of the tanks previously hit and immobilized are beginning to shoot again. Take aim at them! One of them falls silent at the first shot. The other suddenly jerks into slow and ponderous motion towards a nearby hollow, and although it is hit again, with its last ounce of strength it just manages to drag itself out of sight. When the four tanks in the second line see the fate their comrades have met with, they cease firing and push off as fast as possible.

When silence has descended, the gunners examine the last tank to be shot at, finally brought to a halt in the hollow. Five Tommies, including a captain, are trying in vain to get their vehicle started again. They surrender immediately.

Once again the next day the *Oberkommando der Wehrmacht* announces that enemy tank attacks on the lower Somme have been repulsed. And the Pomeranian tank destroyers are able to hand over their sector of the Somme, courageously held for days on end, to the Bavarian comrades who have now arrived to take over. Reinvigorated by a few short days of well-earned rest, they will head for new battles.

By *Leutnant* Alexander Stahlberg

Flak Gun Caesar

Among the thin 'infantry screen' which the riflemen form, stretching out to the south, stands our flak battery. The gun, 'Caesar', is positioned 300 metres (330 yards) to the east of the road that leads south to Huppy. It is there to cover against tank attacks from the south and south-east, the direction of Huchenneville. We have been lying in wait for two days when the first enemy tanks finally heave into view at the edge of the wood.

They are 32-tonners. It would do them too much honour to call their appearance an 'attack'. They approach hesitantly, dart to and fro like grey shadows along the edge of the wood, shudder, come to a halt, and seem not too clear about where to attack.

Quiet now! Our Caesar is going to show what he can do. Raise the sights slightly! Then fire! Completely calm, the Number 2 on the gun takes aim. 'Got the range!' – 'Fire!' After 10 shots, two tanks are in flames, burning fiercely. So much for that! Badly damaged, the third tank withdraws into the safety of the woods. We were firing as though on the range.

Not long afterwards, stronger enemy tank forces prepare for a new attack. And once again Caesar 'speaks', quickly and surely finding his range and flinging shell after shell at the enemy's armour. Don't spare the ammunition! The bright torches are burning once more out there ahead of us! Seven tanks standing at the foot of the ridge are knocked out by direct hits. A few of the attackers, some damaged, succeed in retreating to the village of Huchenneville. The penetrative force of our shells is colossal. If they achieve a square hit on target, they pierce the monsters' armour and send them up in flames. Often, when the impact is too flat, they bounce off – like pebbles skimming a pond – over the tank turrets, followed by a shower of sparks. For the moment, though, we've done it! They are all in chaos over there, and the sight of the burning brutes will not be exactly encouraging for those coming up behind.

We do not realize until later how much we were under the spell of the lust for battle. Just one example: while the lieutenant was kneeling in the singed grass, his eye pressed to the telescopic sight, giving orders, shouting, disappearing occasionally in clouds of gun smoke, jumping into the gunner's seat and sighting the gun himself, while we ignored the enemy fire and pumped out shot after shot, kept a lookout, or hauled up ammunition, gasping and sweating – during this time, our detachment commander had arrived almost unnoticed, had quickly been briefed, and then began without a word dragging up ammunition with us. Nobody had quite taken it in, it just seemed the natural thing to do in a battle.

The next morning more enemy tanks, followed by a strong force of infantry and supported by intense artillery fire, attack in *Caesar*'s sector again. Under fire from our trusty *Caesar*, standing once again exposed on all sides, the first tank daring to emerge from the wood towards the south is set alight by a direct hit. Another one is also hit and put out of action. But this is where it gets lively! Five more machines, 32-ton tanks, break free from the wood, drive towards our free-standing gun and engage it with main and secondary armament.

In the meantime, our own infantry has suffered losses and retreated under the impact of the enemy artillery. On *Caesar*'s left flank the enemy has already reached the village of Villers. We have lost all protection from ahead and to the rear! But three times we throw half a dozen shells into Tommy's face. There are explosions all around us. The shrapnel clatters against the gun barrel and the gun mount, shattering the fuse setter. Explosion after explosion, near us and behind us! Three members of the gun crew are injured. The tractor is knocked out. Then the gun chassis is hit. The steel monsters churn on towards us, getting closer and closer. It is time to break off a contest that has become too unequal. When our gun commander is killed by a shot in the head, the last five men retreat. *Caesar* will never fire again. He himself has been shot to pieces.

But despite everything, on this day the enemy fails to achieve his aim of getting across the bridges. A kilometre further back, still a long way from the

Somme bridges, our three other heavy anti-aircraft guns put a firm stop to his advance.

Berta knocks out 21 tanks by direct hits and damages 10 others that lie immobilized. By 30 May the newly-formed *Caesar* crew had already taken over a new gun, with which we helped to strengthen the German defensive front, that thin line south of Abbéville. It was a line we held until our own thrust to the south.

[The gun that dealt so effectively with the British tanks in this localized action was the redoubtable 8.8cm (3.46in) Flak 18. The tanks were probably A13 Mk III Cruisers of the 10th Hussars, part of the 3rd Armoured Brigade, 1st Armoured Division. The A13 was fitted with Christie suspension and was powered by a Liberty engine (an American World War I aero type), and reached the remarkable speed of 56.3km/h (35mph). This pace produced some mechanical problems and so the speed was governed down to 48km/h (30mph). The tank's drawback was its thin armour – 6–14mm (0.23–0.55in).]

By *Leutnant* Klay

English Gentlemen

Through a series of unfortunate accidents, five German flak soldiers were captured by the British during the advance on Calais on 23 May. The Tommies pulled us out of the trench, ripped off our belts and helmets, and pushed us with hard blows in the small of the back towards their vehicles. The British must still have been scared, because every one of us was surrounded by an escort of three or four men with machine guns and rifles.

They searched our pockets, stealing everything, right down to buttons and the grubbiest handkerchiefs. They tore the boots from our feet and the clothing from our bodies, with as many shoves and sneers as possible. Finally, they bound our hands and feet with rope as thick as a finger, tying our arms right up to the elbows, so tight that our joints seemed almost dislocated. To stop anybody getting away, they went on to tie a rope between our hands and feet. We were lying on our stomachs on the hard tarmac, widely separated, surrounded by gleaming pistol barrels and maliciously grinning faces. Everyone who passed tore a badge from our collars as a souvenir, or pulled off one of our stripes, thanking us with a hefty kick and a few curses.

A number of interrogations followed, where to his great annoyance the German-speaking captain found that we were extremely stubborn, and that we made fun of him in our replies. That was why they resorted to threats. But it did not stop at threats, according to what an English speaker among us overheard.

158

The British captain gave orders that we should all get a last cigarette and a small cup of tea between us. The ropes were tightened still further, even though our hands and feet had already turned blue. Then they broke our identity tags in half, and fixed one half to our epaulets with the mocking remark: '*Germany nicht wiedersehen*' [You won't see Germany again]. We had heard enough, and had already finished with this life.

[German ID tags consisted of a single metal disc with a perforation across the middle. If a man was killed the disc was snapped in half with one section remaining with the body and the other being sent to the unit.]

Suddenly there was machine-gun and gun fire. What was that? We were lying in the middle of the road, completely without cover, unable to move. Were we actually going to be shot by our own side? The firing soon died down again, and the British, who had taken cover behind their vehicles, crept out again.

Hours of painful waiting followed, with nothing happening. Hours of nerves stretched to the limit.

Then a machine gun hammered again, this time from a different direction. A British reconnaissance plane flew over low above us. He must have thrown down a message, for there was suddenly a great stir along the whole road, and from the agitated talk you could make out one thing again and again: 'German tanks, German tanks.' Hastily the vehicles are started up. Ammunition is distributed; the British are getting ready to move out. Messages fly from man to man, and orders ring out down the dark avenue. We are shifted away from the road towards a tree, and we quickly roll a bit further to the ditch, to the camouflage netting that stretches from tree to tree; in our nervous state of anticipation, we don't notice the streaming rain.

One British vehicle after another races past, including six armoured cars, all heading west. And nobody takes us with them, nobody shoots us, nobody bothers about us. Only one asks what to do about the prisoners. But nobody answers. So we stay behind by ourselves.

Had they forgotten us, or did they just not have time? We did not know. An incredible miracle had taken place. We were free, even though we were still tied up and lying on the ground. What did it matter to us that our infantry company comrades who soon found us and cut our ropes, were terrifically shocked by our appearance. What did we care about the blood on our faces and uniforms. Why should we care if there wasn't a dry stitch of clothing on our bodies! We were free, and we were going to see our comrades again!

By *Gefreiter* Ernst Brunner

The Assault on Calais

On the evening of 25 May the southern part of Calais, including the Old Fort, is taken by German assault troops and cleared. Only the northern part of the city is still holding out, including the old town and port areas, within which is the citadel, now turned into a stronghold defended by powerful English and French forces. The commander of the citadel has rejected a parley to negotiate its surrender. A first attack, organized concentrically with two separate assault groups, has just been beaten back.

About 23.00 hours, the division commander holds a conference with all the commanding officers involved. The division orders the continuation of the assault by both attacking groups on 26 May. Stuka attack from 09.00 hours to 10.00 hours, then bombardment by all artillery until 10.15 hours.

At 00.30 hours the brigade moves its command post, together with the commander of the infantry regiment and the artillery commanders, to the fourth floor of the Calais Opera House; the brigade's observation post is set up on the roof. In order to support the attack with direct fire, single artillery pieces as well as the flak guns are moved at night – despite sustained enemy fire of all kinds – to positions by the bridges over the canal separating old and new towns, which represents a serious obstacle because it is constantly raked by fire from about 12 enemy machine guns sited in houses in the old town. All preparations are made in good time, and officers and troops wait impatiently for the attack to begin. No-one doubts that it will succeed. At about 09.00 hours, the first Stukas roar in. With deafening crashes, bomb after bomb does destructive work. Red flames flicker in various places, thick smoke and sand clouds rise skywards, and large chunks of masonry spin through the air. The effect is overwhelming. The preparation for the attack is rounded off by the artillery with its usual superbly directed bombardment, so that the instant the last shell falls, our men charge forward into the attack, confident of victory.

Initial successes are reported, and orders given for them to be exploited immediately. But from our observation post we hear increasing machine-gun and rifle fire; the enemy has come back to life, and is fighting for his very existence. Individual groups of shock troops have penetrated the citadel, but are pushed back by a British counterattack almost to their starting point. On the southern edge of the old town, almost all the enemy's machine guns are back in operation, preventing us from crossing the canal, exactly as before. Courageous and determined officers, NCOs and men trying to cross are shot up. The column on the right in the town faces the same situation. A detachment initiating a pincer movement on the right makes progress, but despite fighting hard it is slow to gain ground. The 2nd Battalion of the infantry regiment, the left-hand part of the pincer, is held down by defensive fire from the bastion.

The mood in our command posts is really depressed. However, the brigade and artillery commanders remain optimistic, trying to put together a reasonably clear picture from the many reports coming in. It soon transpires that casualties are low, but that the failure of the attack has had an unnerving effect. It is therefore important for command to keep its nerve. After a further review of the situation and a discussion with the artillery commander, another concentrated bombardment is ordered, to be followed immediately by a renewed attack. The brigade commander reports this by telephone to division.

There is a break in the fighting. The exhausted assault troops gather their strength, and when the new attack begins at 14.15 hours after a short but effective bombardment, ground is soon gained. Even the initial successes are bigger than they were in the morning, and around 14.30 hours brigade is able to tell division that it believes Calais will fall today.

The 2nd Battalion's attack on the bastion also makes good progress; completely unexpectedly, the garrison surrenders its excellent position. An extremely satisfying outcome, which justifiably gives rise to hopes of a complete victory. Three hundred men are captured; some retreat to the citadel, and others make for the coast. A second breach, perhaps the decisive one, has been made in the enemy defences. The capture of the bastion has an effect upon the citadel; the enemy begins to weaken here, too, so that by around 14.00 hours our attack is going well. But we have not yet achieved final success. The British now seek to attain their objective by trickery. They hoist white flags, only to receive the unsuspecting approach of our brave assault troops with machine-gun fire from various quarters. A new crisis has developed at the very moment that victory seems within our grasp!

But the brigade renews its order: attack, take the citadel, and destroy the enemy! The 2nd Battalion fights its way through to Fort Risban, capturing it after some time, and then lending effective support from the north in the battle for the citadel. The attacking group on the right advances on the eastern edge of the old town, and some of its units reach the southern and the south-western sides of the Bassin des Chasses [docking basin]. The British stubbornly defend the docks. The 2nd Battalion pushes simultaneously into the eastern part of the old town, linking up with units of the 1st Battalion attacking in the north-east. The bulk of the attacking group on the left launches a successful onslaught on the citadel from the south and east.

By 17.30 hours we hold the old town, the citadel and the entrance to the port. A jubilant mood prevails in the command posts in the Opera House. Filled with pride, we think of our brave assault troops, whose indomitable will to win no setback could break. A stubborn and ferocious struggle was needed to wrest this fortress, Britain's gateway to France, from the enemy. It was precisely the unexpectedly obstinate British defence that proved to us how much store they set by the irreplaceable port city, and thus how painfully they must be feeling its final loss.

In the report of the OKW (*Oberkommando der Wehrmacht* – Armed Forces High Command), we soon hear the laconic words: 'Calais has fallen.' People at home heard nothing about the fierce fighting that preceded its fall. The defence of the fortress was tough – but our infantry regiments were tougher, fighting fearlessly and determinedly until they achieved their objective. After the battle, many a hero now lies beneath the cool turf.

But still there was no rest. Immediately afterwards, the troops were sent to defend the coast, since we had to reckon with British attempts to land troops at any time. But the night of 26–27 May passed peacefully. The enemy were not even aware by the morning of 27 May that they had lost this place that was so important to them. British planes flew over during the early hours of the morning dropping considerable stocks of ammunition and provisions on the citadel. They did not suspect what a pleasant surprise they gave the German fighters by supplying such a tasty breakfast. The number of prisoners taken in and around Calais was substantial: around 20,000, including the Commandant of Calais, a British brigadier [Brigadier Claude Nicholson], three or four staff officers, a senior French naval officer, and about 70 other officers. A Luftwaffe major was released from the citadel. He had been shot down in mid-May and taken prisoner.

The British units belonged to a battalion of the well known 'Queen Victoria Rifles' which had made a name for itself in British colonial and military history. Along with Sedan and the Somme, Calais had been added to the division's battle honours. Confident of victory, after a short breathing-space it looked forward to the new tasks that would be assigned to it.

[Calais, attacked by the 10th Panzer Division, was defended by men of the King's Royal Rifle Corps, the Rifle Brigade and Queen Victoria Rifles. Calais is now a battle honour of the Royal Green Jackets.]

By *Oberst* Fischer

The Lighter Side of War

WHEN THE CO'S 'PAPER COLLAR' BURST OPEN …

U nder fierce machine-gun fire and shelling, the CO had suffered a shot clean through the chest and was having a field dressing applied by the unit medical officer, so that he could resume command. A dispatch rider was sent off to bring up guns to help prepare for the assault on the fortress. Armoured reconnaissance cars that had meanwhile appeared on the scene could not make any headway against the fortress, either. While the troops were being regrouped and preparations made for the next attack, the following jolly conversation took place between the medic and the commander:

'You must lie down, Major.'

'You should save your breath, doctor!'

'Major, I have to tell you that the wound is quite serious, and as a doctor I'm responsible for you.'

'And I'm responsible for my men!'

'Major, I must insist on asking you to lie down!'

(Their voices keep on rising.)

'You've got no right to insist, I'll do what I like here!'

'Major, I must emphasize that I am responsible and urgently request you to follow my instructions.'

With that, the CO's 'paper collar' [dressing] burst open, and he shouted at the top of his voice: 'Are you the commander here, or am I? Just clear off and leave me in peace!!'

Whereupon the good doctor, hurt to the core and with his most tender feelings deeply injured, shrugged his shoulders in resignation, and hurried to the next casualty. It was only after the battle that the CO took himself off for proper treatment at the main aid station. His serious wound healed up, and he was fully restored.

SLEEPING IN A GAS-MASK!

We had hardly got to sleep in our foxholes, when there was a sudden gas alert. More asleep than awake, we put our masks on. But when the all-clear came, many of the men forgot to take them off; exhausted, they just went back to sleep.

It was a highly comical sight in the morning when we woke up and were taken aback to find ourselves transformed into prehistoric animals with long snouts – and quite a few could not remember when and why they had put their gas-masks on in the first place. As we later found out, it had not been a real gas alert at all. Pioneers building a bridge had created a smokescreen to foil enemy observers. A nervous soldier had given the alarm, which immediately spread like wildfire.

THEY MISSED THE 'BUS'

There was still heavy fighting going on around Calais when we reached the coast after a sustained march. The area had by no means been cleared of the enemy yet. There were still a number of large and small groups of Tommies wandering around looking for a way to get over to England on their own initiative. We had already succeeded in prising out a few Tommies from their hiding places under the coastal cliffs. It was clearly necessary to comb through the area thoroughly.

Taking three men, I set off to search under every overhanging rock, until I suddenly spotted a large motorboat with a covered cabin lying on the beach below. It looked very suspicious to me, and leaving my men hidden on the slope to cover me I crept up to the boat. Then it was the work of a moment to jump on board, yank the cabin door open, and go in, pistol in hand. I found myself facing a bunch of Tommies, who must have thought I was the devil incarnate. Disturbed while taking a nap, they woke up with a start and stared at me in fright. They put their hands up straight away. At first, I thought I was only dealing with five or six men. But more and more emerged from a cabin to the rear, and in the end I counted 15 of them.

My men and I disarmed the Tommies. Then we collected another seven British soldiers from a boatman's hut about 20 metres (66 feet) away. They had seen their comrades surrender, and decided to accompany them voluntarily into captivity. That was the end of their attempt to take off for England in the motor-boat once the tide came in. Once again, the Tommies had missed the 'bus'.

A PEACEFUL VILLAGE IDYLL IN THE MIDST OF WAR

With two light flak platoons, we took up forward defensive positions against tanks and infantry, 7 kilometres (4.5 miles) ahead of the main front-line, 12 kilometres (7.4 miles) south of Abbéville. Alongside each platoon there was a forward infantry sentry post with 10 men. It was hard to say who felt happier – the gunners or the riflemen – not to be out there all alone.

Admittedly, at first there was no cause for anxiety. The French Army, against whom our defensive line had been put in place, had not yet arrived. We were still seeing the smiling face of Picardy, and the village in which we were billeted was showing a friendly face, too. We really were living in a remote, carefree idyll! Even the farming women, initially so hostile, were now greeting us with smiles. And when they told us through their tears about their men who were far away on military service, and whose fate was uncertain, our words of comfort visibly consoled them. We stroked their children, who had become quite trusting now that they knew we would not chop their fingers off. Even the trouble-making Abbé had lost his influence. He had run towards us advancing German troops with outstretched arms and cries of delight, shouting: '*Des Anglais, des Anglais!*' When he learned from the supposed Englishmen where they actually came from, he had sunk to his knees whimpering: '*Pas battre, pas battre.*'

There were many things for the German gunners to laugh about and many peaceful activities to pursue. They smiled appreciatively when the

French girls asserted with a giggle '*Les soldats allemands sont très corrects*', adding rather ruefully '*un peu trop corrects!*' But the German soldiers went on kindly helping them with the milking and catching horses that had broken loose. There were also a number of funny moments. Once, the driver of the platoon leader's vehicle came under fire from a Morane aircraft flying at 10 metres (11 yards). Instead of braking as fast as he could and looking for cover, he put his foot down and started a mad race with the plane. Luckily, the hunt had a happy ending, and the hostile Morane pushed off. We were all tickled pink when, after the lieutenant reprimanded him for his stupidity, he calmly replied [in broad Low German]: 'Aw, lieutenant, give us a break. Me old bones are still rattling enough as it is'.

But after two days of this enjoyable life, the enemy arrived. They moved into a valley about 8 kilometres (5 miles) away. Suddenly, the war was back.

[The Morane-Saulnier M.S. 406 CI single-seat fighter first flew in 1936. The German driver was lucky that the French pilot was a poor shot – the fighter was armed with a 20mm (0.79in) Hispano-Suiza S9 cannon and two 7.5mm (0.29in) machine guns.]

THE FLAK 'ON THE PHONE'

There was a short break in the firing during the bombardment of Dunkirk. An NCO from an artillery observation post was sent to the rear to find out 'what impressive rapid-firing weapon had opened fire on Dunkirk'. Our chief gunner, with his usual good humour, sent him back with this message: 'Just report that a heavy flak battery is having a telephone conversation with the Tommies here.'

Tank Destroyers in the Dunkirk Blocking Force

It is dark and ghostly, as wearing and nerve-racking as all nights spent facing the enemy. Constantly tense, expecting some surprise. His eyes water in the sharp wind, perhaps because he is tired, too. With all his senses concentrated, the sentry tries to penetrate the darkness, not to miss the slightest thing. His time will soon be up. Then the next man will have to climb out of his stinking hole and take over the watch. He plods up and down, without making much noise. There was a big storm yesterday, making the ground very soft. Caked with mud, your boots hang like lead weights on the end of your legs. If they get too heavy, you stamp hard a few times so that a thick, soggy lump of dirt flies off and hits the ground with a splash.

With every step in the saturated earth, you sink in deeper. The water wells up all round your boots. They used to be black. But that was a long time ago. Your greatcoat is encrusted with mud, wet through and crumpled. Your hands are grey and cracked, your beard too long. Thick stubble on your cheeks and chin, coated with the dust and dirt of the last few days. Over your eyes there is a thin, dark veil of tiredness.

That is the sentry. No different from his comrade whose turn comes next, or from all the others in this boggy trench, dreaming of home.

The corporal on sentry duty after midnight looks exactly like all his men.

He has been pushing on, forwards all the time, without sleep, without rest, always on the heels of the enemy. But this is the sixth night in the same position.

Every day you hoped the attack would start again. But the longed-for order to attack never came. So the time was spent in waiting, listening and staying in a state of readiness. It was not a restful time. The enemy's artillery and heavy mortars constantly battered a defensive line whose position was well marked. That was how it had been for five days and five nights here outside Dunkirk. The half-platoon of tank destroyers have dug themselves in, in the two musty, damp trenches on either side of the track. To the right and left their neighbours are the infantrymen to whom the unit has been allocated. Here there is a tank half buried, so that – hardly visible to the enemy – only its gun barrel shows above the surface; further left there is a machine-gun post. The flat plain of Flanders stretches out into the distance, allowing a clear view. The artillery on both sides fires night and day. Time and again, the enemy mortars in St Georges and Bourbourg subject our trenches to terrible destructive fire. And yet, so far, we have been all right, although craters gape all around us, long since filled with water.

In the trench, too, the muddy, yellow-brown bilge water has gathered, into which we throw ourselves for protection every time the shells comes screaming over.

Out there, the darkness is occasionally lit up. An enormous column of flame shoots up into the sky and for a moment colours everything for miles around a bloody red. Then there are just small flames flickering through the darkness. The oil and petrol tanks in Dunkirk, hit by our Stukas some days ago, are still burning.

The new day dawns, and the shells are coming over again. But soon our own artillery's missiles are whistling over our heads, looking for their targets on the other side. There is a chirping and screeching above us. On the enemy side, bright clouds rise where shells have landed. But they do not hold back with the heavy stuff, either.

The enemy shells get closer and closer. First of all they land in front of the trench, and then behind it. The French are getting their eye in! The shells burst shrilly all around. Shrapnel flies through the air, falling who knows where. This is when we catch it!

And then the artillery fire suddenly stops. But for how long?

During the morning the runner brings up some coffee. He takes back with him the cards on which you have written a few words home. But there is something else he brought, aside from the coffee – a rumour – empty chat? The attack is going to begin again today. Because of the fall of Calais, new forces have been released that can now be brought into play against Dunkirk. Oh God, if only that were true! To be able to march forward again! To get away, out of this stinking trench with its flooded holes! Heavy rain sets in. The canvas is soon soaked through. Once more you get the cold jet of water right through to your skin. The muffled thunder rolls on through midday. Lightning fills the sky. Single-mindedly the Stukas maintain their course to the north-west. Soon afterwards, in between the rumble of thunder, you hear explosions from the port of Dunkirk.

Around midday, the rain eases somewhat. There is a sound of battle quite close. Over in Bourbourg, white signal flares soon go up. The infantry is attacking. We have taken Bourbourg. And then from the right the riflemen, who have fanned out, turn towards the north-west. They look strange with their dripping capes draped around them. New waves of infantry go forward. A cheer from the trench; it will soon be our turn to go forward.

And then the order comes. At last the moment we yearned for is here. The rain has stopped. Panting, a gun crew drag their anti-tank gun through mud and sludge. Ahead of them, the 1st Machine Gun Commando trudges through the morass. They are very heavily weighed down. The gun seems to get heavier all the time, too. The wheels churn in the sticky mud and seem to have swollen to twice their normal size. Beads of sweat break out under the steel helmets and trace light channels down the grime-encrusted grey faces. But they are going forwards.

The evening sun finds a path through the racing scraps of cloud. A bright ray brushes over us, almost affectionately. Resolutely we follow our path forwards, through marsh, bogs and streams, through the enemy's conquered positions and trenches.

Ahead there are more signal flares. The enemy has been overwhelmed.

By *Unteroffizier* Martin

A War Correspondent with the Tanks

[Guderian's Panzer Group reached Pontarlier on the Swiss border on his fifty-second birthday on 17 June, and by so doing trapped General Prételat's French Army Group 2 against the Maginot Line. Two days earlier, two XIX Panzer Corps divisions had made a 90-degree turn near Pontarlier and headed north-east, reaching Belfort on 18 June. Guderian's Panzer Corps had made the largest encirclement of the campaign.]

*D*ay 1, morning: Together with another war correspondent and an infantry sergeant, I have worked my way forward into the hotly contested town of Le Chesne. The Aisne divides the town into two halves, and here as along the whole of the southern front the river has been for days both the main battle line and the frontier. The lively artillery action on both sides creates glaring gaps, and turns blooming villages into heaps of rubble. A glance at our comrades' foxholes, and beneath the piles of stone that were once houses, reveals that a kind of static warfare has developed on the Aisne that is unfamiliar to our generation.

The great hope of both officers and men is – the tanks! Much blood will have to flow to gain the necessary bridgeheads, without which, in view of the situation, even the Panzer Division cannot do anything. Once the tanks get under way, well then …

And what about us in the Propaganda Company? Will we stay with the infantry units, or will we be sent in with the combined tank and rifle brigades again as they brush aside everything in their path? Do we even know whether tanks are going to be used here? No, we don't know anything. Wouldn't the terrain over there, where we can clearly make out the enemy's artillery, rapid-fire guns, mortars and heavy machine guns – wouldn't it be perfect for a tank breakthrough? A great idea: from here our divisions should be able to encircle the Maginot Line. It's time we had a second battle of Flanders …

In whispered tones, these thoughts are being expressed in hiding places on the Aisne, and in battalion command posts further to the rear.

Night-time operations are still taking place. Assembly areas are being reconnoitred. An attack is in the air, like an impending storm …

Day 5: Our wish is granted. We are assigned to the Guderian Panzer Group, which has moved here from the coast in the meantime, first of all to one of its corps, and then to a specific division.

The intelligence officer points to a map. A large arrow shows the direction of the division's advance, from the Aisne right down to the Marne!

My God, how is that possible? During our days on the Aisne, we have become a bit more modest about distances … Then we are released to join an advance-guard battalion of the division. The spearhead of the attack, marching at 08.00 hours, punctually tomorrow.

Marching? We'll be racing. We're going to be asking a lot of our vehicles.

One thinks of the comrades who will make the guns speak tomorrow morning along the whole front; of the comrades who will fight tough infantry battles to gain access to the river and overcome the French defences; of comrades who will build bridges under heavy enemy fire, bridges for us, the tanks …

Day 7: We are over the river. During the night the whole Guderian Panzer Group rolled across the military bridges built at such a high cost in casualties by the pioneers. An unending stream of tanks and armoured troop carriers thunders across. The Guderian Group poised for action! A massive block of steely strength …

The Panzer general stands on a hill. His gaze is directed towards the south. His tanks have pushed through on a very wide front, across country in the chalky terrain. In their rapid advance enemy positions are crushed, some villages simply bypassed. This Panzer arm is fantastic! Like a creeping barrage it pushes forward at incredible speed towards the Marne.

Behind the tanks the rifle regiments work their way forward. We have lost sight of the tanks. Their way of fighting consists of the breakthrough, then pursuit of the enemy, constantly pressing on.

Day 8: Early morning south of Juniville. Two heavy tanks stand near the road, keeping watch. Tank destroyers roll up, and take up positions on the flank.

The tanks' gun turrets point east. In the direction of the Maginot Line, from where a few surprises have come. The southern front proper is held by the most advanced units of the division's rifle regiment. Between us and them are a few burnt-out enemy tanks. From yesterday evening ...

And on we go. Pioneers once again bring up pontoons and inflatable boats. Truckloads of prisoners pass us in an unending stream from the opposite direction.

The Guderian divisions roll on. Firing and fighting, overrunning the strongest enemy positions ...

Day 10: Another 20 kilometres (12.4 miles) to the Rhine-Marne Canal. Sharpshooters and pockets of resistance to our rear have kept the units that follow us busy.

We really only do measure distance in kilometres now. Our dynamic Panzer arm has spoilt us for any other kind of calculation. Would front-line soldiers in the Great War have believed that the Guderian Group could keep up this pace not only in the Polish blitzkrieg, but in France?

Stubbornly fought-over villages go up in flames as a result of pointless resistance. Especially with these small strongholds the division's assault guns come into their own, working together brilliantly with rifle units.

Tanks are pitched against tanks! Nothing can hold up the black-uniformed officers and men. At the end of these contests, the enemy tanks are left as smoking wrecks.

On a narrow front, the tanks and armoured troop carriers tear towards the Marne near Etrépy, giving the enemy no time to destroy the bridges. Ferocious enemy fire does not deter Knight's Cross holder, Oberst Balck, from taking the valuable bridge over to Etrépy, with a handful of officers and men from the leading tanks.

Particularly on the Marne, there are many examples of heroic military actions. Soon a few crossings are secured, and our units push on deep into the region between the Marne and the Sâone.

Day 13: A terrible scene of devastation. We are standing on the banks of the Sâone looking at the burning town of Gray. French military and civilian vehicles were fleeing in panic towards the large bridge, when it was blown up, cutting off their escape. They were cut to pieces by firing from both sides, and burnt out. In one of the houses near the bridge there is a dead French general. He died in Gray, surprised by German fire.

Day 14: Our triumphant progress is amazing. We are outside Besançon. We can see over the magnificently sited fortress on the River Doubs across to the citadel standing on the heights. While a rifle battalion on the edge of the town pushes on in the direction of Belfort(!), our division's heavy artillery (how has it managed to catch up so soon, given our pace?) sights its guns on the bulwark over there. Soon a heavy black cloud hangs over the town, where there are still occasional explosions.

Day 15: Just as we did previously near St Dizier, we see something that is only explicable in terms of the fantastic speed of our armoured units. A few days ago an enemy column calmly drove 'into the arms' of a rifle company that was roaring towards them. This morning at dawn a French Army artillery unit was travelling ahead of us on the road to Belfort. Our tank men shot past it. We greeted each other civilly in the half-light! How could the Frenchmen know that German tanks were approaching from Besançon, after all? Our men play the part of Tommies excellently – but soon explain the true state of affairs ... We have been inside 'the strongest fortress in the world' for quite some time before the enemy decides to open up fierce defensive fire. But what good does it do him? The division's advance units have already occupied the most important points in the city. Despite heavy street fighting, we hold Belfort. The citadel and the forts are soon softened up by the artillery for the assault. Troops coming up behind us do the rest. Meanwhile, the tanks and troop carriers, together with the flak and tank destroyer units allocated to us, have already swept on to the foothills of the Vosges Mountains, into the heart of the Maginot Line.

We left the latitude of Basel behind some time ago. Strasbourg must soon be on our right ...!

And then the day of the ceasefire arrives.

Diary entries from 15 days of battle
By *Leutnant* Werner Schäfer

Panzer Bridges Across the Aisne

A fter the victorious conclusion of the fighting around Hazebrouck, our motorized division was resting by the canal near Boulogne.

The date is 1 June 1940.

We just had long enough to take a good look across the Channel at the steep cliffs of the English coast, and wash off the dirt of the last few weeks.

Shortly after midnight the division was already on the move again, in an incredible forced march, into the area north of Rethel to prepare for a big new mission.

Here my pioneer battalion was allotted the task of building, near Rethel, one of the bridges required for Guderian's tanks.

First of all, the infantry had to establish enough of a bridgehead to enable Guderian to launch his final deadly assault on France.

Building a river crossing beneath the eyes of the enemy is no simple matter!

Reconnaissance by night and day gives us the necessary information about the best places to gain control of the Aisne and the Ardennes Canal that lies beyond it. The pioneers of another division have done some good groundwork for us.

At first light on 9 June we are ready to go. The first shells rudely disturb the enemy's sleep. Pioneers and infantry attack along a broad front. After fierce fighting, we succeed in getting a few people across the Aisne, as well as the Canal. The essentially undamaged enemy artillery and the skilfully sited machine-gun posts along the southern banks of the waterways prevent our troops from making progress, however tireless their attack. New fiery abysses are constantly opening up in front of them.

The crossing has not been achieved at the first attempt, and when the natural and man-made mists clear, the assault troops are not well placed.

But the outcome of the first day's attack cannot be left at this.

The order reads: 'The objective is to gain a footing on the southern side of the Aisne with such speed and in such depth that by this afternoon at the latest the Guderian Group's tanks can be on their way to attack beyond the Aisne.'

In this situation, something special is required.

Things do not look any better with our neighbouring divisions.

So forwards, no matter what it costs!

After reporting on the situation at our divisional command post, I set off by motorcycle – in a different direction from that of our crossing area so far – further to the west of Rethel, desperately looking for alternative crossing points. The Frenchman's unpleasantly noisy bombardment of the approach roads here is not promising, either – he is placing his shells at the entrance to the town, as well as within it. Roofs are collapsing into the streets, the church has been half destroyed, and the orchards and meadows running down to the Aisne are under constant, ferocious artillery and machine-gun fire. Actually, it is very surprising that the French sharpshooters are happy to operate in this inhospitable terrain. Happiness is hardly the right word, of course, they are simply going on doing their duty for a while. That is something we respect.

The racket of war around Barby forces us to get the motorbike into top gear. A bike that was accompanying us has already dropped out of the race.

Then it seems expedient to dismount and enjoy again for a moment some of the advantages of a pedestrian with regard to negotiating the terrain, cornering ability and adaptability. We go through some bushes, along the bed of a stream to the river. Early this morning an attempted crossing by the infantry and pioneers was beaten back here too, with heavy casualties. There is plenty of evidence of that earlier attempt. However, even though this hardly seems a more auspicious place for our purposes, it does have the advantage that the line of sight of the enemy observers, and all the fire that comes over in this direction, is impeded by a line of poplars and a sparse wood on the southern side of the Aisne. This is where we are going to have to risk it, otherwise we'll never get across the Aisne and the canal!

It is 12.00 hours.

According to orders from the corps, bridge-building is not to start until we have secured a bridgehead line about 2 kilometres (1.25 miles) south of the Ardennes Canal. Despite not achieving this goal with our first attack, and in spite of the enemy's attentions, we've got to risk building the bridge, whatever the loss of men or materials! The advance detachment of the divisions and units of the tank division urgently need the completed bridge; that justifies my decision.

The result is that directly after my successful return from reconnaissance, parts of my 1 Company – who happen to be available – are sent off in great haste to clear the terrain on the south bank of the Aisne. They also must clear the canal itself and the village of Nanteuil south of the canal from enemy machine-gun nests and riflemen, and so create at least a small bridgehead. Every officer, NCO and man knows what is at stake now, and how much our commanders depend upon our action. That is why they are prepared to put their lives on the line.

The track to Nanteuil is mined. The ground has to be cleared of 64 mines. At about 13.00 hours. The battalion's command post is moved to the bridge site, and at the same time a company of riflemen from the infantry regiment who have just arrived are sent in to reinforce and extend the bridgehead. Gradually, the pioneers are more able to devote themselves to their main task of bridge-building. The company commanders, orderly officers, adjutant and platoon leaders have their hands full. Under heavy enemy fire, it is difficult to shift the bridge-building site from its original planned location near Rethel-Acy. In the face of the enemy, three platoons of pioneers have to fight their way to the new site from their previous position, where they had dug themselves in after the last failed attempt to cross.

It appears that our intentions are not lost on the enemy's artillery observers. Their fire is directed at the terrain on both sides of the Aisne. We are in great difficulties. Fortunately, some of the shells explode in the poplar trees without doing our men much harm. All the same, it is uncomfortable enough to operate in all this vicious enemy fire. It demands iron nerves and absolute concentration. It is much easier to defend yourself, fight back or attack!

Via the line of departure established near Sorbon, the combat vehicles, ordered forward from their assembly area carrying some pioneer units and the bridge-building gear, are moving towards us. Unavoidably, their route takes them along one of the highest ridges in the region, and then down into the Aisne valley through Barby to the bridge site. A few of our vehicles made it unscathed into the valley, but eventually this brazen impudence became too much for the French artillery observer, who was able to watch the entire parade. The French artillery, singing their swan song during these memorable days, subject this rewarding target to thorough treatment, and it is incomprehensible that they do not do more damage.

About 80–100 metres (87–109 yards) apart from each other and at top speed, our drivers – wonderful chaps who have proved themselves in the Sudetenland, Bohemia, Poland and northern France – bring up their vehicles through the impressive display of firing.

Thus, with the arrival of these first vehicles, bridge building is able to get properly started at around 15.45 hours. The enemy artillery constantly butts in, however, creating many a gap in our ranks. But our casualties could have been much greater, and we can count ourselves lucky that the shells exploding in the Aisne next to the bridge throw up more water than shrapnel. We have to cut a path through the wood on the southern bank of the river. There is extensive earth-moving work to be done, as well as the reinforcing of the road on either side of the bridge with special equipment. The problems pile up! But still – our work makes progress, and soon we can start building the second bridge, over the Ardennes Canal, although flanking machine-gun fire interferes considerably with the pioneers' activities.

Towards 16.00 hours we are able to report that both bridges will be serviceable by 18.30 hours. Soon afterwards, the advance detachment of the division begins to cross, and during the night the entire tank division is able to cross the Aisne sector at this point.

We feel sincere and un-envious pleasure on behalf of our comrades when we hear that, after days of laborious and difficult preparatory work, the pioneer battalion deployed to the left of us near Château-Porcien has succeeded, just a few hours ahead of us, in completing another tank bridge. In the knowledge of duty done, we look back on our day's work. We grieve for the painful losses that death and injury have wreaked in our numbers, but they are justified by our great success in creating on time a crossing facility to launch part of the Guderian tank group on its breakthrough to the Swiss frontier! The 9th of June 1940 has become a day of honour for our pioneer battalion!

By *Oberleutnant* Hecker

The Tanks are Coming at Last!

We are resting in a wood north of the Aisne near Charleville when – finally – on 10 June at about 15.00 hours I receive orders to take the company up to the Aisne, in the direction of the small town of Rethel, and report to the divisional commander to await further orders.

'Early this morning the Guderian Group crossed the Aisne to attack to the south. Here, too, the forces built up along the Aisne front during the battle of Flanders will move into the attack, and after the infantry have established a bridgehead south of the Aisne and the pioneers have completed a temporary bridge, our tank division will begin its thrust through the enemy positions west of the Argonne and Verdun towards the Swiss frontier, in order to encircle the French on the Maginot Line and destroy them.'

My task is to cross the Aisne in the Rethel area, reach the village of Perthes, 8 kilometres (5 miles) south of Rethel, and from there to reconnoitre to the south and west, linking up with the infantry divisions attacking there.

When I issue my orders to the company, every single man is pleased to know we are going to engage with the enemy again and proud that we have been selected once more for a special mission. On the roads and tracks leading to the Aisne endless columns are marching southwards – a glorious sight! I soon take off with my company across country, to get to the Aisne as quickly as possible. A pioneer officer reports heavy fighting around

Rethel, and says that the bridge has not yet been built yet. So I drive further to the west and find military bridges over the Aisne near Château-Porcien and over the adjacent canal. The endless columns of another armoured division are pouring across them to the southern bank. The officer in charge at the bridge sympathizes with my plight and slips my company through between the columns. I heave a sigh of relief, because I now have freedom of action for my tanks.

I reach Acy via Taizy and Nanteuil; here, too, the roads are choked with vast columns and baggage trains. There are many delays. Nanteuil and Acy show signs of heavy fighting, and they cannot have been in German hands for more than a few hours. Gaps have been blown in the brick barriers at either end of the village, and behind them stand shattered anti-tank guns. Large groups of prisoners come towards us, and the dead from the battle still lie unburied. From here we can see the town of Rethel, picturesquely situated in the Aisne valley, but now with tall flames and columns of smoke rising from it in many places. Artillery fire can be heard very close by. At the eastern exit from Acy isolated machine-gun and rifle fire whistles over our heads, and near the road is an aid station where the doctors have their hands full, with more wounded men being brought in almost every minute.

I spread out my company by a field's width, so as not to offer a concentrated target for enemy planes and artillery, and go ahead with a motorcycle to reconnoitre. On a railway embankment infantry, are pinned down in an attempted assault on the village of Sault. A large brick factory is the main centre of the enemy defence, and every attempt by the infantry to renew their attack is immediately stalled by defensive fire from there. Even German artillery cannot break down the resistance. The infantry recognize me from my black uniform as a tank man and call out: 'The tanks are coming at last!'

The infantry battalion commander explains the situation to me. He requests the help of my tanks, because his objective for the day is still 6 kilometres (4 miles) further on. He has to reach it without fail before dark, but his company is pinned down by the defenders in the brickyard and a few other strong pockets of resistance in nearby farmyards. I tell him that my objective is Perthes! He informs me that another regiment of the division is still involved in heavy fighting there. I order Sergeant K. of my company to take his platoon around the defensive positions and attack them from the rear; after reporting by radio to division, I myself will go on with the rest of the company to Perthes. There is no time to lose, because it is already 19.00 hours.

Despite a number of road blocks and mines, by outstanding leadership Sergeant W. succeeds in approaching with his platoon under cover quite close to the brickyard. Suddenly the five tanks open fire with machine guns and main armament, slamming volley after volley at the brickworks. Then the firing dies down. Two of the tanks roar at breakneck speed towards the brickyard, flattening a gateway, and firing a number of shells into the yard and the buildings. There are only occasional shots ringing out now, and the tank commanders wave to the infantry to follow them. But the infantrymen do not come. They cannot believe it is safe at last to storm the defences in the brickworks, which have kept them pinned down for so many hours. The tank crews jump out of their tanks, pistols in hand. The first Frenchmen walk out with their hands up. The other tanks now move closer in and help to clear the factory. The French are no longer putting up any resistance. A French captain is surprised in the act of burning his orders. Six officers and over 100 men are captured, as well as many machine guns, mortars and infantry guns, mountains of ammunition and hand-grenades. The infantry cheer the tank crews, and then they attack with the tanks to break down the last pockets of enemy resistance. That, too, happens with surprising speed.

During this fighting around Sault, I continue across country with my company in open formation towards Perthes. After we have crossed the railway line, a platoon leader reports: 'French sign in the cornfield: *Danger de mines!*' – The company follows in my tank-tracks. The church tower of Perthes is visible in the distance. From a hill I see our infantry attacking Perthes. Artillery and anti-tank guns are firing. A battalion adjutant comes up to my tank and asks for assistance, as his battalion is held back by heavy flanking machine-gun fire from the eastern edge of the village. I give radio orders to Lieutenant S. to neutralize the machine-gun nests, help the battalion get on with its attack, and then proceed to the Annelles road.

I myself propose to take the last platoon round to the west of Perthes, to attack the enemy there from the rear. Then a dispatch rider comes up to me: 'Careful, Captain, our anti-tank guns have just fought off an attack by heavy enemy tanks that came out of the woods south of Perthes. About 10 tanks managed to get away. Also, the tracks and fields are mined!' Out of sight of Perthes, we feel our way forward. I creep with my tank up to a hill to stop and make observations. There, off to the right, is our anti-tank gun position, about 600 metres (655 yards) away. Suddenly two of the guns start taking aim at my tank! I fire off flares, and my radio operator signals with his flag: 'We are German tanks!' The anti-tank people understand our signals. As I later discovered, the gun crews involved in this fast-changing battle had believed themselves to be surrounded by the surviving enemy tanks. They no longer knew exactly where friend and foe were.

Perthes is burning brightly and, as it is getting dark by now, the flames light our way for the next attack. In the background we see the enemy tanks still burning, but on our side too we can see that a fierce battle must have raged here in the afternoon. Shot-up guns and vehicles, dead and wounded men. The defensive fire from Perthes continues unabated. Despite the approach of darkness, I take the few tanks I have and make a wide detour around Perthes to attack the enemy from the rear, and join up again with Lieutenant S.'s platoon.

As I stop south of Perthes, with the tanks still shooting towards the village, the enemy fire slackens off. Using flares, I have already made contact with Lieutenant S.'s platoon. Then I see against the glow of Perthes a crowd of people surging out from the village. I aim a few shells into the middle of this crowd, and shots from my machine gun whip through them. The other tanks see this and race towards the target I have indicated – the enemy fleeing from Perthes. Despite the darkness, my tank soldiers pick up from the cornfields and ploughed fields some 30 Frenchmen, including a number of officers. The enemy gives up all resistance when he sees the tanks have circled round to his rear.

The riflemen then move on into fiercely burning Perthes to clear it of the last remaining enemy troops.

By *Hauptmann* von Arentschild
From the Führer's Order of the Day for 5 June:
'Soldiers! Today our forces on the western front
are back in action.'

We Hit the Enemy from Behind his Barricades!

After some hard and stubborn fighting, on 10 June the attack across the Aisne west of Rethel was successful. Thus the Weygand Line had been penetrated in yet another sector. The tank division poured through this open gateway on 11 June and reached Machault around noon. However, barricades and well-fortified positions in houses on the edge of the village brought the attack to a halt. Reconnaissance troops who had been sent in suffered heavy casualties, although wounded men were returning with reports that the defence force was not strong. A company of motorcycle riflemen was sent into the attack, and pioneers were to mount a shock troop assault on the barricade – visible from some distance – blocking access to the village from the north, and thus opening the way for the motorbike troops. The platoon of pioneers was to push forward along the main street to the middle of the village, then strike off to the right to secure the railway line behind it.

The attacking force was assembled about 1000 metres (1093 yards) outside Machault, while the artillery opened up a brief but intensive bombardment. During the shelling, the pioneers and motorbike troops worked their way forward. They succeeded in getting to within 200 metres (218 yards) of the place without being spotted. But then came the 'tack tack' of machine guns; our opponent had noticed the attackers. The pioneer platoon was coming under heavy fire from the left side of the village, as well as from ahead of them, and – as it later transpired – from the church tower.

The group worked their way forward in stages. About 50 metres (54 yards) from the entrance to the village stood a French tank that had driven over mines laid by its own side. It was still burning as the pioneers pushed on past it to get to their first objective, a solid barricade just before the entrance to the village. A house standing next to it had been fortified with defences that were obviously intended to cover the barricade. The latter consisted of bales of straw, agricultural equipment, rocks and beams, all enclosed by stout planks, a method of construction often employed in the defence system of the Weygand Line. These barriers were very dangerous because they often incorporated mines lying deeply buried in hay and straw, and detonating when the barricade was torn apart. Just after the barrier, there was a street leading off into the heart of the village. As the pioneers discovered in working their way forward, this street too was blocked by a barrier.

The platoon leader, Sergeant R., decided to distract the barricade's defenders by getting a few of his men to concentrate heavy fire on it from the front, while he took another group round to the back of the house to surprise the occupants from the rear. Working forward quickly, he reached the north side of the house without being seen. As he was peering cautiously round the corner of the house to see how to proceed, he found himself staring straight down the barrel of a 7.5cm (3in) gun about 50 metres (54 yards) away, poking out from the second barricade, which lay across the street leading into the village. With lightning speed he threw himself down, called over his group and then crawled with his men, keeping close to the ground, around the corner to burst into the house. The defenders, about 20 Frenchmen, were utterly astonished and surrendered without resistance.

It was clear to Sergeant R. that his next objective must be the 7.5cm (3in) gun in the next barricade. For if the following groups started to remove the first barricade and the enemy gun opened up, there would be heavy losses. Once again he succeeded in moving round to the rear of the enemy. Taking a look from behind a projecting wall, he noticed that the crew of the 7.5cm (3in) gun were getting ready to open fire. Leading his group from the front, he charged with long strides towards the gun crew, seized the gun layer from behind and pulled him to the ground. The pioneers racing up behind him threw themselves upon the other crew members and instantly overwhelmed them. The entrance to the village had been secured. Sergeant R. gathered together the two groups of his platoon – which had meanwhile reached the first barricade but had not been able to start dismantling it because of intense enemy machine-gun fire – and continued with his mission. The place would have to be taken before the barricade could be removed. His orders were to reach the middle of the village, before turning right and securing the railway line. When the platoon reached its line of departure and was launching itself forward, it came under heavy machine-gun fire. A lance-corporal was badly injured, and a medical orderly corporal, determined at all costs to get help to his wounded comrade and bring him back, was killed by a shot to the head. Another lance-corporal trying to rescue both comrades was caught in a burst of machine-gun fire, and also badly wounded. But Sergeant R.'s resolve did not weaken. His stubborn attack subdued one house after another.

At last, there was some relief for the pioneers. Motorbike troops had penetrated the village at right angles to the pioneers' line of attack. Together with a bicycle squadron from a following division which had joined in the motorbike soldiers' attack, they advanced into the middle of the village. This gave the pioneers a breathing space. The enemy's resistance ahead of them crumbled. The occupants of the houses surrendered their positions one after another. The attackers shook hands in the middle of the village. They could not get over their astonishment. It had not been a small force of defenders at all, as the wounded reconnaissance troop leader had reported: nearly 600 men had occupied Machault, and in a short time had been forced to give in to the determined and careful assault tactics of the attackers.

By *Hauptmann* Dr Walter Menningen

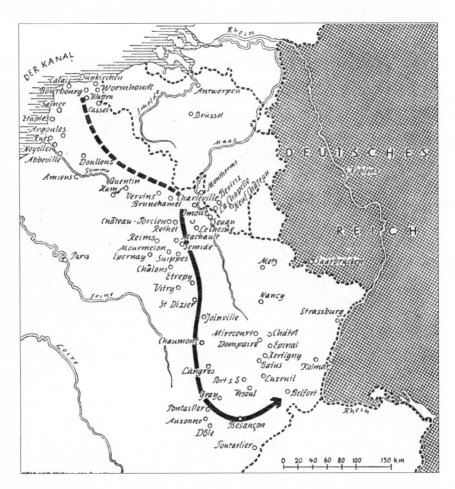

The German conquest of France launched from the line of the rivers Somme and Aisne on 5 June was a spectacular demonstration of the blitzkrieg *tactics advocated by Guderian.*

Behind the Maginot Line and to the Swiss Frontier

Everything is Going Like Clockwork Today!

The battle must be fought boldly and audaciously – that is what it said in battlegroup orders. And in lengthy discussions, the battlegroup commander, Cross holder Colonel von Ravenstein, explained as follows: 'The great firing power of our vanguard force must spread fear and destruction during the advance. Even the slightest enemy resistance should be nipped in the bud by instant and relentless fire from all weapons. If they cannot be bypassed, then – without investigating the details – the enemy, barricades, or suspicious areas on the edge of woods or villages, should all be subjected to massed destructive fire. The *furor teutonicus* [teuton's fury] must shake the Frenchman to the core!'

The reason for these instructions was made clear at the same time. Unlike in the first stage of the battle for France, it was no longer a matter of charging at an enemy presumed to be obstinate, and capable of putting up a tough defensive fight. The mission now was to push on past the already demoralized enemy (to be dislodged from his position on the Aisne by the German infantry) far towards the south, in order to sever the important links between Paris and eastern France, the Rhine front.

The offensive had begun on 8 June. News of it arrived at the same time as the order to prepare to march. Everyone was agog with anticipation. 'The hunt is on again!' But then nothing happened for a while. We spent two endless days on standby while the infantry were crossing the Aisne and the Aisne Canal. Yesterday afternoon we got the longed-for order to march.

'Step on it', shouted Lance-Corporal Edi to his comrade, who like him had been serving in the same vehicle for three years, and had led it through all the vicissitudes of the march into the Sudetenland, the desert-like tracks of Poland, and the vicious artillery onslaught in France. He would have liked nothing better than to roar southwards at 80 kilometres (50 miles) an hour. But it was clear to everyone that our farsighted leadership could still not afford to increase the pace. So it was not until the onset of darkness that the river was reached.

The pioneers' bridge was crossed by the light of burning farmhouses. 'Hey, there's been some heavy stuff going on around here!' exclaimed Edi during one of the frequent halts the column was obliged to endure because of difficult conditions at the crossing point. This appreciative remark had prompted a pioneer on duty at the roadside to describe in a few words what a heroic battle the East Prussian infantry had fought as the first troops to force a passage here near Rethel, and break through the unusually fierce defences of the Weygand Line.

Long after midnight, when they passed the most forward infantry pickets, a shout of 'Halt!' had rang out. The companies had driven up side by side on to the broad fields of the Champagne area, which had resulted in a few casualties through mines. However, that did not prevent the drivers and crews from falling into a short but deep sleep next to their vehicles.

And now, at just after 04.00 hours, the morning of 11 June is beginning to dawn. 'On your feet!' the command rings out across the broad field. Everywhere, figures drunk with sleep are stretching themselves. The blankets are stowed away and vehicles readied, and in between there is a quick gulp of coffee. The order to fall in has already been given.

'Take it easy', says the veteran Edi, 'we've got plenty of time; it'll be at least half an hour before the advance guard gets going.' The 6th do not belong to the advance guard, so the comrades can observe in the early morning light the familiar spectacle of the head of the great dragon being lifted with a rattle and the column creeping forward: lead tanks, riflemen, many heavy weapons, the massive colossus of the assault artillery, a battery, anti-tank guns, and pioneers. It all trundles forward, harmoniously arranged, back on to the route of the advance. The outlines of the various vehicles are sharply silhouetted against the brilliantly clear eastern sky.

The vanguard's progress can be clearly followed. They have just reached the outskirts of Perthes. Then the lead tank gives a jerk, and immediately afterwards there is an explosion. Damn, the French have been laying mines again. The leaders stop. 'There, can you see that car moving so fast up to the front? That's the colonel. He'll get it sorted out.' And sure enough, the vanguard are on the move again, sweeping round to the left and bypassing the village in a wide arc.

'So who's going to take the village, then, with all those road blocks and barriers?' asks a replacement crew member. 'You can attack it all by yourself. But you'd better hurry up so you don't fall behind and get overtaken by the clean-up unit of the Labour Service.' The conversation is interrupted because the bulk of the column is now on the move again. Precisely at this moment there is a brief noise of intense fighting up ahead. The spearhead troops have met with enemy resistance in the next village, Pauvres. A short burst of fire is enough to shock the weak enemy force into silence. A group of prisoners marches towards us. Pauvres itself is bypassed. You can clearly identify a number of mined barricades here. The French obviously did not have time to camouflage the mines.

On we go, without further hold-ups. The mood improves. 'It's all going like clockwork today, mates.' The vanguard does not even go near the next village, standing in open, empty terrain. The whole column rolls past it across country, a few hundred metres from the village. At this moment the spearhead is reaching the next village, Leffincourt. There is the same scene here of barriers and mines at the eastern end. The place is passed to the right. Just as the first vehicles of the bulk of the column draw level with the village, they come to a standstill, and some fairly loud fire is audible from the south east. The lead vehicles have run into a cleverly camouflaged enemy position on the edge of the woods. Some impressive French anti-tank fire causes serious casualties among the advance-guard tanks. There is a hail of enemy fire from a variety of weapons. The commander of the rifle company orders his men to dismount, and tries to find cover for its vehicles in a hollow. The leader of the advance guard, Captain Löwe, another Knight's Cross holder, orders an attack on the little wood. There are isolated successes. One rifle platoon, going in boldly, manages to capture an anti-tank gun complete with ammunition tractors, and seven heavy machine guns. The forward battery is already in place, and it puts a 7.5cm (3in) gun out of action that was subjecting the German tanks to direct fire. Nonetheless, the attack as a whole is bogged down by superior enemy fire, particularly by the powerful fire of the French artillery. Löwe gives the order to 'dig in!' In the course of the day, he is to conduct a stubborn and fluctuating battle at this point before the enemy is finally overcome.

The men of 6 Company at the head of the body of the battlegroup do not have a very clear view of this tough battle the vanguard are engaged in.

Isolated shots meant for the advance guard whizz over their heads. Anti-tank shells, at the end of their trajectory, flop down like tired birds into the field next to the column. The French artillery now starts sending over its greetings. 'As you were – just relax!' says Edi to reassure his young comrades, who show every sign of buckling at the knees. 'It just sounds worse than it is.' That's right – the shells are landing in the middle of Leffincourt village. There are grins all round because the French are keenly and skilfully pounding their own village, in which no German soldier has set foot so far.

'There'll be work to do soon', calls out Edi. While his comrades have been enjoying the display of French artillery and putting their capes over their heads because of a light shower, he has been watching the spot up ahead at the side of the road where the colonel stopped his vehicle. 'Look, the General is there now as well. And that's the tank commander coming up.' – 'Wow, just wait till you see how his tanks tickle the Frenchmen's tummies!'

There's a short discussion in the vehicle. Cards are being dealt out, when suddenly there is a lot of shouting; officers and dispatch riders are coming back. The news spreads: there's going to be a big tank attack! 'Company leaders to the commander!' – What's going on? A few moments later the orders for action come through. The advance guard will be left to fight its own tough battle. The bulk of the force will turn towards the south and attack the enemy on this very favourable terrain. First wave: a tank detachment, minus the lead tanks. Second wave: rifle battalion – 6 Company in front with the heavy weapons under its command, and a reinforced 7 Company behind. Third wave behind them: a complete tank detachment.

Preparations take place behind a crest, undisturbed because out of sight of the enemy, and take half an hour. Then the large battlegroup moves forward slowly. The sight of it alone fills everyone with enthusiasm and happiness. As far as the eye can see, from one slope to another and well spread out, the vehicles are rolling over meadows and fields, each of them leaving visible tracks in deep clover or in fields of ripening corn. The various units are travelling in a V-formation, like a flotilla of fishing boats putting out to sea. Everyone is filled with feelings such as may have inspired those squadrons of cavalry at [Frederick the Great's battle of] Rossbach, when the wide-cuffed white glove of a cuirassier general signalled them to charge into the thick of the enemy.

The attack rolls over the brow of the first hill. There is artillery fire from a copse on the right. The tanks do not notice it, but just continue. The platoon of 6 Company on the right dismounts. One or two heavy mortar shells land in the French battery's position, and the momentum of the attack overwhelms the battery. But now the enemy are firing from the left as well. The rest of 6 Company is forced to dismount and clear the edge of the wood. The French retreat. Again they are raked with efficient fire from the heavy mortars. They surrender. Prisoners are sent to the rear. 'That feels good' is the comrades' comment as they board their vehicles again.

Hey, look how far the attack has got in the meantime! 7 Company drove on a long time ago to catch up again with the first wave of tanks. The reinforced 6th follows in the midst of the second tank detachment. The attack overruns a light French position. Some of the enemy are literally flattened in their foxholes. The attack makes use of a broad sweep of land between two wooded ridges, and its path goes through wheat fields. The vehicles cut a swathe through the tall corn. The riflemen fire from their vehicles with everything they've got. Anything that escapes the tanks is caught in this way.

'Look, over there – the general in his half-track command post!' Like all the commanders involved, he is travelling in the midst of the attacking troops. Everyone is gripped by wild enthusiasm. The soldiers shout to each other: 'Like on the training ground!' – 'Same as the display at the Party Rally.' The tank guns bark at the edge of the wood. There are only isolated pockets of enemy resistance. When it occurs, a vehicle stops, and the riflemen open fire as though out hunting for hares. The Frenchmen emerge totally distraught from their holes. 'Our opponents are depressed', observes our Lance-Corporal Edi.

By about 12.00 hours, we reach the hill east of Machault. After a short breather and a check on our position, the attack rolls on as far as the St Etienne sector. In the midst of the artillery fire, General Guderian himself appears. He seems satisfied.

By *Leutnant* Stahl

On the Old Warpath in the 'Lousy Champagne Country'

We were marching on the left wing of the Guderian Group, covering its open flank. When our route was announced, I shouted for joy – it ran through the Champagne country. But, dear reader, do not leap to false conclusions, what I mean is 'the lousy Champagne'. Yes, that is how it is: some think of Épernay [famous for the sparkling wine], and some of Ripont and the Butte de Tahure [sites of World War I battles].

My joy at the prospect of seeing the old battlegrounds again after 24 years, and probably fighting over them once more, was put to the test by numerous alterations to our route. But finally, after conquering the Aisne, that is where it took us – into the chalk soil of Champagne. Literally into the soil, as it soon began to rain so much that the dispatch riders spent more time sitting on the ground than in their saddles, and the mud nearly tore the boots from our feet.

My men were certainly not too enthusiastic about my 'old war homeland'. But I was, all the more so. 'Pauvres', read Gunner Meyer, former law student, at the entrance to a small village, thinking to himself 'poverty in the plural'. For Gunner Meyer, that was the end of the matter. The fire-control NCO, on the other hand, had a closer relationship to the landscape, spying out the undulating terrain for good artillery positions. But for him, too, this artillery angle was the extent of his interest in the Champagne country. So I was alone in my love for this miserable region. I was desperate to take up a position in my old division's area, which we had now reached. My wish was granted; we soon had contact with the enemy. At a full (motorized) gallop, the howitzers sought cover behind the nearest undulation in the ground, and took general aim at the church tower in Semide. Meanwhile, I set up my observation post with the battery troops in a small wood still showing evidence of a hasty retreat. Much as I peered through the telescope, there was no sign of the big bad enemy. What I could see, though, were the old sights from the World War passing in front of me: the barracks in camp, the stalls for horses and limbers within Semide. While I was looking for the site where they used to be, and was just thinking what calibre gun the French had used then to reach this 'rest area' with their shells, the order came: 'Change of position; forwards, we're pursuing the retreating enemy towards Orfeuil.'

My battery and I were marching in the advance guard. According to its commander, the village, with its post-war houses once more turned into torches of war, was free of enemy troops. But just as we were turning into the hollow leading to Orfeuil, bullets started whistling round our heads. I just had time to cast a glance at the fork in the road where the small house containing the local sick bay stood in 1916, and where the Swabian medical officer Ludewig used to cheer us up with his frequent inoculations and an encouraging: 'Cough through your nose, then you won't catch cold'.

In a few minutes the battery was off the road and ready to fire. It was an unforgettable sight, the way the barrels of the howitzers rose above the tall luminous poppies. When I returned on my motorbike to the place where the leading troops had first taken cover, I found that the enemy's resistance had become stiffer. The firing was mainly coming from the German cemetery honouring our World War heroes, where the irreverent poilus had set up their machine guns. So I was forced – with great reluctance – to aim my guns at it. Fortunately, the shells that landed in front of and behind the cemetery were enough to put the enemy to flight.

Soon we were marching, or rather sliding, towards Aure. But before we reached the village, in terrain that was so familiar to me, we were met with such heavy machine-gun and rifle fire that we detached the limbers on the spot and began shooting, sometimes with direct and sometimes indirect fire, at Aure and the hills beyond it. The enemy's observation posts must be over there. They were determined to prevent us from advancing right up to Aure. But in vain! We took Aure, and then started bombarding Manre as well, from where our infantry were being shelled. We managed to put an artillery OP sited there out of action. Our position in the Aure gorge made it imperative for us to secure our exit during the night. We succeeded in doing so. But Manre itself was initially stubbornly defended.

It was only towards morning that enemy resistance began to flag. The French started to give way, pursued immediately by our forward units. The regiment followed at first light, fully expecting our opponents to make defensive use of the old battle ground left unchanged since the World War to serve as a military training ground. However, recognizing that they had an armoured division to deal with, the French pulled out in one move.

So I arrived rather sooner than I had expected on Hill 194, our old 'Isberth Hill', where I set up my observation post, precisely in the bunker which had served me in 1916 as both vantage point and shelter. All that was missing was the reinforced roof over the bunker. I looked around at reference points in my former observation sector, said hello to the 'gun mountain', thought about the nightly casualties to the columns moving up the 'Karcher Road' from Gratreuil to Ripont, remembered the soldiers who used to stand on the slopes of the 'Dormoise Valley' below me with fixed bayonets, waiting to hasten the death of any 'light railway ox' that a French shell might happen to hit – and I was happy with my memories.

My head was still full of them as I went down into the 'Dormoise Valley' to reconnoitre a new gun position, passing the sign indicating the site where Ripont used to be. I stopped by the stream playfully used by the pioneers to drive a little water-works, paused, and turned into the thicket to find, half hidden by luxuriant new growth, the German soldiers' grave with a cross whose barely legible inscription says that seven unknown German soldiers lie there. There was no time now for more than a moment of silent homage. I went on, up to the heavily shelled slope behind which my battery had stood in 1916. And I found the spot again. Yes, there stood, as though built to last for ever, the cement dugout with the inscription: 'Bombproof dugout, built by Sergeant Schümann, 2./R.Pi. 52, May 1916.' German workmanship!

What a contrast between the two wars! In 1916 and 1917 we fought for every square metre, whose value lay not in the ground gained, but in the improved position it offered. To think how much artillery was deployed in the area around Ripont in February 1917 in preparation for the assault on the '*Ferme de Champagne*' [French World War I fortification]. What an effort for an operation involving such a small gain in terms of territory! However, the tactical purpose that justified these extensive preparations must not be overlooked: the infantry went in behind the artillery's rolling barrage. Operation 'Cuckoo's Egg' was a complete success. The French infantry, accustomed to leaving their dugouts only after the German artillery had stopped firing, were captured at the instant when the barrage had just passed over their position.

While I was wondering where I might find the graves of my comrades killed in this wasteland, orders arrived: 'Division will take up pursuit; route will be Butte du Mesnil – Beau séjour Ferme – Valmy – Givry en Argonne …' So I had lost the chance to re-enact from my old firing position that powerful shot in the direction of Beau séjour Ferme that we had pulled off in 1916. The No 2 gun-layer, having just finished his preparations, pulled his four marker pennants out of the crater-strewn ground in front of my old position 614, remarking: 'A pity we couldn't manage it.'

During the drive through the 'Kitchen Gorge' I would like to have taken another look at the 'Debus and Ditfurth Tunnels', the shafts that ran right under the enemy position at that time, each with room for a whole battalion plus canteen and shop etc. Another site I would like to have visited was 'Dora', our old observation post in the 'Duck's Bill', but new duties called.

We drove as fast as the bad tracks and the old craters would permit, between abandoned ammunition and discarded equipment, in pursuit of a fleeing division of French colonial troops. We caught up with their rearguard near historic Valmy, and quickly captured them.

And now there began a veritable steam-roller operation. The battles were short but fierce. The enemy's guns never had a chance to get into position, and their artillery fire directed at our flanks did not bother us. We were forced to attack, however, when black troops heading the fleeing division dug in again at the edge of the Argonne Forest.

After artillery bombardments had paved the way for the infantry, the villages of Remicourt and Givry en Argonne were taken, although there was very fierce fighting for possession of the forest itself that night and the following day. Here too it was above all the Senegalese, especially as snipers, who put up the stiffest resistance.

So it was that after a few days we had put 'the lousy Champagne', my old World War battleground, behind us. And we continued our thrust to the south – to the Swiss border!

By *Hauptmann* Hilsheimer

Attacked by Negroes

The regiment's task was to keep the routes clear, i.e. to protect the roads reserved for the Guderian Panzer Group. Every day new sectors were allocated to the regiment for security duties, and the faster the advance progressed, the longer they became. For example, in a single day our 1st Battalion was distributed along the stretch from Hirson via Rethel to Suippes.

It was not easy to take care of the sanitary and medical needs of a battalion that was so extended. As a military doctor, I often faced difficult questions. I could not be everywhere at once. There was no question of setting up a regular aid station or a local sick bay. The enemy might appear at any point. Even companies placed far to the rear could suddenly be sent into action. Medical care was certainly needed everywhere, in any case. With the furious pace of the advance, accidents were common, as well as sudden illnesses. The superhuman physical and mental achievements of our cycle troops during those hot days – they rode as much as 180 kilometres (112 miles) in a day – frequently made medical assistance necessary.

To keep on top of my duties, I had to be very mobile. For the purpose, I had the use of a captured vehicle I had acquired by barter in Brussels some weeks earlier. I drove long distances in this car, together with my driver and an NCO medical orderly. We had to plan the route ourselves, and were often completely isolated. On both sides of the road there were extensive woods which, as we later discovered, were still full of enemy troops. On the other hand, we often had the greatest difficulty in getting through on the crowded supply routes. It required much skill, and sometimes cunning, for a solitary vehicle to get past those long columns. But I always succeeded in reaching the most remote unit and carrying out my duties. My 'saloon car', which was often made fun of, was a true comrade to me, who never let me down despite the most difficult road conditions.

One day our commander wanted to identify a place for our supply convoy to cross the River Suippes. In glorious summer weather we drove – one is tempted to say peacefully – through the broad fields of the Champagne country. We could see the towers of Reims in the distance. Shortly after Pont Faverger, the wide landscape ahead of us flattened out into a plain across which we had a good view. A few hundred metres ahead of us, there was a sudden movement in the cornfield. The car slowed down, and we found a group of stragglers, Negro soldiers. They did not seem to be armed.

The commander stopped to take the stragglers prisoner. He summoned the Negroes over. One could see that they were undecided. Two responded to the challenge and came towards the car, while another tried to run away towards the rear. The commander then ordered the driver to shoot at the fleeing man. In the meantime, the two black devils had reached the car. The commander made clear to them that they should drop any weapons they had. I had got out of the car, and was watching the two closely as they took from their boots and uniforms long knives – some of them saw-edged – and hatchets, and threw them down at my feet.

As the third Negro had not yet stopped running, the commander took the rifle himself and aimed a shot at him. As though by pre-arranged signal, the Negroes now fell upon us. There was a fierce hand-to-hand struggle. It all happened within a few seconds. One of the Negroes had thrown himself upon the driver and was about to cut off his hands. I had released the safety catch on my pistol. A bullet to the heart laid the Negro low, and the driver sank down badly wounded at the side of the road. A few metres away the commander was wrestling with the second Negro. They were rolling on the ground. The Negro's knife flashed dangerously close to the commander's uniform collar. I saw the black head emerging from the scuffle, and put an end to this horrific scene with a well-aimed shot. There had only been two rounds in the pistol's magazine …

The commander and I carried the wounded driver to the car. While I sat in the back bandaging his wrists, the commander drove. Knife cuts to his uniform and equipment showed the danger he had been in a moment before. But with great self-control he drove the car out of the danger zone where there were not only Negroes, but even scattered enemy tanks driving around.

We had not expected combat, and this little episode is a good illustration of the kind of situation we could get into at any time as medics.

By *Oberarzt* Siems

The Dispatch Rider

H e is not often mentioned, but his achievements are many and valuable, and in action he is a great but silent hero – the dispatch rider.

There is no-one in command, from the highest staff officer down to the humblest corporal, who does not know the valuable services this soldier has rendered.

With complete self-sacrifice, in the most difficult conditions, giving his last ounce of energy, the dispatch rider was the bringer of orders that were often decisive – perhaps the message to subordinate officers in every kind of combat situation, telling them that relief was finally on the way. And he was always alone in battle, alone with his machine and his mission.

Exhausted, his eyes swollen from the dust through which he raced, his face encrusted with dirt, man and machine forming a single clump of dust – that is how we always see him standing before us. Past hundreds of vehicles, past columns on the march, he made his way forward with orders. He had only one thought in mind: to deliver orders to their destination with all possible speed.

I can still see him in front of me, near a makeshift bridge completely inaccessible even for pedestrians, dragging his machine through the stream, always concerned to keep the engine above water so that his faithful helper will not let him down on the other side. He is utterly exhausted when he gets there, but after sitting down, taking just a short rest, he presses on again. He must get on – the blocked bridge was no obstacle for him!

I can still see the dispatch rider coming back from Rethel on a captured motorbike to report briefly that he had run into enemy infantry fire. His bike had literally been shot away from under him. For two hours he had taken part in the battle alongside the motorcycle troops. However, having fulfilled his mission, he had felt it was a matter of honour not to return to his unit without a motorbike. In the next village he had mobilized an enemy bike. He carried out his demanding duties on this machine until the end of the campaign in the west.

Whenever you glanced sideways during an advance, you could see the dispatch rider moving up over rough terrain. In his mouth there was the piece of paper bearing his route and his objective, so that he had this all-important aid always at hand. Setting off without proper roadmaps, working from the simplest of sketches, he always reached his goal.

A dispatch rider badly wounded near Rozoy would not let his wounds be dressed until he had safely handed on the written orders and oral explanations entrusted to him. And once he had seen his replacement driver roar off at last, despite all the pain, the blessed smile of one who has done his duty spread all over his face, stiff with dirt and fatigue as it was. It was only now, knowing that a comrade was completing what he could no longer fulfil, that he would consent to be taken to the aid station.

Where the intelligence units with their telephones cannot go, where distances are too great for telephone lines to cover, the dispatch rider does his duty as a human link. Rest is an unknown concept for him. The message he brings nearly always needs a reply: he shuts his eyes briefly at the roadside or on the machine itself, and then he is off again with the new order! The same hardships once more, the same dangers he was previously proud to have put behind him. I have never heard a dispatch rider say that he is tired, even when he has only had a short rest after a mission, and can hardly be roused when he is needed once more.

The dispatch rider displays again and again the highest sense of responsibility towards his comrades – one of the finest characteristics of the German soldier. He knows precisely what a valuable service he performs for his comrades in scrupulously fulfilling his mission.

Many examples could be given to illustrate the dispatch rider's willingness to serve and his selfless devotion to duty. He belongs to those who, in the enormous organization that is the *Wehrmacht*, without expecting any recognition, do their utmost to help bring victory to our colours. The dispatch rider of today is descended from the World War [1914–18] runner in the trenches. He does his difficult duty as an unknown soldier and messenger – the very duty performed by our Führer silently and with distinction in the World War...

By *Hauptmann* Ferdinand Weissmeier

The Supply Convoy Wangles its Way Through

O ne characteristic of the headlong push to the south was a kind of persecution mania. I am not thinking of the way we persecuted the poor French poilus of the '*grande armée française*', but the way our baggage trains and supply services were left gasping by the speed of the advance troops, the fighting men.

I was put in charge of the combat supply convoy of my tank detachment, and so I was smitten with the said mania. The job of such a unit is to deliver to the fighting troops at the right time fuel, ammunition, food, spare parts and essential items of that kind.

All our vehicles were marked with a 'G' (for Guderian). Our Viennese other ranks always understood this G to stand for '*gehn'ma, gehn'ma*' [Viennese dialect for 'let's go']. Until we crossed the Aisne, your place in the great long snake of the German Army, including mine, was fixed by orders from on high. But after the first big battles beyond the Aisne, I chose my own position in this pack, and I was only stopped a few times by higher authority.

I want to mention just one example among many.

In Mourmelon-le-Petit, a senior commander told me to halt and let an entire rifle brigade go past. I mused sadly about the supply convoy leader of an artillery detachment I knew who could not reach his fighting troops for three days. It's your turn to suffer the same misfortune, I told myself, as column after column trundled past me.

At 13:30 hours a dispatch rider comes back from our detachment staff headquarters. He sees me sitting in my car, stops his bike, raises both hands despairingly to heaven, and shouts at me in his Viennese dialect: 'Well, why don't you go up to the front?' I ask him tersely for a report on the situation up ahead, and hear that our brave tank crews have been fighting in Châlons-sur-Marne since 10.30 hours, and are reported to have run out of ammunition and fuel. Ignoring the order not to clog the road up with my convoy, I take it forward and overtake other columns. In the next village there is a jam, complete standstill! I manage to slip through on our captured motorbike. In the village square, I see three officers in agitated conversation. Each of them is trying to prove that he has priority. With this lengthy hold-up, they have had plenty of time for their debate, and now as a Johnny-come-lately I start asking to be let through first! It is clear to me that my request would be turned down, since they are suffering from the same 'persecution mania'.

Now for my tactics in the battle of words. I park my motorbike, march up in parade-ground fashion to the most senior of the three officers, and ask for his support. I am met by critical and pitying looks; they obviously assume I'm not quite right in the head. I am asked what my problem is. I roll off my concise report: '1st Detachment Tank Regiment X in combat since 10.30 hours in Châlons, all vehicles out of ammunition and fuel. The dispatch rider sent back to me is as black as soot from the dust and too exhausted to ride any further.'

The only answer I get is: 'That could happen to us as well, running out of ammunition; we're at war, and everything is possible in war.' I bristle up, and say very loudly: 'Herr Oberst, I can't let my comrades die when I've got ammunition and fuel here and just need to get to the front!'

That works, and emerging with pride from this battle of words, I reach Châlons and my troop via Les Grandes Loges.

By *Hauptfeldwebel* **Wilhelm Richter**

Crossing the Marne at Night

West of Rethel, the riflemen had fought to open a crossing over the Aisne. We crossed the river during the night of 9–10 June, to be ready for the start of the attack towards the south next morning. Drawing upon their experiences of the early days of the war, the French had deepened and fortified the Weygand Line. Every village had been turned into a small fortress, defensive positions constructed in every scrap of woodland, every road mined and barricaded. Here the French regiments put up a stubborn and desperate defence. Every village had to be stormed, and the enemy overcome in every wood. It was an unusual sight for us to see infantry divisions marching to our right and left. Infantry, motorized and horse-drawn artillery, tank and rifle regiments, among them the nimble, mobile bikes of the motorcycle rifle battalions worming their way through: all these troops, no longer limited to roads and tracks, were moving south in long columns across farmland and fields. Nothing could have demonstrated the strength of the *Wehrmacht* and the might of its attack more conclusively and convincingly than the unforgettable sight of these tank and infantry divisions advancing from the Aisne to the Marne.

At a rapid pace, then, we reached the fateful river, and wheeled towards the east on the German side. It was tempting to mount a surprise attack on St Dizier. Only if we could manage to capture the bridges over the Marne intact would it be possible to push on over the high plateau of Langres and then further south, to complete the bottling up of the troops in the Maginot Line.

The road from Vitry to St Dizier, near the Marne, is like an avenue. The battlegroup motorcycle battalion rode off at speed toward St Dizier. In the wonderful landscape of this area, showing no sign of destruction, you might easily have been able to forget you were at war, if the deep and monotonous drone of German aircraft overhead had not reminded you of the military purpose of your journey. Like little silver fish, the bomber squadrons moved from south to north in this ocean of sky. The last rays of the setting sun made their bright fuselages shine so brightly that you could hardly pick them out against an evening sky flooded with light. But there – a sudden jolting and flashing between the planes. They were under fire from enemy anti-aircraft guns probably sited, as a glance at the map told us, on the St Dizier airfield, south of our march route. Those were the last shells they were to fire against German aircraft. They had probably heard about our approach, even if they were still waiting in vain for their officer, who at breakneck speed had tried unsuccessfully to overtake our column, carrying their order to withdraw.

Meanwhile, the advance troops of our force had reached St Dizier and had been met there by anti-tank and artillery fire. The tanks stood closely packed together on the road. We rode down onto the meadow on the left, where cows were grazing quite peacefully. Surprised and curious, they stared at the unwelcome guests in their meadows, but were otherwise not in the least disturbed. There was a constant whistling of bullets around our ears, and you could clearly see the gun-flashes on the western edge of the town. In the meantime our own artillery had moved up, and was firing off shell after shell at pockets of enemy resistance. The tanks were placed wide apart and aligned with bushes and hedges, to keep them out of sight in this flat landscape.

The day slowly ebbs away, and the sun is already worryingly low in the west. The situation requires speedy action. On no account must our opponents be given the chance to blow up the bridges on the Marne. The best idea would be to cross the Marne at Hoëricourt, and then attack St Dizier from the south. That is a job for which no-one is better suited than us, the motorcycle battalion, who can detach themselves quickly from the body of the march, and form a new advance guard. In an instant, the commander of the lead company has informed his platoon leaders of their new task, and ordered them to fall in immediately.

Even as he is running back to his vehicle, he is giving the signal to mount and start up, and handing over to the leader of the advance troop a map marked with the route of the march. Then the motorbikes take off. Once again we drive around fences and enclosures – upsetting the cows – because we are in a hurry to get out of this meadow, where the bullets are whizzing around so uncomfortably.

Now we are once again leading the column, as we did so often in the early stages of the campaign in the west, and once more we are in that strange mood that comes from pride in knowing that you are up front, combined with the uncertainty of anticipated enemy resistance at any moment. The advance troops sit in their sidecars, ready to leap into action, rifles across thighs, keeping a sharp watch to right and left. The first village is approached with caution; there is nothing out of the ordinary about the houses or gardens. Is the village clear of the enemy, or are they simply luring us on, letting us get as close in as possible? The leading troops ride into the village, but no shots ring out, and the advance continues undisturbed. The terrain now becomes very unfavourable: completely flat meadows with the occasional row of bushes which obscure our view. We have to be particularly vigilant on the left, because we are now behind the airfield whose occupants thought themselves so safe just a short while ago. But more than one pair of eyes also casts a suspicious glance at the woods on the right, where the French can so easily hide their movements from us. The pressure of time and our allotted task make it essential to move on fast, however.

The first bike stops, and its crew jump off to examine a small bridge over a linking canal. In the middle of the bridge a beam has been let in to the surface, and on the other bank a number of sandbags are piled up. It looks as though the bridge has been prepared for blowing up. But then a dispatch rider crosses the beam, and the group resumes its progress.

There is another village ahead of us. This is where the Marne Bridge must be, that is why we do not quite trust this village, however peaceful and harmless it may look in the evening light. The leading troops dismount and cover the last hundred metres on foot, up to the edge of the village. Are our suspicions unfounded? Slowly the lead platoon rides into the village. It is empty, abandoned. They reach a bend in the road and take a corner to the right. There – Frenchmen! The bullets are whizzing around our heads. But just as fast, the leader of the group whips out his submachine gun and empties the entire contents of his magazine. Not anticipating such a rapid and eloquent response, the Frenchmen disappear like the wind among the houses. But at the same instant we hear the barking of a very heavy machine gun, and think it advisable to clear off the street with all possible speed. To the right of the street, the lead platoon prepares to attack. It makes its way through gardens and over fences. The many bushes and shrubs give perfect cover. The houses are grenaded. The shots constantly whistle over our heads.

We never catch a glimpse of the enemy, who finds it all too easy to stay out of sight here. But we must stay on his heels and not give him a chance to blow up our bridge at the last minute.

Meanwhile, it has got dark. The moon begins to supply us with the pale light we need for the next few hours. Now and again we catch the faint sound of flowing water gurgling and splashing. That must be the Marne. But where is the bridge? Sometimes bullets go on flying around unpredictably in our vicinity. We have left the village houses behind us, but there is still no sign of a bridge. And bushes and shrubs block our view completely, in any case.

We now pick up, somewhere to our right, the characteristic rattle of tracked vehicles. The sound can only be reaching us from the other side of the Marne. The noise increases the further forward we get. You can clearly distinguish within it the familiar clattering sound of tanks driving up and braking. But then somebody shouts: 'German tanks, don't shoot, we've sent up white flares.' We ponder this – can German tanks really have got to the opposite bank and be trying to link up with us? Somebody keeps on yelling: 'Don't shoot, German tanks.' It all seems a bit fishy to us.

In the meantime, a machine gunner has carefully worked his way out to the left to get a clear view of the road. And down there the mysterious source of the shouting is moving about. 'Are you from the tank regiment?' somebody asks him from the other side of the road. The fellow then indulges in some rabid cursing of Germany, and starts firing his rifle wildly all over the place, probably to demonstrate his warlike attitude. That settles the matter, and the next second he is silenced by our machine gun.

And now at last we can see our bridge. It stands out sharply in the moonlight against a dark background. On the opposite bank we can see the houses of Moëslains. Above them stands the disc of the moon, casting a ghostly light upon the bridge, and shrouding everything else into mysterious darkness. An eerie silence has meanwhile descended. The noise that was coming from the other side has faded away, and finally disappeared altogether.

The monotonous melody of the quietly flowing Marne has the effect of strangely heightening the solemn mood. And in this mild, peaceful summer night, German soldiers are standing by the Marne. Thoughts of hunger and fatigue have long since been banished; all their senses and nerves are concentrated on ending and crowning their day's work with the securing of this bridge. Are there watchful French soldiers on the other side of the bridge, ready to defend it, determined to forestall our success, which is as important symbolically and militarily for France as it is for us? The first two men of the group move cautiously on to the bridge and edge gingerly forward. Stop, what's that? A fuse runs right across the road and along the railing of the bridge, to disappear under it. It is cut without hesitation. Now we can see the lower part of the houses, too. The road runs dead straight through the village. The tarmac glistens like dirty lead in the moonlight. The silhouettes of the houses and trees stand sharply outlined against the night sky. The heavy tread of our hobnailed boots echoes alarmingly through the night. If the enemy opened fire now, there would be nowhere to hide …

But not a shot is fired, no hammering machine gun disturbs the sublime stillness of this night of full moon, nobody makes a move to oppose our crossing. Just a few more steps, a leap into the trench, and we're across. We have traversed the Marne, the bridge is in our hands! The machine gun is quickly set up at the fork in the road.

By now, the rest of the company has followed us over the bridge. The company forms a bridgehead, being reinforced with an anti-tank gun and a submachine-gun platoon for the purpose. Only a few of the men are able to get some well earned sleep; the bulk of the company is needed to guard the bridge, for this crossing-place over the river that is so fateful for both nations must on no account be lost again.

By *Leutnant* Heinz Peter Huppert

Two Fast-moving Days with an Armoured Reconnaissance Unit

O ur orders came by radio during the night: cross the Rhine-Marne Canal at dawn; reconnoitre on the left flank of the division and ahead of it. The idea is that our detachment should later be reinforced and deployed as an advance detachment.

At first light on 15 June 1940, it is actually freezing cold, though the engines of our division's many vehicles are humming quite contentedly in this – for them – pleasant coolness, after the terrible heat of the previous day.

Our bones creak and our fingers are stiff, however, as we bump along out of our night-time cover, from woodlands and behind hedges, and across the fields to reach a rutted country track.

But for a while now the rolling ribbon of road beneath us has been wider and smoother, and the sun has sucked the mist out of the meadows and hollows by the time we cross the Rhine-Marne Canal on a small bridge in our neighbouring division's sector. Everywhere, we still come across traces of yesterday's battle as we drive through shattered villages, swathed in clouds of acrid smoke drifting across the street from the burning remains of houses. – There is no sign of life anywhere; the Frenchies have decamped en masse once again. Fine, we'll just go on keeping them moving!

Now the sun stands high above the fertile country, blazing down relentlessly. Soon the open, undulating face of the Champagne country begins to change, giving way to large areas of woodland, with lakes between slopes that are becoming steeper, lending the landscape a new aspect. Deeply coated in the white dust of the Champagne soil, we have finally reached the front. Our armoured reconnaissance detachment has been augmented by a motorcycle rifle battalion, a tank company, half of a tank destroyer company, an anti-tank gun, and a heavy infantry gun.

Our scouting units, who since early morning have been looking for the enemy on the left flank of the division as well as ahead, and have found them, send in radio reports. The reports contain references to the floods of retreating enemy infantry, the capture of whole French columns, the roadblocks found in almost every village, and their removal, the capture of a demolition squad next to a bridge heavily defended on the other side of the river by enemy tanks and infantry (the fact that the bridge was blown up under their noses, all the same) … Reports, reports, reports! In the armoured signals vehicles the sweat is running down the faces of the wireless operators. The dispatch riders, roaring along to find the commander, the fluttering report pads in their mouths making them look like hunting hounds, are hardly recognizable with their swollen eyes in faces furrowed by dust, heat and sweat beneath the dust-white helmets. But the commander can form a comprehensive overview of all contacts with the enemy, and is able to pass on to the division the intelligence it wants.

Now the smooth flow of the advance has been halted. The commander is going up to the front. But after he has driven a few kilometres, the column starts moving again. Just before the next town, where the road begins to curve down towards a pleasant river valley, the smoking wrecks of two Renault tanks stand on the left of the road. Behind them in the roadside ditch and in the open field are a dead man and, among the captured crews, a few wounded who stare at us wide-eyed as we pass. Our troop scouting ahead of the advance guard, together with the tanks coming up behind them, quickly crushed this resistance. Now they are well to the fore, having driven through the town, crossed the still intact bridges, and pursued and shot at the enemy, who are fleeing on motorcycles.

A little later our reinforced detachment is rolling with all possible speed towards the south. Our direction and objective is the town of Dôle. Another 130 kilometres (80 miles) as the crow flies! We have covered some 100 kilometres (62 miles) today already.

It is late afternoon. Along the floor of the valley there winds a serpent made up of endless columns of diverse units, to the uninitiated a scene of hopeless confusion. The leading troops of our neighbouring division have wedged themselves into our ranks. Artillery tractors pulling their guns rattle along past refugee carts piled high; ammunition lorries, heavy tanks, the occasional dispatch rider weaving his way up to the front through the two or sometimes three lines of traffic; now a motorbike company, next to them an armoured reconnaissance car overtaking, while an orderly officer's vehicle dashes across country – all heading to the south, to the south!

Nobody has a proper map any more. Unit commanders are given their routes for the march using small black and white copies with a scale of 1:300,000. We meet French soldiers, at first singly, then in groups, then hordes; their hands are raised, their faces brown, white, and black, their expression appalled, hate-filled or apathetic.

It is high time we refuelled. A heavy armoured reconnaissance car has already pulled up at the roadside. 'Fuel's finished!' shouts the commanding officer to us as he drives past. But this jam-packed road is hardly the place to stop. At a big fork in the road the adjutant suddenly appears, calling, waving and yelling at each vehicle: 'K. Battlegroup straight on!' Like foaming water parting round a rock, the hundreds of vehicles in the oncoming stream divide. Our neighbouring division breaks away, and we are once again just 'by ourselves'. An orderly officer is darting to the front, commanding the head of the column to halt for refuelling.

Tired and drained, with red inflamed eyes, the drivers crawl down from their tanks. The leader of the reconnaissance troop cools his driver's eyes with a wet handkerchief, although he can hardly keep his own eyes open, and tears are rolling down his blackened, dirt-streaked face. The radio operator drags up fuel containers, the last canteen of water is circulating, and some English biscuits are shared out – nobody is really hungry, despite not having eaten properly all day. Somebody is handing round German cigarettes, someone else passing on greetings from home.

Then the heavy anti-tank guns are rattling up behind us. Our 30 minutes refuelling rest are up. 'Get mounted, start up engines!' The hatches are closed. The vehicles roll into the twilight, 10, 20, 50 of them, to the south, to the south – hundreds. Once again we are dutifully devouring the kilometres.

The vanguard crosses one of the great *routes nationales*; this one leads straight to Paris. Automatically, two anti-tank guns pull out, covering the column against surprise attack from left or right.

Hundreds of refugees with their jumble of possessions stare in astonishment at '*les allemands*', some fleeing into the fields, while others cower fearfully in the ditches. From a number of the vehicles, cigarettes, chocolate or biscuits rain down upon them, which greatly increases their astonishment. Suddenly a train approaches from the left on the nearby stretch of railway, easily identified even from a distance. The vanguard stops. The pioneer troop throws beams and large rocks onto the track to form a barricade. Tanks take cover, turning their turrets, and two groups of motorbike troops get into position.

'Fire on my whistle signal!'

The train is now only a couple of hundred metres away. The whistle blows! One or two machine-gun volleys to his right and left warn him to stop. By way of reply, the engine driver speeds up. There is a shot from a self-propelled gun; smoke, steam and spouts of water shoot up from the iron colossus. It hisses and puffs, and a thick cloud of smoke rises from it. The engine's speed drops; slowing all the time, the train rolls as far as the barricade – and then stops. Five figures jump down with their hands up and walk over to us: French railwaymen, their faces as white as chalk.

The leaders of the column get under way again; dusk is well advanced. The vanguard has put the next village behind it, with the bulk of the group following about 2000 metres (2180 yards) behind.

There is a huge forest that seems to go on for ever. 'You know, if the Frenchies were up to it, they could give us a great deal of bother here!' – 'Yeah, if! But they're not!' Red torches flash: pull in to the right and stop! 'We are going to laager up for the night!'

There are isolated pistol and rifles shots from ahead, and now a German machine gun is hammering. Silence again!

An hour later, the great army juggernaut is at rest in the open fields. A cold night wind sweeps across the many sleepers in the furrows and by their vehicles.

The staff officers are still busy; the radio orders for tomorrow have arrived: continue to the south east! Then the successes of the day are discussed, while the sweetish smell of British cigarettes dissipates in the night air.

And the chronicler writes in the war diary the words of his commander '… no significant contact with the enemy, a few dispersed French troops. When pulling up [for the night], advance guard runs into the end of a marching infantry column which – as far as darkness permits – is taken prisoner. The exact number of enemy soldiers captured by the forward detachment cannot be established because of the speed of the advance; all were sent to the rear along the route of the advance. General impression of the fighting is that Guderian Group broke through the effective parts of the enemy forces previously stationed on the Aisne, and the feeling is that we are now encountering only weak rearguard groups and reserve troops hastily assembled and thrown into action.'

A nasty thick mist lies over the whole landscape next morning.

But we are already on the move. Three units have been scouting ahead for some time; the road is wide and wonderfully smooth. Now the sun is breaking through. Soon there is not a damp spot on vehicles, jackets or spectacles, and the road is running away as smooth as butter beneath us.

Extravagant in its variety, the countryside constantly presents us with new charms – hills and fields, villages and woods in motley succession and in the early summer light – how far removed we are from that monster, war!

There are constant situation reports from the reconnaissance units: 'Ch. Clear of enemy!' – 'G. clear of enemy. Road barrier removed!' – 'W. full of refugees. Clear of enemy!' Suddenly from ahead of us there is the muffled thud of an explosion, and a whirling column of smoke rises into the sky. We race to the front, come to a bend in the road, and find a seemingly endless goods train stationary on the railway running alongside the highway. It has a variety of wagons, and as we roar past we can see military equipment and heavy weapons, furniture wagons, agricultural implements, and enormous bales of straw, interspersed with horses and refugees with their sparse possessions. The tracks in front of the locomotive are torn up and twisted. Our people have blown up the track to bring the train to a halt. A little while later we can see, from a bridge beneath which another railway line runs through a gorge far below, a hospital train standing at a small station. Complete astonishment among its passengers, lightly wounded and convalescent soldiers from a field hospital behind the Maginot Line. They did not expect us here! They have been travelling for two days, trundling from station to station, nobody knew where to –

We are now in the middle of the Langres plateau. The lead vehicles have been several kilometres ahead of the rest for some time now, travelling through heavily wooded terrain. Suddenly, our reconnaissance plane flies over very low, sees the first tank reconnaissance group and begins waggling his wings like mad. There – the observer is now waving, too! What does it mean? The leader of the advance unit stares after him. Now the plane is turning steeply, coming back and waggling its wings again dangerously! What is our good old 'Gertrud' trying to tell us? Obviously, she will have told the radio operator at Staff all about it, but that's so far to the rear! The road emerges from the woodland, and at this instant the Henschel 126 zooms very low across the small town up ahead. Shooting is coming from there! Stop, switch off engine! French machine guns can clearly be heard, answered by tracer bullets from the aircraft! This answers our questions. Three military troop-trains, already under full steam, are trying to leave the station. But our tanks are in amongst them, shooting up the approaching locomotives. Riflemen give supporting fire; there is a short skirmish; 300 prisoners and some rich booty are left behind under guard; in the post-office the switchboard is put totally beyond use. Onwards, onwards: the following battlegroup's advance units have already caught up with us!

There is a scorching sun blazing down on us once more. When we stop, breathing becomes hard work! Then our divisional commander pulls up in an open car, stopping to inform our commander about the latest intelligence concerning the enemy, and his own intentions. Breakthrough to the Swiss frontier, seal off the Maginot Line! So let's get on with it!

After continuing for a while, we are halted again. About 6 kilometres (4 miles) ahead there is a gigantic pillar of smoke. The recce unit comes back to the advance guard to report: 'Straight ahead, village of P.; stubborn resistance, bridge destroyed. Our neighbouring division to the left is attacking now!' A glance at the map. We are very close to the River Saône, the first of the three river sectors that will have to be overcome before we get to the Swiss border.

No sooner has the commander issued the order: 'Swing round to south west to secure minor bridge', than the battlegroup is moving again, disappearing into the nearby forest.

In just under three hours, the first vehicles are trundling across a small antiquated bridge over the Saône, closely followed by the long chain of the division. Our general is there again, hearing a report that the bridge was taken in a surprise attack by advance units after they had crushed weak resistance from the village. Charges had already been put in place to blow it up, and barricades laid across the road, but a resolute first-lieutenant of pioneers had cut the fuses. His men had thrown the explosive charges into the river, with a small bridgehead force of motorbike riflemen providing cover while they worked.

Securing the bridge was a real stroke of luck, because the division has only 16 metres (17.5 yards) of bridge-building material left: the rest has been used further back or is still on its way to us. After the splendid success of the Saône crossing, our commander has decided to use minor bridges for all subsequent river crossings, too.

So the advance units rush on, over winding, bumpy tracks through forests, over meadows. They pass through dirty villages, travel along a short stretch of highway, then diagonally through an isolated farmyard – towards the south east. It is essential to reach the other two rivers before the enemy can blow up the bridges. That is why telephone connections everywhere are put completely out of action, to prevent any possible 'welcoming ceremony'.

Some time ago the steering of tanks, trucks, motorbikes and tractors was taken over by driver's mates: officers, NCOs, other ranks. The drivers themselves are those strange-looking figures dangling their legs over a windscreen, or sleeping behind the turret of a clattering tank. Here an arm hangs out of a tank, there a young lieutenant acting as a dispatch rider dashes by with a fluttering note in his mouth, while the young comrade he is relieving slumbers exhausted in the shaking sidecar. But many drivers take a pride in holding out, and are lovingly supplied by their travelling companions with ready-lit cigarettes, chocolate, and the fulfilment of every wish that can make their work easier. Their collars are wide open, colourful silk scarves are wound around their raw necks, and they wear green sunglasses, British protective goggles or blue eyeshades as they roar, dirty and sweaty, through enemy country, their skin peeling beneath the stubble. They are the knights of the road, 20th-century reincarnations of the *Landsknechte*, the lusty soldiery of the 17th century.

Once again the sun is disappearing in the west; we are getting near a town. The inhabitants stand gawping in the villages; we have seen no refugees for quite some time. Well, no evacuation was thought necessary here! After the terrible realization that these are not English but German troops, real German soldiers who are rushing towards them, the people out strolling in their Sunday best simply stand thunderstruck. That's right, today is Sunday! Onwards, onwards … The town is a garrison town, and the French soldiers – reservists – quickly find their leisure-time being supervised by Germans.

The road is wide and smooth. The lead troops drive as a matter of course over a canal bridge, and then run into a railway crossing blocked by a long troop-transport train. The engine whistles, and the train jolts into movement, its open wagons full of French soldiers. Time to go into action! The SP gun again briefly addresses the engine, seconded by the lighter voice of the machine gun. Thus addressed, the locomotive replies with a malevolent hissing and spitting. Once more it has to be spoken to sharply. Then it gives a loud puff: the engine, station, sheds are all enveloped in a black cloud, and the lucky NCO commanding the lead tank, to whose support many others have hurried in the meantime, is able to establish after taking possession of the train that he has prevented the flight of over 2000 men, a general and 12 other officers.

But now the motionless train is blocking the railway crossing! However, shortly afterwards we are bumping over the platform, crossing the tracks, knocking over a tree, and squeezing out on the other side between the waiting room and a goods shed. A fence collapses, and we are rolling down the loading ramp – and on we go. We pass an airfield with many burnt-out machines, a small village, the River Doubs, the bridge – we're across! – another bridge over a branch of the river, and on and on! It is twilight. Just one more bridge, and the road to the Swiss frontier is clear! Forward! Forward! The advance guard hurries to the front. Everybody knows that in the next half hour the day's success must be crowned!

The narrow country track has now reached the bridge. Just two more kilometres upstream – the bridge, the bridge! – There it is! And it's still in one piece! A lovely concrete bridge with high arches. The reconnaissance unit edges forward cautiously. The motorbike troops stand ready to dismount, their weapons already in hand. Now – top speed! Two or three reconnaissance cars race across the bridge, firing into a group of fleeing enemy soldiers. A figure in light brown, no doubt a French officer, falls to the ground mortally wounded.

From the woods on the other side of the bridge, enemy anti-tank guns are suddenly firing, but their aim is poor, and the shells are whistling over the heads of the reconnaissance unit. Events crowd in upon each other. Heavy and medium tanks have joined in; mortar and motorbike troops are firing into the woodland on either side of the road; a pioneer unit inspects the pillars of the bridge; the anti-tank guns rush up and are soon hurling their destructive missiles into the pockets of resistance until the sparks fly. Dismounted motorbike troops fan out to consolidate the tanks' bridgehead.

We have secured the bridge! The way to the border is clear!!

At 22.50 hours the tank radio operator at staff headquarters puts together the daily report from our commander to the division: '22.50 – after fighting three bridges taken – one general, 19 officers and over 2500 men captured – numbers of weapons and equipment items not established – objective accomplished.'

By *Leutnant* Wolf-Max Ostwald

The Bridge on the Saône

After a stormy advance along the Marne valley towards the Swiss frontier, on 15 June the advance guard of a tank division came across a blown-up bridge over the Saône. There is no other serviceable crossing-point to be found, either upstream or downstream! A start is made on building a bridge across the wide stream. But it is taking time. Every hour is precious. The French Army is pouring out of the unplugged gap in the Maginot Line north and south of Besançon, and heading south-west.

During evenings and nights, reconnoitring goes on continuously along the river. Finally, at 00.30 hours we get a report from the reconnaissance unit of the motorcycle rifle battalion that 15 kilometres (9.3 miles) upstream, near Quitteur, has come across a big, intact road bridge. Concentrated enemy columns are crossing the bridge towards the south.

The motorcycle rifle battalion fall in. Their objective is to: 'Take the bridge near Quitteur by surprise attack and form bridgehead to south.' After a long day on the move, they have only had an hour's sleep, but the cold night air soon wakes them up. After 10 kilometres (6.2 miles) the lead company dismounts in what is thought to be the locality of the bridge. They need to reconnoitre to establish their exact position. The bridge is not marked on their only map, an out-of-date one with a scale of 1:300,000.

By the river there is a mist and the first glimmer of morning light, but no sign of the bridge. They walk along the river. The sound of engines here would give them away. After a kilometre of wet water-meadows, it has become lighter. There is a brief gap in the mist, and suddenly, 400 metres (438 yards) away, the outline of a large arched bridge becomes visible. Has it been prepared for demolition? Will we be able to get hold of it undamaged?

Spreading out, the lead platoon runs across the open plain towards the bridge, where everything is still quiet. Two French sentries can be seen. They seem to be watching us, but at first they do not seem to know what to make of the grey figures in front of them on the meadow. One is calmly answering the call of nature.

The lead platoon reaches the road embankment, climbs up on to the road, and with the platoon leader at its head, charges across the roughly 150-metre (164-yard) long bridge. Not a shot is fired, even now. The French sentries run away. When their people reach the far side bank, a machine gun starts rattling away from that direction. The enemy has woken up. From a nearby hill facing the bridge the enemy rake it with anti-tank and machine-gun fire. Only the platoon leader and a small group have succeeded in getting across. They have taken cover over there, next to and beneath the bridge. The others, some wounded, are forced to retreat behind the embankment on our side of the river.

But the enemy have been unable to prevent the most important step. During a pause in the shooting somebody calls out from the other side: 'Demolition cables have been cut!' At least we are free of our greatest worry. But none of us dares raise his head, either on this side of the bridge or the other. The enemy are very well placed, but they fail in their efforts to detonate the explosive charge attached to the pillars of the bridge by firing at it from the side. A few of our group on the other side are wounded. In the end there are only three men and an NCO with a light machine gun left fighting over there. We keep in contact with them by shouting across the river.

However, our opponents do not dare to attack them and throw them into the river. We can hear the enemy shouting and arguing volubly. There must be differences of opinion among them.

Other, newly arrived companies go into action. The well-directed fire of a half-platoon with heavy machine guns brings the first relief. It is now possible to raise one's head and assess the situation.

A report is drawn up, including a sketch and a request for heavy weapons. The runner races back to the battalion. Without cover on the open meadow terrain, we see him throwing himself to the ground time and time again. If only he can get through! Lacking heavy weapons, we are powerless lying here directly up against the embankment. At last, the runner disappears behind the railway embankment. Not long afterwards, there is a new sound. Shells are landing among the enemy. Our own infantry artillery, with our own mortars joining in later. They silence two of the enemy's guns. But there is still heavy firing on, behind and in front of the bridge.

Then, just half a metre (20 inches) over our heads – as it seems to us – the sharp crackle of bullets. Somewhat confused, we look around. A new enemy? No – 400 metres (437 yards) to our rear we see the fire-flashes of our own heavy-machine-gun platoon. The salvo was accurately aimed at the enemy's position on the slope.

The runner returns from the battalion bringing a sketch: 800 metres (874 yards) downstream 3 Company is crossing the river in inflatable boats to attack the enemy from the flank.

The enemy begins to yield.

No letting up now, and 2 Company is ordered to advance across the bridge. The first group surges forward. Hardly have they leaped down the embankment on the other side, when an enemy 7.5cm (3in) gun fires at close range over open sights, but too late. The group have found cover; 2 Company charges forward. The bridge seems almost endless. They too get across. But seconds earlier there had been a flash of fire from the enemy. The shell lands in the middle of the group. The group leader and two men fall.

After another explosion on the enemy side, two *poilus* run away. They have blown up the last surviving gun covering the bridge.

Everything happens very fast now. The company goes forward up the hill, and the remaining French troops are captured. Heavy machine guns are placed at the top of the hill to hasten the enemy's flight. Dispatch riders and the battalion staff cross the bridge, followed shortly afterwards by our commanding general. The division is ordered to resume its advance. The way is clear! We are quite proud of ourselves.

We still have the most difficult task of all to carry out. While the chains of the tanks clatter over the bridge, we dig two graves and fashion two crosses. A few hours later we take our place in the continuous moving column. The battalion takes a break at midday. A swim in the Saône wipes away the traces of battle.

By *Oberleutnant* Baron von Frydag

The Street by Street Battle for Vesoul

A fter a blazing hot day which has brought different enemy contacts and strenuous physical exertion, at 21.00 hours the 1 Platoon of 1 Company of our infantry regiment is deployed on a hill south east of Pusey to cover the village against a surprise attack from the direction of Vesoul. The men are just digging in, for our orders are to hold this position at all costs during the night. On the left is a platoon from 4 Company, but there is nobody to our right. However, about 1500 metres (1640 yards) to the south of us, a battle is going on for control of a village. Through my binoculars I can clearly see our own artillery putting down a heavy barrage on the place, and a detachment fighting its way forward with hand-grenades against isolated farmhouses.

Then our situation changes suddenly. A runner bringing the latest intelligence for the battalion reports that the regiment is pressing for faster progress. The neighbouring platoon from 4 Company is withdrawn, and soon I too receive orders to mount and set off from the eastern exit from Pusey to follow my own company.

After a few kilometres, we catch up with the company. It had stopped when its leading vehicles reached a fork in the road north-west of Vesoul. On the hill above, enemy machine guns are rattling, and down here the bullets are zinging around our ears. So we dismount and take to the ditches on either side of the road. Around 23.00 hours, I am summoned by the battalion commander. I find the battalion command post on the road to Vesoul a good

221

100 metres (109 yards) ahead of us. After being briefed on the position, I receive the following orders:

'You will form an assault group, with an anti-tank gun [3.7cm *Panzerabweherkanone* 35/36] in support. After a short artillery barrage you will push forward as far as the barriers at the entrance to Vesoul. You will take and occupy these barriers, and you will demand the surrender of the occupants of the place. If you succeed in subduing resistance, push on through the place and secure the bridge at the eastern exit.'

Unfortunately I do not know the terrain or the barriers, or the entrance to the place, let alone the place itself. To judge by the kinds of roads running to it, Vesoul must be a town. But is it a town of 5000 or of 50,000 inhabitants? I do not know. Nobody has a map. But the order has been given, and will have to be carried out according to the commander's instructions. NCOs and men volunteer to take part. They are wonderful chaps, with whom you can really get things done. Three groups are formed. The night is pretty dark, which rules out making the groups too large; they each consist of an NCO and six men. But each group has a machine gun, and three machine guns commanded by first-class men amount to considerable firepower. All superfluous kit is jettisoned. But each man is issued with four hand-grenades, which he tucks in his belt or his boot-tops. About 00:30, I report that the assault troop is ready. The leader of the company is ordered by the commander to follow immediately behind with 2 Platoon, the heavy-machine-gun group, and another anti-tank gun to provide cover and follow through if needed.

We move towards the town on the road along the western slope of the hill. After 200 metres (217 yards) we run into our last picket. It is held by our 2 Platoon. The platoon leader briefs us further about the situation. It seems that three French machine guns command the road. Thus there is a risk that we will not be able to take the anti-tank gun forward with us. At the very least, it appears there is no question of taking the enemy by surprise. The leader of the company therefore decides to inform the commander in person about the situation. But the order to carry out the shock-troop operation remains in force. So, here goes!

We proceed along the left-hand ditch, bent double or crawling. The ditch on the right runs along the foot of the slope and is particularly exposed to enemy machine-gun fire. The shock-troop leader and an interpreter crawl on ahead, and the groups follow. The anti-tank gun follows at a distance of about 100 metres (108 yards), manhandled forward. Everything is done in absolute silence. Orders are whispered and passed on from man to man. As the enemy machine guns are still hammering away, the anti-tank gun moves up unnoticed, too.

We have covered about 150 metres (165 yards) when a runner from the battalion reaches me. The commander orders me to hold the operation, stay where I am and await new orders. We quietly build up some defences to right and left. There is a direct danger from the left, particularly, for the enemy machine-guns are hammering away level with us on the hillside. The nearest seems to be no more than 30 metres (98 feet) away from us. After about an hour and a half we get new orders to proceed. Earlier, however, about 1000 metres (1090 yards) to our right on the railway line an oil tanker wagon had gone up in flames. All that damned light, making it more difficult for us to get forward.

So – carefully and quietly onward! After 1000 metres (1090 yards), the first barricade can be seen. It consists of two French trucks placed across the road. Whether the barricade is occupied, and in what strength, it is impossible to tell. There seem to be large farmhouses to right and left of it. The anti-tank gun is ordered up to the front. Then the gunner is instructed: 'Two shots into the truck on the left, two into the one on the right, then fire at the farmhouse to the left of the road.' The gun is quickly made ready, and it fires. Enemy machine guns reply from all sides. The Frenchman seems to be taken totally by surprise. I plunge forward with my infantrymen at a quick pace. On the left, in the farmhouse garden, there is a machine-gun nest. Its gun-flashes are immediately in front of us. In go the hand-grenades! The machine gun falls silent. The same thing on the right-hand side of the road. First of all fire from our own machine gun, then hand-grenades again. Fleeing figures jump back. Order to the anti-tank gun: 'Move up!' Next order to the gun: 'In front garden of first house to the right of the road, fixed enemy position. Fire at house and position!'

This well-constructed position gives us trouble; we can't get near enough to it yet to use hand-grenades. Another machine gun is deployed next to the anti-tank gun. Two French anti-tank guns reply, their shells landing with a crash among us. Again and again. Somebody falls face down into the ditch. … He's had it! A head wound. In the darkness I can't see who it is. I myself am slightly wounded in the right thigh. It's like a blow from a hammer. The blood trickles down my leg, but the leg is still useable, so on we go.

Once more there is an enemy machine gun in the farmhouse garden on the left; more hand-grenades are lobbed in. One group is ordered to search the house. There are no enemy troops in the house, but Frenchmen bolt out of the garden. Meanwhile, the anti-tank guns are engaged in a duel. Our advance is halted. I get all three light machine guns quickly into position. They pepper the French anti-tank gun positions. Under cover of their fire, grenadiers charge forward, hurling three or four hand-grenades at each position. The anti-tank guns are silenced.

Massive barricades made of tree-trunks block off the streets. We machine gun them, and hand-grenades follow. We have to take five or six barricades in this way. A French anti-tank gun stands behind the second barricade. Danger of mines! Careful! Look out for trip-wires! It is still dark. The street has now narrowed. Heavy rifle fire is spraying from windows and gardens here and there. A few men are wounded. The anti-tank gun cannot follow us because of the tree-trunk barricades. The assault troop has to go it alone. All the houses are locked up. All you can do is fire at random into the windows, and then onward! The first prisoners are taken. We force them to shout: 'Comrades, give yourselves up, we are surrounded.' But it does not help. The only reply is more firing. And you can't make out where it's coming from. I shout in vain for the interpreter. He was the man killed earlier. An order comes through from the battalion commander: 'Keep up the attack!'

We have passed the last barricade. It is particularly strong, built from iron rails and cars. I push on for another 100 metres (1090 yards). Then we have to stop. There are only 15 of us left. We have lost one dead and four wounded; I have sent two runners to the rear to bring up the rest of the company, to help the anti-tank gun get past the barricades and to search the gardens.

It has become lighter by now, just a pale glimmer of dawn, but it gives us some light to shoot by. In front of us, in the town centre, there is the clatter of French tanks. The noise gets louder all the time. The tanks roll towards us. We have to pull back to the last barricade, because the locked houses, facing directly on to the street, offer no chance to get out of the way. Fortunately, our anti-tank gun now arrives, and there is even a second gun with it. Now the French tanks can come on! The street curves gently about 150 metres (164 yards) ahead, and as the tanks pull out of this bend, the anti-tank guns blaze away at them. Shot after shot rains down on the steel giants.

Suddenly we are taking heavy fire from a three-storey house. There are also shots constantly ringing out from gardens and from the vineyards on the slope. At this point, our chief infantry gunner appears in the guise of guardian angel, bringing an infantry gun [7.5cm *leichtes Infanteriegeschütz* 18]. Together with the anti-tank gun, the infantry gun gives the house a proper pounding. Meanwhile, a heavy mortar placed on the southern slope of the hill directs its fire into the high-walled gardens. At the same time, 2

Platoon has been sent in by the company commander to provide security. They gradually scrape together a large number of prisoners from houses and vineyards. Now we have reached the point where we can continue our advance. Two assault troops are formed. Cautiously working our way forward from one property to the next, we climb over walls, cross gardens and farmyards, jumping from house-corner to house-corner. We take individual prisoners, but we haven't got time to search the houses. Cellars and flats are bound still to be sheltering Frenchmen.

The anti-tank and infantry guns follow us, giving us firing cover. In the courthouse we take 40 French prisoners at once, forced out of the air-raid shelter in the cellar by hand-grenades.

Is this town going to go on for ever? On our right there are extensive grounds, on whose eastern and northern edges enemy machine-gun nests are sited. The grounds are searched and the gun nests taken care of by our heavy weapons. The enemy flees. Many houses and gardens are now systematically cleared. Finally, we are able to set up machine guns on the river bank, as we have identified enemy machine-gun positions by the big bridge.

There are numerous Frenchman under the bridge, between its great pillars. It appears that they are preparing to blow up the bridge. High time we got them on the run. Light and heavy machine guns, infantry artillery, and mortars concentrate their fire upon them. The Frenchmen can only take this intense fire for a few minutes, and then they bolt in wild panic. The fleeing troops have left countless dead and wounded men behind. This is a dreadfully vivid demonstration of the destructive force of our combined heavy weapons. I give a walking wounded man the job of alerting the hospital to send out stretchers, and getting the fire brigade to provide help.

The shock troop, however, pushes on right to the end of the long bridge. In the process, once more, a number of prisoners are taken. We secure the exit from the town, and I report to the company commander that my orders have been carried out. It is now about 07.00 hours.

Now, however, our stomachs begin to make peremptory demands. Suddenly, we all feel terrifically hungry. It then occurs to us that the field kitchen did not come up at all yesterday, and that we have not eaten for 24 hours. So we buy up all available bread supplies in a nearby hotel. We get the landlady to make coffee, and everybody thinks it is the best meal he's ever had in his life.

By *Leutnant* Heher

... *And We Were Planning to Get some Sleep Tonight!*

O ur repair squad spent the whole of last night until the early morning hours repairing armoured reconnaissance cars and other vehicles that had been put out of action the previous day. Finally, we had them all ready for returning to the detachment. At top speed, they rolled out one after another to join the reconnaissance cars fighting in the front-line.

Meanwhile, another order has come in for us: 'J Squad to go on immediately to Recey.' So, 'J Squad, quick march!'

We finally get to Recey at 23.00 hours, and move straight into large premises next to the route of our advance. Our fuel tanks are empty; we need to fill up. But where can we get the 'juice'? The detachment's tanker column moved on ages ago. Will our motor transport sergeant be able to sniff some out again?

The loyal fitters of J Squad, who are nearly all drivers as well, have performed superhuman feats in the last few days. They all worked right through last night, and today they sat behind the wheel for nearly 20 hours. The driving by itself would not have been too bad, but they were all towing another vehicle. We had collected four armoured recce cars and two trucks that had dropped out during the advance, some of them through enemy action, and towed them to Recey. But now the loyal chaps were completely done in. The glaring heat of the day had played its part, too. They all dropped where they stood; blankets or straw were not needed tonight. Just to get some sleep at last, to finally shut your inflamed eyes ...! But somebody had discovered a stream, and that revived their flagging spirits. Even sleep had to take second place: we're going to have a wash, at 23.00 hours! Water! Imagine being able to wash off the filth at last, the dust of the day that covered your face like a thick crust! Everyone is prepared to sacrifice the quarter of an hour it will take. Then, losing no more time, get your head down!

But even this well-deserved sleep was not to be granted us. Like clockwork, at 23.15 hours we get the regular report of damaged vehicles from the detachment: 'Three light tanks, one eight-wheel armoured car out of action in the Recey-Auxonne-Dôle sector. J Squad to follow on immediately. Repair vehicles. New base, Besançon.' For us that meant giving up the sleep we so desperately needed, getting the towed vehicles repaired straight away, and being back on the road by first thing tomorrow morning.

… and actually we were planning to get some sleep tonight…!

I quickly review the work we will have to get through by the morning. We'll be taking new vehicles in tow tomorrow, and so we've got to get today's haul back on the road first. We've got at least seven or eight hours work to do, and the only chance of getting through it by early tomorrow morning is if everybody, master mechanics and fitters, drivers and drivers' mates, puts their backs into it 100 per cent. The men's keenness to avoid towing tomorrow, or being towed, puts some pep into them. We immediately get to work on the ailing vehicles, four men to each wagon.

The first of the light armoured vehicles took an anti-tank shot in the engine, which means: remove engine, put in replacement engine, weld armour. Verdict on second tank: damaged transmission, defective clutch, one driveshaft joint sheared off. In this case, we take out the transmission, replace gear-shift lock, re-line clutch, change joint at front wheel. The eight men work like crazy; they want to be the first to get finished. They manage it by 06.00 hours. You won't find many to compete with that. Working right through the night, by the feeble light of a torch, after the terrific exertions of the last few days and nights, they have pulled off this exceptional feat.

The third vehicle, a six-wheel armoured car, was damaged by shell splinters: fuel and oil pipes broken, radiator leaking, electrics shorted. Radiator, fuel and oil pipes have to be removed and repaired. The fourth vehicle, an eight-wheel armoured car, has a damaged transmission, gears out of action. Action: take out gearbox, do welding job, since no spare gearbox is available at the moment. The same result here as with the first two tanks; by 05.30 hours they are both ready to go back into action. The two lorries don't give us so much to do. The first needs a new cylinder-head gasket, the second has to have a new camshaft and its radiator welded. The men have them ready by 03.00 hours. A few of them have to go on sentry duty, which is also carried out by drivers.

The following morning was to prove that sentries were necessary, even though we were 80 kilometres (50 miles) to the rear of the detachment. The night had been pitch black, lit up only by the torch and the flickering green arc of the welder. In this light the men's naked torsos glisten, covered in sweat and oil. The night is warm and the work is hard. Towards 04.00 hours daylight begins to return. This helps the work to go faster. I can already see that we will have all the vehicles finished by 07.00 hours.

In the meantime our motor transport sergeant has arrived, and with a truck full of fuel! He found it in a village 40 kilometres (25 miles) east of our march route; he has a perfect nose for such things, absolutely priceless. He had already given up looking for us and was about to find somewhere to sleep, thinking he would resume his search at dawn, when he was drawn by our welder's flame. When he got closer, he saw that everyone was working flat out, and learning that we would have to get going again first thing in the morning, he – completely on his own – had refuelled all our vehicles. Then he hit the sack, and after two minutes some powerful snoring indicated that he had taken his saw to a massive branch.

By 06.00 hours we're finished; everything is in working order. To stop the men from dropping off at the wheel, I let them have a couple of hours rest. They immediately stretch out, and in the same instant they are all deeply asleep. Not one of them has so much as closed his eyes for 36 hours.

I am not yet asleep, perhaps I'm over-tired, when I suddenly hear the sound of engines on the road, first of all distant, then getting closer. And our sentry has sounded the alarm. What's up now? More vehicles to repair? They can go and …! But I am soon undeceived. A column of French lorries is roaring along our march route! The road runs very close to our workshop site. The blighters are driving as though the devil himself were at their heels. They disappear into the distance as fast as they appeared.

The alarm and the racket have woken everybody up, of course, and they are all on their feet. The motor transport sergeant jumps on to his motorbike, taking a man armed with a rifle in the sidecar, and they are off in pursuit. A driver, a machine gunner and I jump into our 'sunshine limousine' – an Adler machine-gun carrier – and chase off after them. We confirm that we are on the right track when we see a broken-down motorbike on the road, with two Frenchman. As we have one man too many with us anyway, we drop the machine-gunner off to prevent the two from escaping. After about a quarter of an hour we catch up with the French column. Their vehicles are standing on the road, their occupants lying in the ditch and firing wildly at a German lorry convoy standing by the side of the road. Our sunshine car has barely poked its nose around the corner – our machine-gun has not yet fired a shot – when the guys start throwing away their weapons without another shot, and surrender. Our sunshine limousine turned up a little too suddenly behind them. A colonel and 50 men – quite a decent catch. We hand them over to the crews of the lorry column – which has now drawn up near us – for transporting to a prisoner-of-war camp.

We turn round straight away to go back to our J Squad, but not before helping ourselves to a French truck and a motorbike.

Our motor transport sergeant has done well, too. He has come back from his early morning outing with a French car and three prisoners. He had taken a wrong turning, and unexpectedly came across the car, which hastily attempted to escape. But the occupants underestimated the speed of our BMW bike, and after a few minutes the sergeant's sidecar passenger, firing while moving at full pelt, had put a shot straight through the back window of the car. That was enough for the Frenchmen. Attended by the sergeant, they drove off to the prisoner assembly point.

By now it was 08.00 hours. We would have to get under way at last if we were to reach our new goal, Besançon. In the meantime, the others had drunk some coffee and got the vehicles stowed ready to leave, so we were able to drive off without delay. Nobody could be too annoyed about the Frenchmen making us lose even the two hours sleep we should have had. Everybody was too pleased about the success of our sunshine limousine.

By about 17.00 hours, we reached Besançon, joining up with our detachment there. We laid the vehicles up for the night immediately. During the trip we had picked up another four tanks and taken them in tow. But the drivers managed all right. Everyone was looking forward to Besançon, for there was a faint hope that we could stay there for a few days. No effort was too great, nothing was too much to ask, because we knew that, as long as nothing went wrong, tonight we were finally going to get some sleep. And nothing did go wrong. No, today it all worked out. We stayed for a while in Besançon. The repairs to the tanks we had towed were put off until the next day, and the men were allowed the luxury of a whole night's sleep at last. Finally they had what they had done without for the last two days and nights: sleep, sleep, blessed, well-earned sleep!

By *Kriegswerkmeister* **Leonhard Fichtl**
Senior Fitter

A Hazardous Mission
to Parley in Belfort

S ome years ago, when with a bleeding heart I read Binding's novel *We
Call upon Reims to Surrender*, I never dreamed that I myself might one
day drive into a great enemy fortress with a parley group, in an adventure
that was stranger than fiction.

In the late evening of 17 June, our armoured reconnaissance unit stood
20 kilometres (12.5 miles) south of Belfort, on the big highway that leads
from the village of Héricourt into the city. This fortress in the depression
between the Vosges and Jura mountains, the 'Gateway to Burgundy', was
famously built up by the French in the World War as the main stronghold of
the Alsace front. It was now held to be the strongest southwesterly corner-
post of the ring of French fortresses.

As the detachment crept towards Belfort under cover of the woods, a
radio operator was spreading the news that Marshal Pétain had just told the
French people in a broadcast: 'The strength of France is exhausted, and I
have approached Herr Hitler to sue for armistice terms.' During a break in
our advance, this information spread like wildfire. Our joy knew no bounds.
We almost forget that the war was still on. Champagne corks were popping,
and we drank deep to our victory.

As we were just pulling another bottle of this noble liquid from our
baggage, we were given an order that was greeted with a loud whoop of joy:
'Manpack radio group No 1 will drive with a captain and an lieutenant to
Belfort to call upon fortress to surrender.'

The camouflage was quickly removed from our vehicles, and we were off before we had time to think about it. 'We will be driving at around 70 to 80', called out Lieutenant S., 'so keep up at all times. We want to get to Belfort without stopping!'

We are a parley group! What a ring that has to it! A captain, an lieutenant, an NCO and five private soldiers calling upon Belfort to surrender!

We peer keenly ahead. The dark figures of numerous deserters emerge from the deep twilight. We ignore them. The journey continues. Soon it is completely dark. At times, the only thing we can see ahead of us is the red taillight of the officers' car. Suddenly we see the lights of oncoming lorries, coming nearer, then sliding past. Nothing happens. We enter a large village, Héricourt. As our car passes the entrance to the village, there is a demand to 'Halt!' in French from the side of the road, but we are already through.

On the village, street a column of men is marching wearily towards Belfort. We drive past without them taking any notice of us. At a crossing behind a bridge a barricade has been erected across the street – it is flanked by two anti-tank guns, and in addition the street is choked. Enormous ammunition and fuel trucks are jammed together, complete chaos. We cannot get through, we have to stop. What now? People are looking at us critically, and some groups are coming towards us. Then to our astonishment our captain manages to unnerve the *poilus* with powerful curses in French. He jumps down on to the road and directs the traffic. Nonplussed, the French make way. Meanwhile, a sentry guarding the bridge has approached us to ask his compatriots coming from the west – as he thinks – for information.

'*Avez-vous entendu où se trouvent les Allemands?*' (Have you heard where the Germans are?)

We must not reveal now what darkness has so far concealed. My comrades stare rigidly at the *poilu*. My knowledge of French comes to my aid.

'*Non, je n'ai pas entendu.*' (No, I haven't heard anything.) And pointing to my headphones, I add: '*Mais nous pouvons pas causer, il nous faut entendre.*' (But we can't have a conversation, we've got to listen.)

At that moment our cars start to move again; the way is clear. On the highway we report these developments to the detachment by radio. Soon we reach the fortress city of Belfort. Once more we come up against a barricade. But in the darkness we are able to pull back unrecognized and try to find an alternative route. Then the outline of a large barracks with its casemates stands out against the dark sky. We drive up a slope and stand in front of its walls. A French tank stands in the gateway, groups of soldiers of various branches are trying to get in, and columns of vehicles are pushing past; a lively scene so late at night. The NCO in charge of the guard at the gate has recognized us as Germans. Soon we are surrounded by a number of *poilus*.

Our captain immediately asks to be taken to the commandant. He is absent, so his deputy is sent for. It takes him a good hour to appear. In that time we have plenty of opportunity to observe our surroundings. In the light of the gateway lamp, the sentries stand around us. We start conversations with them; being Alsatian, many of them know German. A few stay in the background muttering imprecations like 'German swine' – 'Murderers'. But most of them are more accessible. They want to know why we have come. The news that we (the Germans) are just outside the gates of Belfort causes general consternation and horror. There is not much fighting spirit around any more. Several say openly that they wish the commandant would surrender the fortress so that this miserable war would end. They also want to know what life is like as a POW under the Germans.

This friendly atmosphere, which we of course are eager to cultivate, enables us to keep up radio contact with the detachment. Looking out of the window, we both chat and take radio messages at the same time. The leader of the radio unit acts as courier between us and the captain. Nobody objects. Our officers are generally more disliked by the *poilus*. The communists among them are quite hostile. The officers have to put up with many a threat. As far as we are concerned, however, they automatically assume that like them we regard our superiors as tyrants, and they consider us practically their suffering brothers of the fourth estate.

A car now draws up. A young French general staff officer in a white coat steps out, and then our parley representatives are taken into the building. A little while later – we have just finished decoding a radio message – there is a knock on the car window. They want to take us away for interrogation. Secret radio documents quickly disappear into a crack. Kurt, the driver, who did not understand what the Frenchmen wanted, was used to taking a nap whenever we stopped. He is asleep at this moment, and when we wake him up he is reluctant to go with us. Then we follow the sentry into the barracks. When we step into the dirty guardroom, lit only by a few candles, we find our superiors and comrades in a less than pleasant mood. We suspect that the enterprise has come to nothing. Belfort is not going to surrender. 'Your affair looks to me more like a surprise attack', says the general staff officer mockingly, 'I'm sorry, gentlemen. Whether Belfort surrenders will soon be decided. Meanwhile, you will stay here at my disposal.' We are searched, individually interrogated – naturally to no effect – and then taken one by one with a three-man escort to a barrack block. We are placed in two separate rooms, one for officers, and another for us lower ranks.

We look around. The state of the quarters confirms our previous impression of the French military. There is a large amount of litter lying about, the beds are disgustingly filthy and the furniture is sticky with months of dirt. Even we hardened warriors, used to dust and soil, find the place uncomfortable. We can't stop ourselves pointing this out to the French. We demand a broom and sweep the rubbish into a heap. The captain drops in again and calls out to us: 'Good night, chaps; we won't be here tomorrow night.' As usual we click our heels and roar: 'Good night, Captain!', making the French stare at us in amazement. Tired out, we lie down on the beds and sleep securely, for in the corridor outside our room nearly 20 *poilus* sit guarding us in the light of two candles, rifles between knees and pipes in mouths.

Next morning I wake up at about 08.00 hours. Machine guns are chattering. It becomes very lively in the building. Men are running up and down stairs, ammunition is brought up, hasty orders sound shrilly through the building. Restraining my joy, I register that the battle for Belfort has begun. The shots get slowly nearer. Artillery joins in. The clatter of tank treads can be heard. My comrades now wake up, too. We listen intently, trying to distinguish enemy fire from our own.

It is not long before the first shells begin to shake our barracks; things are getting a bit tricky. 'Hey, what if the artillery drops one on this room.' – 'Let's hope they don't bring in the Stukas!' somebody else remarks. We can sympathize with our guards, who have been left alone with us. They are standing in the corridor, white with fear, whispering anxiously. Even if we don't feel particularly happy about being wiped out by our own side, none the less our hearts leap for joy at every shell that falls.

A French first lieutenant dashes in: 'Gentlemen, go to the room across the way, here on the left. You're right opposite the gateway that is being shelled.' He speaks fluent German. An Alsatian with the good old German name of Müller.

We follow him. Then the officer dashes out again, and we are finally left completely alone with our guards. The increasingly heavy and frequent explosions have a more and more visible effect on the *poilus*' state of mind. Our captain notes this with satisfaction. He tries to help them, using his powers of persuasion. His confident manner with them is brilliantly successful. When he puts it to them that 'If you value your lives, you should go with us out to the barrack square', and immediately – followed by us – gives the lead, in their naivety the guards all obediently trot along behind us. We stop where the steps lead down into the square, and squat there. As I can tell from our captain's alert gaze, our safety is not his only concern; he wants to see and hear. The *poilus'* fear makes them confide in us, and their innocence leads them to give away a lot of information.

One company is involved in fighting over by the wall, using heavy machine guns and hand-grenades. The other soldiers and civilians are sitting in the casemates; they come from the most varied branches of the service. As scattered troops who only arrived yesterday, they are difficult to deploy in action. Their only weapons are their rifles. And what a bunch they are! Next to us is a young Alsatian, 17 years old, in a civilian suit, with only his rifle and helmet to indicate that he is a soldier. The captain begins craftily, with reassuring words, to persuade them all that resistance is useless, promising them that he will do his best to put a halt to this dreadful shelling, if they will do what he tells them. First of all he asks them to lay down their arms.

But what would their superiors say to this? At that moment we are joined by an NCO. He is put in the picture. But he completely rejects our demand. On the contrary, he rips his rifle from his shoulder and points it threateningly at us, shouting: '*Comment, deposer les armes? Ah, messieurs, moi, je suis Français et je défends la France avec ma poitrine jusqu'au dernier moment!*' (What, lay down our arms? Ah, gentlemen, I, I am a Frenchman and will face the enemies of France until my dying breath!)

Is this the ruin of everything we have so carefully built up? Luckily, the corporal soon turns his back on us and goes away. Then a second lieutenant comes dashing up to us from the casemates, imploring us to follow him to the shelters, for the sake of our safety and that of his men. But with quiet authority our captain succeeds in persuading him that a complete surrender is necessary. Distraught, the officer now runs from one casemate to another, giving orders for weapons to be dropped in the middle of the square. He also allows our officers to approach the first lieutenant conducting the fighting at the wall, and call upon him to surrender, too. It makes our hearts laugh to see the poilus jumping out from the casemates, throwing their weapons down in the square, and then hopping like rabbits back to safety! We are beginning to see our plan fulfilled, until the Alsatian first lieutenant appears. Out of breath, with his pistol aimed first at us, and then at the poilus, he roars: '*Qui vous a donné l'ordre de déposer vos armes?*' (Who gave you the order to lay down your arms?) Discovering that the second lieutenant himself was responsible, he turns on him in a fury. The second lieutenant stutters some confused words about pointless resistance. Giving a strict order for weapons to be picked up again, the first lieutenant rushes back to a company engaged in the fighting, whose resolution he has reason to doubt.

Hesitating and cursing, one or two of the poilus pick up their weapons; but the first lieutenant is hardly out of sight before they are throwing them away again. While we irresolutely await the next developments, a tragi-comic scene is enacted before our eyes. The NCO who a moment before was going to defend France until his dying breath, appears near us again, and finds himself surrounded by nothing but rebelling comrades. Undecided about what to do and bright red with anger, he trots up and down, suddenly stops, pulls his rifle from his shoulder, smashes it down with the others, reaches into his tunic pocket, throws away his ammunition, and goes off, accompanied by the not particularly gentle 'blessings' of his men.

Almost at the same instant, the first lieutenant charges round the corner, again with pistol drawn, but he no longer points it threateningly at us. You can see that he is physically and mentally exhausted. 'Captain, I am surrendering my weapon to you, I am your prisoner, I can't go on, my company has been wiped out. Just make sure that this terrible bombardment stops!' he blurts out in desperation. Then he breaks down, crying and sobbing. They are the tears of a brave soldier who has fought a losing battle to the last. The captain holds out his hand, but the Frenchman refuses to take it. He is wounded, and we offer to bandage him, but he proudly rejects our help. German blood! But fighting for France.

We have to do something quickly. The shooting has become even fiercer; roof tiles and masonry are flying around our heads. The assault tanks are firing directly at the barracks.

We pick up rifles and ammunition, and then herd the 600 or so *poilus* that have responded to our call and crept out of their various holes, into a corner that is as far from the firing line as possible. Then a shell falls there, too. We are in danger of losing our prisoners again; they are beginning to be hostile. Just in the nick of time, Lieutenant Seidel succeeds in raising a white flag. The firing stops.

On his orders, I jump with the captain into a gap between the barrack blocks, opposite the gateway. Our pioneers are leaping and crawling through the entrance. I wave, hurry over to them and report to the first-leutenant in charge: 'Everybody within the barracks area has surrendered.' The prisoners are led off, and we look for our vehicles. To our great joy, we find everything more or less as we left it. The slight damage can soon be repaired. There is an assault tank standing in front of the gateway. My friend Kurt cannot believe his eyes when a friend of his pokes his head out of the tank roof. He has not seen him for months. 'Was that you shooting, mate? Lucky for you you didn't hit me!' – 'How long have you been here, then?' – 'Since yesterday evening! You know what I told you; the reconnaissance detachment always gets there first!'

In the square outside Montbeliard railway station, the detachment receives news over the radio from division that we have all returned alive and unhurt. As he later says, the commander, who has had a sleepless night on our account, feels as though a heavy weight has been taken off his mind.

By *Obergefreiter* Hütter

Behind the Maginot Line – the Push Towards Épinal

Do you remember, comrades, when we were in that little village north of Vesoul? Dusk was descending on the evening of 17 June. The mood was celebratory! Marshal Pétain had sued for an armistice …

Hour after hour we stood, the grey bulk of our vehicles pressed against the houses – we stood and sang, sang the songs of our homeland. The French listened and smiled. Their children gathered round the men in field-grey. We gave them chocolates and biscuits. Didn't we have the right to be generous, after all – we, the victors?

An old man rushed out of one house, asking excitedly: '*Est-ce vrai que la guerre est finie?*' (Is it true that the war is over?)

'*Oui, oui*', replies the soldier nearest to him. Perhaps he had not understood what the old man was saying. Or perhaps he did not want to spoil his pleasure.

Suddenly the old man is in the midst of the field-greys, clutching their arms, shaking their hands. 'Two sons … I've got two sons out there … They'll be coming back … oh …' – and he turns towards his house, raising his hands as though in prayer – 'Oh, mother, we're going to see them again!'

The grey 'barbarians' are motionless. All are somewhat affected by the father's joy. At this moment, they would all really like to see the sons return. And they are all remembering that back home, a loving heart is thinking of them – a father, a mother, a wife or fiancée. How wonderful that is … Orders ring out. 'Get ready'! The command is passed from vehicle to vehicle.

'Mount!' Yes, we are going on. The situation? Nobody knows. The mission? Nobody knows. We have taken Vesoul, and have wheeled round to the north-east. Are we going to attack the Maginot Line from the rear?

A short break during our night-time advance on 18 June. Our column is standing on a lonely country road. The men are sleeping like the dead. How many nights have we spent without rest, how many nights of fighting? We can no longer recall. A milky mist is rising from the valley on our left. The sentry's tread rings out heavily on the road.

The company commander has nodded off, too. No more than four hours sleep in three days and three nights – it's too much … Shouting from up front. 'Commander of the 5th to battalion'. He is immediately wide awake. His vehicle pulls away at speed. The orderly officer standing by the roadside shouts: 'Go right on to division, quickly, quickly'.

So we have our orders. They simply say: 'Surprise attack on Épinal!'

The intention is for two rifle companies, supported by an allocation of armoured reconnaissance cars, field-howitzers, anti-tank guns, machine guns and pioneer shock troops, to breach the fortress in a sudden onslaught. They will all advance together initially, and then split up to cross various bridges over the Moselle.

'But it's all got to go fast, very fast', says the general. 'We've got to fall upon them like the devil himself!'

The mad dash begins. The platoon leaders and the commanders of the heavy weapons assigned to us are brought up by motorcycle. Clinging to the running boards of the command car as it careers along, they are told the commander's plan of action.

What kind of orders is it possible to give when everything is unknown – the situation, the terrain, the enemy – if you have had no time at all for reconnaissance? All you can do is what the general said, fall upon them like the devil himself. You can only trust to your luck. You can only show guts. Somebody once said: 'If the courage is there, the weapons will not fail!' Courage and weapons – they are not going to fail, damn it …

There is shooting. Machine-gun fire is whipping down the endless, dead-straight Chaussée. Out in this exposed country, columns of earth are sent flying up, and grey-black puffs of smoke explode over our heads. With a clatter, shots are falling all around us.

What is the name of this damned backwater from which we are being bombarded so impolitely at this unearthly hour of the morning? Oh yes, it's actually two places: St Sauveur, and to the left just behind it the spa town of Luxeuil. It's half past six by the clock. A lovely day, a lot of sun, hot. Very hot, in fact. In every sense. So we jump down from our vehicles, and take cover. The commander goes forward to reconnoitre the situation.

The situation is very simple: 7 Company has run into a barricade defended with all kinds of weapons and what seems to be a strong force. The whole nest is spitting fire. The 7th attack, but cannot manage it alone. Heavy weapons are in action on our side, especially artillery.

The enemy is all around us. We have to guard our flanks – 5 Company puts out some men to give cover on the right, towards the railway embankment. And on the left that village, lying there so peacefully in the glare of the sun, we really ought to … The battalion commander, too, thinks we must take the village of Breuches!

An order: 'The 5th will advance on Breuches with one platoon, secure village and bridge over stream and form bridgehead.'

The 2 Platoon leader, a young second-lieutenant, is very happy with his mission. 'Thank God', he says in his earthy way, 'at last we can get out of this shit and do something!'

Now 2 Platoon mounts, and taking a slight detour it quickly gets to the village. The enemy strews the terrain with a few shells, without hitting any of our vehicles. Motorized infantry roar to the front. Time gained – bloodshed saved …

The men jump down only just before reaching Breuches. The vehicles move into cover.

Meanwhile, the struggle for St Sauveur has reached its climax. A mighty artillery duel is raging. Enemy fire, with heavy weapons of all kinds, is still dominating the no-man's-land between the two forces. All the vehicles have to be taken to the rear. Our artillery, partly firing from exposed positions, suffers casualties. 6 Company, pushing forward to attack Sauveur-Luxeuil on the left of 7 Company, loses a machine-gun crew through a direct shell-hit. Shots continuously crack and whistle around the battalion command post. The orderly officer is badly wounded. The regimental commander stands unmoved behind an aircraft hangar. Shells exploding, machine-gun salvoes hissing; for him they are just the necessary background music of battle. With icy calm he issues his orders.

In this situation, the battle for Breuches acquires decisive significance. A flanking attack by the enemy from the village, perhaps even using tanks, would catch the troops fighting for St Sauveur, including the artillery, deep in the flank. The reverse case would mean that, in possession of Breuches and the bridge over the stream, we could roll back the enemy near Luxeuil from the west, and thus relieve the other, hard-pressed units of the 2nd Battalion.

At this time, about 10.00 hours, intense firing can be heard from around Breuches. Have the enemy occupied the village? What has happened?

The 2nd Platoon found the village free of the enemy. Cautiously the various groups feel their way forward to the bridge. Between the village and the stream there is an open area. The bridge must be beyond it.

For heaven's sake, there are a few Frenchies running about over there! A light machine gun is quickly positioned; a couple of short bursts of fire, and one Frenchman pitches to the ground, the others disappear.

But now the enemy have been thoroughly alerted. A withering fire hits 2 Platoon from well-hidden positions on the other side of the stream. Two heavy machine guns and an anti-tank gun are identified. Two comrades are killed. Four more are wounded. The butt of a light machine gun is shot away.

It would be insane to charge the bridge directly. Without hesitating, the platoon leader directs his mortar fire at the enemy beyond the bridge. One group is sent forward in a wide sweep to the right. The platoon leader himself advances towards the stream with two other groups, largely under cover of houses.

Terrific work by the mortar crew! Their rounds are superbly placed. The small shells hammer away incessantly at the enemy, forcing him to take cover completely. He passively awaits the disaster that is about to befall him. And perhaps at this moment a bold assault on the mortar's position would have been enough to give him mastery of the situation again. But the enemy lacks the drive for that …

So the men of 2 Platoon 'steal' their way (to use the platoon leader's graphic expression) towards the enemy pockets. Silently, Red Indian style, they trudge through the water that runs swiftly away like a white-water stream, dotted with little islands covered in thorn bushes. Behind it is the road, then a dense wood.

Now for it! Hand-grenades rain down from both sides. Like the devil himself the German soldiers leap into the midst of the enemy. A short hand-to-hand struggle ensues, and then the French give way. Two officers and three men, uninjured, are left in the hands of the victors. The haul includes one armoured machine-gun carrier with fully loaded ammunition trailer, two heavy machine guns, and an anti-tank gun.

Our losses are heavy, unfortunately: four dead and five wounded are testimony to the boldness of the attack. But the success achieved outweighs the casualties. As would soon become evident, the enemy has been deprived of a decisive position.

'Breuches village and bridge firmly in our hands!'

The battalion commander breathes a sigh of relief. He orders that the position must be held at all costs. For the moment he can stop worrying about his left flank. Just as well: he has plenty on his hands up there by St Sauveur.

The commander of the 5th sends his brave 2 Platoon a rifle unit and a self-propelled anti-aircraft gun. The reinforcements are greeted with relief.

For the moment, however, the area around Breuches is profoundly quiet. The sound of fighting is a long way off. Thus they have time to establish their bridgehead properly. The anti-aircraft gun is excellently camouflaged, sited so as to dominate the road to Luxeuil. The machine guns are set up. Will the enemy launch a counter-attack? Just let him try!

Let's have a look at this French anti-tank gun. The second-lieutenant, a sergeant and a corporal fiddle around with it. A nice weapon. And plenty of ammunition ...

Old soldiers can deal with anything. In no time at all they have worked out how to fire the French gun. It is turned towards the enemy. You can never tell when it will come in handy.

The silence is broken by the clattering of an engine. A motorbike. A Frenchman roars up, obviously believing the bridge still to be in French hands. Nothing stirs. The Frenchman slows down. Where are his comrades?

Then, 30 metres (98 feet) away from him, a machine gun spits fire. Motorbike and driver crash. The tank explodes. A sea of flames on the road. Finished! A soldier's fate ...

It goes quiet again. The French heavy machine guns are made ready, too. The platoon leader is determined to defend himself with all the means available.

'D'you think we'll get anything to eat today?' Machine gunner H. is deeply interested in the question of his stomach.

His comrade, P., mocks him: 'Well, start running; just after the bridge there's the Hotel Atlantic, they're waiting for you!'

Laughter breaks out among the hungry men. H. himself joins in.

The eternal essence of the German soldiery: in the midst of the enemy, thrown back on their own resources, a handful manning an important post. They all know what is at stake. They all know this bridge must be held at all costs. And yet they have not forgotten how to laugh ...

This is it: loud engine noises from up ahead! In feverish anticipation the men lie behind their weapons.

There – 500 metres (546 yards) away a colossus is coming over a rise in the road. More follow – two, three, four, five tanks!

This is the flanking attack our leadership had correctly predicted, intended to relieve the defenders of St Sauveur. Now, even before reaching Breuches, it is running into the iron resistance of a reinforced 2 Platoon.

The anti-aircraft machine guns rattle away. The lead tank wants to turn, and gets stuck; blue smoke pours out of it.

The anti-aircraft gun now gives up the ghost completely. Perhaps as a result of enemy fire, which is now pretty accurate.

The machine guns fire for all they are worth. All the same, the tanks are closing in. The situation is becoming critical. At this moment the sergeant, a corporal and a private jump on to the French anti-tank gun. The lieutenant calmly gives the order to fire. And the three of them, as though to the manner born, load and aim the gun. Round after round is fired, and round after round hits the enemy.

Flames break out in the first tank. Soon the second and then the third are also enveloped in smoke. The fourth and fifth decide to avoid the fate of their companions. They just manage to escape over the rise in the road.

But they do not get very far, either. Later, when the great attack on Luxeuil is carried out, they are found abandoned by the side of the road. Giants with a stomach wound, robbed of all their terrors.

Five tanks destroyed, a decisive flanking attack thwarted – that is the proud tally of the reinforced 2 Platoon. Once more, motorized infantry had beaten and destroyed the enemy.

By evening, their vehicles are again on the move. Rolling towards new action – new battles and new victories.

By *Oberleutnant* Dr Hans Berenbrock

We Can't Move for Prisoners

The order was: 'Pursue and overtake the enemy to the east!' Our tank division had moved up in two battlegroups, and on the afternoon of 19 June its advance units reached the west bank of the Moselle north of the fortress of Épinal. Here the division was ordered to secure the north flank of the corps. While the southern battlegroup was attacking across the Moselle towards the east that same evening, the northern group was settling in to provide security along a line running roughly from Portieux via Rapey to Dompierre.

Two sectors were formed. In charge of the sector on the left was the commander of the Panzer Pioneer Battalion, Colonel von B. Considering the area of the sector, his firepower was not exactly overwhelming: staff, 3 Company and Bridging Commando from his own battalion, plus three companies of tank destroyers. Running via the towns and villages in the sector, the security line was soon established and manned.

In any case, the leadership had no cause for concern. The day's march had been characterized by thousands of prisoners streaming out of every nook and cranny. It seemed that the enemy no longer had any will to fight. Right up until nightfall, endless hordes of French soldiers, having thrown away their weapons, flooded from the north towards the new security line. It was a familiar scene of complete disintegration.

To keep the stream flowing, small bands of German troops ranged far out to the north beyond their own lines. These troops were called 'collectors' by the men, and there was indeed a constant gathering in of prisoners of war for processing.

The night passed peacefully. The influx of prisoners ceased during the hours of darkness. But it started promptly again at dawn on 20 June. Thanks to encouragement from the 'collectors', by 10.00 hours many thousands of men, including complete motorized columns, had crossed the security line. Security? At times it now literally just consisted of the battle headquarters of the units concerned, because the men themselves were nearly all on escort detail, taking prisoners back to the assembly point in Dompaire. The guards for the PoW camp also had to be drawn initially from front-line troops. The situation was becoming quite grotesque. The division had been informed and had agreed to send over a rifle battalion.

Then, around 11.00 hours, the flow of prisoners ceased abruptly. A few 'collectors' had come under fire in woods near Ahéville, 6 kilometres (4 miles) north of Dompaire. Under artillery fire! When the Pioneer Company's tanks forcibly reconnoitred the woods, their surprising conclusion was that both there and in Ahéville itself there must be strong concentrations of enemy artillery. The latter were not undertaking any offensive operations, but neither would they allow anyone to leave. Prisoners who were eventually brought in reported that there was a whole detachment of motorized artillery stationed in Ahéville. The men had wanted to make a surrender bid yesterday, but their commander, a colonel, had refused; he wanted to fight on. Colonel von B. decided to keep the detachment under close observation, but leave it alone for the time being. Those men would come over eventually. Meanwhile, the flow of prisoners was turned on again, but from other directions.

At the same time, the division had a serious worry. It had received reports that an enemy column about 20 kilometres (12.5 miles) long was marching from the north towards Mirecourt, a town north of Dompaire. The division therefore released a detachment of artillery and a detachment of tanks for von B.'s battlegroup, which had meanwhile been joined by the requested rifle battalion.

The staff of the security group were not too impressed by the enemy column to the north, however. It just meant that the 'collecting' business would become even livelier. That seemed to be the only real threat, because by now prisoners were proliferating like locusts. The prospect of their numbers possibly doubling was not at all attractive. Where to put them all? For the next few hours, there was no news about the enemy column to the north. God knows which way they might have turned by now. No light was shed by the assiduous questioning of prisoners. The latter did not come from the north, but from the woods south of Mirecourt, which seemed to contain an inexhaustible supply.

A situation conference held by the divisional commander with von B.'s group that afternoon led to the decision to send someone to Mirecourt to parley. The delegate was to call for the surrender of the French troops still in the area south of Mirecourt, and to get them to march to Dompaire. He was also to find out what was going on in Mirecourt itself, and see whether there was any sign of the column reportedly marching down from the north.

I was entrusted with this mission. By order of the general, Colonel von B. had a handwritten pass made out for me, with the official stamp of the Panzer Pioneer Battalion. A bugler was quickly brought in, and a sheet attached to a long pole served as a flag of truce. The divisional interpreter would be travelling in a second car. Two groups of riflemen were also assigned to me, to act as escorts for the prospective prisoners. But the riflemen were not on the spot; my mission was urgent, so I set off just with the interpreter. After passing our forward pickets, I had the flag of truce fixed up in my car, and then we drove hell for leather towards Mirecourt. Shortly before the entrance to every village, the bugler sprang into action, with more noise than musicality. Since I saw no reason to stop the car or even slow down, it was not easy for the bugler to hold the instrument to his lips as the vehicle shook and swayed.

To the right and left of the road sat large and small groups of Frenchies. Others were skulking rather than marching along the path next to the road. A commanding gesture towards the rear got the motionless ones moving again. The places we passed through had been remarkably deserted so far. We had established as much by a quick tour of their streets. Now, several kilometres to the right of the road, Ahéville came into sight. The bugler must long ago have been heard by the Ahéville garrison, and they must have spotted the flag of truce, because the country hereabouts was as flat as a board. We would soon be getting to where the road forked. How would the current lord of Ahéville react? The question was quite nerve-racking, it had to be said. But even before we reached the fork in the road, there came a drastic reply: a flash from over there. Seconds later, a fountain of earth spouted up in the field about 500 metres (546 yards) to the left of the highway to Mirecourt. There was an undeniable disinclination to parley. The shell, landing so far from the road, was saying in effect: 'I don't want to shoot at you, but I don't want anything to do with you either. If you try it on, I will have to take further steps.'

I told the driver to make straight for Mirecourt. The colonel of Ahéville could wait; his time would come. The next place we got to was Mattaincourt. Even from a distance we could make out a grey-brown crowd of Frenchman milling about. Drive towards them! Suddenly the car braked fiercely. In the nick of time, my driver had noticed that the road ended abruptly just before the village. The 10-metre (30-foot) wide bridge that had formerly stood there had been blown up. This explained the crowd on the other side of the explosion site; the Frenchies could not get across the little river with their horses and wagons. We had no choice but to get out, leave the car behind on our side, and cross in a swaying boat. My 'negotiations' with the French, who immediately surrendered, were short and consisted of pointing the way to Dompaire. As the two groups of riflemen had meanwhile turned up at the site, the prisoners – about 400 of them, with a few horse-drawn vehicles – were quickly formed into a column and led off via a detour.

However, I had no more time to lose. I borrowed a small French civilian car and set off again with the interpreter, the bugler and a flag-bearer towards Mirecourt, still about 3 kilometres (2 miles) away. The scene here was much the same as in Mattaincourt. The road was full of French soldiers of all complexions. I asked a French Army medic where to find the officer in charge. Before I could get an answer, a wounded German soldier limped up to us, gesticulating vigorously. He was beaming all over his face, and reported: 'I belong to a reconnaissance detachment, and got captured 10 days ago, after being wounded when the French shot up my vehicle. German soldiers are at the other end of the town, too. There are about 1500 Frenchmen in this hole.' I left the man in the care of the French doctor, and promised to pick him up on the way back.

In front of the town hall there was a busy scene. A few German soldiers were assembling long columns of captured Frenchmen ready to march off to the north. I reported to the German officer in charge, a major. Astonished, he looked up, exclaiming with pleasure: 'I'm supposed to be making contact with your division. Where are they now?' After I had briefed him, he asked: 'And where are you heading from here? I'm sure you'd like to take some prisoners along with you?' I palm him away in horror. 'Major, we've been unable to move for prisoners since yesterday.' Laughing, he replies: 'Yes, it's amazing! Well, goodbye; I'm needed here.'

My mission as a 'parley delegate' was over. The drive back to Dompaire was completed without incident. Our wounded man from Mirecourt was beaming with pleasure when we picked him up. In Mattaincourt the borrowed civilian car was returned, and our vehicle was waiting on the other side of the river.

I discovered in Dompaire that the lord of Ahéville was still holding out. By the morning of 21 June, however, the battlegroup had run out of patience. The attack on Ahéville was ordered for 07.00 hours. In the midst of preparations for the attack, a report arrived that the Ahéville garrison, all its officers and men, with vehicles, weapons and equipment, was on the march towards Dompaire. The news was brought in person by the commander of one of the tank-destroyer companies manning the security line. In the early morning he had driven towards Ahéville to try to find the body of a member of his company who had been killed outside the town the afternoon before, and could not be recovered because of heavy fire.

At the same time the company commander decided to use the opportunity, if at all possible, to try peaceful persuasion once more upon the garrison of Ahéville. He found the Frenchmen all ready to leave for Dompaire. Another surrender, then. Shortly afterwards, the column set off for PoW camp. All in all, a sad and – after they had stood out so long – a moving and pitiable end.

By *Hauptmann* Dr Walter Menningen

Hand-to-hand
Fighting for Xertigny

O n 18 June 1940 our battalion, combining with tank, artillery and anti-aircraft units to form a battlegroup, was marching from the south towards Épinal. The old fortress had become particularly important because beaten and scattered French troops from the Maginot Line were falling back upon their security zone in order to build a better defensive position. Thus there was a little skirmish in nearly every village or town, where the enemy fought stubbornly and determinedly, but where their disunited leadership always quickly decided the battle in our favour. We reached the area 2 kilometres (1.3 miles) south-west of Xertigny relatively rapidly. But here our advance company was driven off the road by heavy enemy machine-gun, anti-tank and mortar fire, so that they were obliged to move straight into an attack on what seemed to be greatly superior enemy forces.

A battery which had now moved up into position dealt very effectively and quickly with the main targets, and we had also succeeded in eliminating some of the strongest pockets of resistance; but about six or eight enemy machine guns had been installed so ingeniously that their locations were impossible to determine. My company, being in the lead, was diverted from the advance and ordered to circle around the hills south of Xertigny and attack it from the south-east, thus catching the enemy unawares in his flank.

With machine guns and rifles at the ready, I led my company's vehicles forward. Under cover of the various small hills, driving along tracks and over meadows, we reached the approaches to the town, the terrain about 500 metres (546 yards) south-east of Xertigny. Ahead lay one last hill, protecting us and the vehicles from the enemy's view. The slope running down towards Xertigny was wooded, offering us a chance of reaching the edge of the town unnoticed. We hoped that the enemy was so tied down by our advance company's frontal assault from the south-west that we would encounter little resistance.

Our artillery fire was falling on the nearby houses of Xertigny. To avoid frittering away the strength of the company too early, and to ensure that the dismounted troops were in contact as quickly as possible with the enemy, the platoons were echeloned as they advanced through the sparse woodland, with the men spread out widely. Our first objective was to occupy the edge of Xertigny. We used flares to indicate our position to the artillery. They shifted their fire to the northern exit from Xertigny, and 1 Platoon, which had briefly halted in a clearing, continued the advance. Up to this moment we had seen no sign of the enemy, so that the sudden onset of machine-gun fire temporarily stopped the charging men in their tracks. Our opponents were firing from a brewery on our left at about 10 o'clock, whose top storey must have given them a good view of our clearing. Individual Frenchmen could be seen at the windows and in the courtyard of the brewery. They seemed to be just a covering force, however, unlikely to put up serious resistance. Corporal Waegele's shock troop, which also included the platoon leader, was ordered to attack the brewery and clear it with grenades. A platoon of heavy machine-gunners assigned to us took up their position on the edge of the wood to give covering fire. The shock troops now pushed on skilfully, using every inch of cover, to the entrance to the brewery. From that moment onwards all we could hear was grenades exploding, and rifle and submachine-gun fire. It told us that our assault group was doing its job well and making short shrift of the enemy.

The 2 Platoon and the other two groups of 3 Platoon were soon able to risk venturing on to the road, which turned into a sunken way running between high walls. Meanwhile, 1 Platoon had worked its way forward through the wood and followed the same route, which led to the town market place. The penetrating echoes of our hand-grenades and the high-pitched shriek of bullets soon drove frightened French soldiers towards us to give themselves up, unresisting and trembling from head to foot.

Our troops had reached the market square. There were weapons and equipment lying around everywhere; about 80 saddled horses were tied to trees. The enemy force here seemed to consist of mounted units left behind to act as a rearguard covering the retreat towards Épinal. From now on we were bound to enjoy the advantage, because the loss of his horses deprived the enemy of mobility. Between and behind us followed the prisoners the Waegele commando had taken in the brewery. The brewery forecourt was likewise littered with great quantities of weapons and equipment.

The heavy-machine-gun platoon, its mission now accomplished, was brought forward, and its new task was to shield our next advance from attack on the right, where an extensive area of meadowland offered our opponents a good view from a distance. It soon became clear how well chosen this machine-gun site was, because after a short fire-fight three enemy 7.5cm (3in) guns which had been targeting our advance company, attacking from the south-west, were put out of action.

The company's half-platoon of heavy-machine-gun operators had also caught up, and installed their guns in the upper storeys of the first building taken. From there, they were able to cover the southern part of the town. A little while later, they gave covering fire for the riflemen attacking in that area.

Now 1 and 2 Platoons and part of 3 Platoon were tasked with rolling back resistance in the whole of Xertigny, on both sides of the road – 2 Platoon was to take the northern side of the road, while the other side would fall to 1 Platoon, which would thus enjoy the advantage of the machine guns that were already firing. But when the leading troops of 2 Platoon attempted to cross the road to the northern side, fierce machine-gun fire started up from the west along the road. It was impossible to cross it for the moment. The enemy, who no doubt wanted at all costs to prevent our attack from reaching the northern area, opened up with ferocious fire at the slightest sign of an attempt to charge across. The 2 Platoon's advance was therefore temporarily brought to a halt. The 1 Platoon, which seemed to enjoy better prospects, would have to overcome this obstacle first; 2 Platoon would then be able to carry out its tasks more easily and safely.

Through a small gate in the walls, 1 Platoon found its way into a park that ran parallel with the dangerous road, separated from it by houses providing cover. The park stretched as far as the centre of the town, was well tended, planted with old trees, and belonged to an enormous château hidden from our view till now by the tall trees. Here too the enemy's presence was apparent from weapons standing around, and unsaddled horses grazing on the big lawns. The enemy himself was not visible apart from the very few sentries, clearly left to guard the horses. After a few hand-grenade explosions, they were no longer a threat. But now the whole of the park as well as the château became very lively. The enemy had clearly felt very secure here, but had now noticed us and was going to try to save what could be saved. Isolated shots from rifles and pistols zipped through the air. The advancing riflemen were constantly facing fierce defensive fire from unexpected angles. The enemy were gradually recovering from their surprise, and concentrating on improving the accuracy of their fire in order to bring our advance to a halt. The few Frenchmen here conducted a desperate defence. They were fighting a losing battle. They lacked leadership. Their actual battlegroup was tied down by our advance company, and the troops left holding the fort here were grooms and batmen who had very little clue about how to deal with the attackers. Even so, they left no doubt that they were French soldiers on active service, for they acquitted themselves well, but they simply did not know which way to turn.

The château is reached. The platoon leader can be heard giving commands, and soon our troops disappear into the building, to bring out any enemy soldiers still hiding there. The interior of the building presents a sight of dazzling luxury. Superbly furnished rooms, glorious carpets and old paintings lend the place a friendly air, despite its dimensions. For an instant you forget that you are caught up in a very tough battle, and you would like to linger. But the moment demands otherwise.

Our 1 Platoon has to make its way to the church. Lance-Corporal Heuell sets up his machine gun on an upper flight of the château steps to cover their further advance. Suddenly, there is a completely unexpected development: through a deep-cut road leading from the main road to the château, a French officer has crept up and is now trying to reach the château in leaps and bounds. Shortly before he gets to the steps, he sees the machine gun and fires at the rifleman. One of his shots hits home. Heuell falls forward momentarily, but soon has himself back under control, and uses his last ounce of strength to fight back. A hand-grenade flies over, landing at the officer's feet, but he adroitly takes cover behind one of the château's decorative pillars. The short duel is brought to an end by the intervention of the leader of the group, who mortally wounds the Frenchman with a well-aimed rifle shot. Within a few short minutes, a dramatic struggle had been played out between two men both fighting for their lives and their cause, and both paying with their lives. Lance-Corporal Heuell succumbed to his grave wounds shortly afterwards. For the company he became a shining example of self-sacrifice to the last.

Meanwhile, the bulk of the platoon has reached the church, whose small, walled forecourt offers a view in all directions. Isolated enemy machine guns are yapping, but there is nothing to be seen.

Sergeant Waegele's squad, whose courageous raid on the brewery had enabled 1 Platoon to make progress, has now also moved on and reached the main street. The remaining enemy troops unearthed in the process hardly resisted capture, thereby swelling the ranks of prisoners assembled in the market square. Units of 6 Company had moved up on the other side of the street. Thus it now became possible to continue rolling up the resistance throughout the whole place. It was still difficult to establish a direct link between the two groups, because the enemy was keeping an extremely sharp watch on the road. For the time being, the physical distance between the two companies could not be bridged. Sergeant Waegele's group had fulfilled its task here, however, and Waegele attempted to link up with 1 Platoon, which had by now also reached the church. Here he was intending once more to throw his weight into the battle. But when he reached the street leading from the church to the market place, which had already proved fateful for 2 Platoon, with his first step into the road he received a mortal wound in the head.

1 Platoon's rapid and effective advance soon became apparent from the market square. Enemy fire along the road diminished, and 2 Platoon could now carry out its task as directed. The groups pushed forward, keeping close to the house-fronts; house after house was searched. A few Frenchmen were brought out of almost every building. The cellars were chock full of civilians seeking shelter. Individual soldiers tried to maintain resistance, but our grenades and the swift intervention of the riflemen took care of them. Thus, without too much difficulty, 2 Platoon was able to draw up level with 1 Platoon.

The lead company, with which contact had meanwhile been established, was still having great difficulty on the western side of the town. We had the impression that all the enemy forces not yet in our hands had gathered in the north-western corner of the town to fight to the last, thus fulfilling the duty of a rearguard. The key position in this area was a hotel situated opposite the church, and from which we had so far, as it seemed to us, only heard isolated shots. The building's significance had not really occurred to us until this moment. Now, with 1 and 2 Platoons sited opposite it and very close, it transpired that the very uncomfortable isolated sniper and machine-gun fire we were taking must come from this building. All we had to do now was to capture this one house, and the whole of Xertigny would be ours.

My company command post was located just behind the most advanced units, when suddenly a sigh of relief went up from all of us at the rumbling sound of approaching tanks. A tank platoon rounded the corner by the church and drove up to my command post to be briefed. Soon the last obstacles would be removed. Unfortunately, however, the tanks' ammunition was insufficient to destroy an enemy who was so well sited in the building. We needed assault guns to achieve the decisive outcome. I personally drove back with one of the tanks to the battalion command post, requesting an assault-gun unit and simultaneously getting briefed about the situation of the advance guard company. They too had made much better progress, thanks to our intervention, and had exploited our latest successes to move up close up to the north-west part of the town. Their most forward troops linked up with my 1 Platoon to the west, so that the dangerous hotel building was encircled by a ring of three platoons.

Our tough opponents claimed one more victim. A second-lieutenant of the assault battery, asking for directions on the road, fell mortally wounded by a sharpshooter's bullet. But now the guns were rolling up, smashing round after round into the hotel. The riflemen of both companies hurled in hand-grenades, and after a short battle in which shell after shell, hand-grenade after hand-grenade had done their deadly work, the building went up in flames. Very few Frenchman were able to escape the hail of fire by surrendering. Most of them fought to the last and perished in the flames. At the last minute, two captured German flak battery soldiers were rescued from the burning building. Two brave lads, whose first request after their rescue was for a weapon so that they could take part in further fighting. It turned out that they were dispatch riders who had lost their way and fallen into enemy hands.

After the hotel had been taken, the battle for Xertigny was more or less over. The French came flooding in from all the streets that had not yet been searched, to give themselves up. Their will to resist was broken. Shaken, they bowed to the brave resolution of their attackers. Right up to the last moment they had shown that the French soldier, too, can live up to his reputation.

Now we were to discover at last the secret of why we had so far not caught a glimpse of the enemy or his weapons. In the rooms, about 2 meters away from the window, heavy machine guns were fixed to tables, shooting out through a very narrow slit in the shutters. That way, the fire-flash and the smoke stayed in the room, and only the death-dealing bullets were perceptible to us.

Our assault troops gradually emerged from the houses, and assembled in front of the church. The blazing hotel and the burning church tower, ignited by flying sparks, illuminated the square. A lurid scene: the grimy figures of our soldiers in their steel helmets standing in front of the church, with the experiences of this day written upon their faces. Once again it had been shown how the commitment of every individual – especially when fighting in built-up areas, which fragments a company completely – can gain the victory, won by the bravery and resolve of individual German fighters.

By *Oberleutnant* Kulok

France is on the March – to a Prisoner of War Camp

France was forced to lay down its arms and sue for peace. What a development in the 10 days or so that it took us to push from the Aisne down to Switzerland, beating one French force after another, leaving the enemy no time to re-group, and finally, by the Moselle in the Vosges, preparing not only a reception for the enemy troops flooding back from the Maginot Line, but prison accommodation as well. The events of these few days of fighting came in a headlong rush. And thinking about that advance now, in quieter times, it is almost impossible to piece together the details of that unique experience in their proper sequence.

In the 40 days of the German offensive, France suffered a defeat without historical parallel. This defeat will one day enter history as the 20th century equivalent of Cannae. It is a terrible and destructive defeat; it is as total as the way we have conducted this war. That stream of prisoners flooding towards Germany between Épinal and Colmar is the complete expression of an absolute collapse. By the time we had sealed off the Maginot Line and broken down the last stubborn resistance along the line Chatel-Thaon-Épinal, our picture of the French loss of nerve was receiving its final touches. French cavalry units wandered into our security zone believing they would be able to link up with their regiment. Lacking any knowledge of the situation, the next day a whole motorized medical detachment arrived among us, complete with a number of wounded. Equally hopeless was the position of the French artillery regiment suddenly discovered to our rear.

This powerful column naturally did not escape the spying eye of our reconnaissance planes. The regiment held out for a day-and-a-half, and then it was all over. An infantry platoon coming from the west, and a tank company from the east, sealed off the French position, and then they surrendered with their colonel, 80 officers, and 1700 men, all their guns, and 250 motor vehicles. Their small arms and rifles were collected, and then the regiment was led off to captivity intact. 'We couldn't go on fighting', the regiment's commander told me. 'We had no infantry with us.'

That was the most striking feature of this stream of prisoners between Épinal and Colmar. It did not consist only of tens of thousands of poilus marching on foot, but gigantic French columns, motorized and horse-drawn, with poilus as drivers – where could we have found enough drivers to move this vast booty? – rolling over the Rhine into German captivity.

The picture of a beaten people! And this is the picture presented to the crowds of French civilians gathering everywhere. Women are asking anxiously after their men, the younger generation watching with curiosity this French *Völkerwanderung*, the migration of peoples from Europe, Africa and Asia. Their minds receptive, the generation growing up now has lived through this unique military collapse. It is a picture that will be seared into their souls for the rest of their lives and appear before their mind's eye whenever anyone threatens the peace of the world.

Once more we must recollect the occupation of the Ruhr. A comparison arises when our people offer the PoWs water. Could anyone have tried that on during the shameful occupation of the Ruhr, when many prisoners were being led past? Blows from rifle butts and kicks were what our women and children had to expect. Our few soldiers accompanying the endless moving columns do not intervene to stop the population. Neither do they mistreat the prisoners when they tire in the hot sun, or when their feet refuse to take them a step further. 'German soldiers, good comrades', in the prisoners' own words. You can read it in their eyes, and perhaps this bitter lesson they are now being forced to savour to the last dregs is the best and only way for millions of Frenchmen to get to know Germany, its people, and its convictions.

By *Wachtmeister* **Alfons van Bevern**

Index